THREE PHILOSOPHIES

OF

EDUCATION

THREE
PHILOSOPHIES
OF EDUCATION

A Radical Re-examination
of the
Basic Assumptions Underlying Education:
Matter-centered; Idea-centered; God-centered

HENRY J. BOETTCHER

PHILOSOPHICAL LIBRARY
New York

Printed in the United States of America

CONTENTS

FOREWORD

This volume is a response to several specific incentives. There was first of all a long-nurtured desire and a felt need on the part of the author to clarify, unify, simplify and intensify his own ideas and actions about educational goals and how best to attain them.

Then there were two provocative recommendations among the articles which appeared in *Modern Philosophies and Education*, the *54th Yearbook of the National Society for the Study of Education*. Dr. John F. Brubacher, in the keynote article, "The Challenge to Philosophize about Education", focused attention on the various sources of *"anxieties"* among Americans interested in education. He expressed the belief that American educators should frankly take a second close look at these anxieties, to determine their causes and to initiate remedial action. Similarly, Theodore M. Greene, in an article titled "A Liberal Christian Idealist Philosophy of Education," voiced an equally strong suggestion. "What is needed now, especially in these times of crisis, is a *radical re-examination* and re-assessment of our entire educational structure, its ultimate objectives, its fundamental pre-suppositions, its basic procedures," and thus to spell out the implications of this philosophy in terms of the living products.

The Supreme Court decision outlawing any teaching about God, the word of God, and prayers to God, has made it crystal clear the answer to God-in-Education? is No! at least not in tax-supported schools where 90% of American children and youth get their basic education.

Furthermore, a systematic inquiry brought to our attention that nine free nations in Europe not only tolerate, but support financially church-sponsored elementary and high schools; that in some provinces of Canada the parents have a choice, to pay their school taxes either to the public school or to a church-supported and sponsored school.

The Federal Elementary and Secondary Education Act of 1965 provides among other benefits for education the possibility of all children, in all recognized schools, whether tax-supported or church-sponsored, to receive benefits intended by this act, for children and youth of low income families. In this connection the Northwest Ordinance of 1787 is being quoted: *"Religion,* morality and knowledge being necessary to good government and the happiness of mankind, schools and the means of education shall forever be encouraged."

Also, in both the Nebraska case (Meyer v. Nebraska) and the Oregon case (Pierce v. Society of Sisters), the Supreme Court ruled that *parents* have the primary duty and privilege to say how their children should be educated. These and other facts prompted this radical re-examination of the basic assumption of education in the western world.

For whom, specifically, is this volume intended? Who are the likely readers?

First of all, the readers and potential readers of the National Society for the Study of Education yearbooks may be counted on as potential readers.

Furthermore, practically all colleges and universities offer a course in Philosophy of Education. In a democracy it is self-evident that such a course will introduce the student to various options among variant philosophies of education. This volume will serve them either as a textbook, or at least as a supplementary text and reference book. It offers them someone's answer to the questions, Where are we in education? How did we get to where we are? Why should we and how could we improve on the total program of education in America? Each of the three options presented is seen in its historical setting.

After a recent four week seminar on "Trends in European Theology and Philosophy," where the writer had occasion to confer ecumenically with pastors, priests and educators of all segments of the Christian Church, he is more than ever persuaded that these men are not at all prepared to go along with naturalistic approaches to the deepest problems of life, as recommended by theologians such as Bultmann and Robinson, to mention but two. God is not dead. And God in Education is not an anachronism. But how keep or re-introduce God into the purposes and curriculum of tax-supported schools? Or how allow the tax dollar for education to be used also for education through other than state-sponsored agencies?

Except for those teachers, pastors, priests and rabbis who have accepted the current trend toward a God-less religion, and propagate a sociology in place of a theology, the large majority of leaders in American religious culture are deeply persuaded that God is still the core of both significant communications from the pulpit as well as in the classroom. Hence the timely readings offered in this volume, by way of undergirding them in every possible way, will be read avidly by them and by all who share the anxieties of the dean of American philosophers of education, John S. Brubacher.

A growing percentage of Americans are now college trained. It is particularly parents who are among those who are groping for a better solution to the current inequitable distribution of the tax dollar for education. Americans are fair-minded. They are resourceful. On university campuses they are accepting the concept of religious pluralism. Courses in theology are being offered at state universities. It should be possible to apply this principle to the elementary and secondary levels of education.

We have presented three options, each being unique and different conceptions and basic assumptions concerning the nature of *reality:* matter-centered, idea-centered, God-centered. The author has given, he believes, an objective image of the other two options. He found the other two options to be based on a fragmentary conception of reality, and therefore operating with a fragmentary conception of man, of truth, of morality, of values, of the good life, and therefore offering an education which does not meet some of the crucial needs of human beings. He found only the God-centered philosophy of education to be adequate for the education of the whole person, in his total environment in all dimensions of space and of time.

This volume provides encouragement and guidance for others to make their choice and to state their preference. In every case the choice will be made, philosophically speaking, on the basis of their conception and their basic assumption, or belief, concerning the nature of reality. At this time when man stands, not only in America but in European countries and in the Middle and Far East, at the crossroads leading to extinction or survival, he must make a choice. Heirs of historical Christianity, teachers, clergymen, parents, must ask with Sienkiewicz: Whither goest *thou?* Especially leaders in American education, from pre-school through graduate studies, must ask: Whither America? With God, or without God? Whither Western culture? Whither mankind?

Henry J. Boettcher
Springfield, Illinois

INTRODUCTION

TOTALITY OF REALITY: A good education is based on the belief that education should be designed to develop the whole learner, to the greatest potential degree, in his total environment. The totality of time, past and future, the totality of space, and the totality of reality, as well as the totality of the community, should be brought to bear on the learner as far as this is possible. This emphasis on the totality of the environment and culture is in contrast to the fragmentary conception of reality, much of which underlies education in America. Still more emphatically does it contrast with the fragmentary conception of reality as seen in current totalitarian views of existence. Freedom is essential and freedom is unknown in totalitarian education.

With equal emphasis a good education is based on the belief that also the nature of man, of truth, of ethics, of values, of the good life, must be seen in their totality. Only with these ingredients will education come close to being a good, and the best possible, education.

GOD: This means that some informed parents and educators believe that *reality* includes not only the physical universe, but also the non-physical: God. God is real. This in turn means that God and the soul *of man* have an important place in good education. As they as Christians[1] see it, eternity and the total welfare of man, of all men, occupy key positions in the goals and the curricular experiences of the learner, experiences designed to attain those goals.

MAN: The heirs of historic Christianity are wholeheartedly persuaded that man's development and functional efficency in body and mind are of great importance. Yet they consider the fact that "man does not live by bread alone" so important that they are determined to maintain an educational system that is unique,

xi

different, adjusted to the fact that *man* is a creation of God; made in God's image; that he is indeed dust, but that he has a destiny; that he is by nature and maturation far from what the Creator intended him to be, particularly in the field of ethics; that man was the object of God's historic thrust into the life of mankind through the incarnation of Himself in the birth, life, teaching, death and revival of Jesus Christ; that through faith in this God-given Redeemer, man is born again, in God's image; and that he progressively, through relevant and purposeful teaching-learning processes comes closer again to the status and role of what the Creator originally intended him to be: the crown and apex of creation, an organism permeated with LOVE, active love of God and neighbor. Leadership in Christian education is intent on providing optimum conditions, for maximum growth in Christ, for the greatest number of persons.

TRUTH: The Christian emphasis on the whole *truth* sets its educational purposes and program off from much of education throughout the world. The scientific method of discovering has done phenomenal things, but to base education on the assumption that only the method of physical sciences can establish valid truths leads to a fragmentary conception of truth. To limit truth to whatever is experimentally established is unwarranted. Certainly history, to some extent tradition, inner experience, and more definitely, truth as it is found in the Judeo-Christian heritage, i.e., the Scriptures, Old and New Testament, belongs to a complete and whole picture of Truth. In contrast to an over-emphasis on truth as found in tradition and in the dicta of the Church, Protestants hold to the basic belief that Scripture is the one valid arbiter of truth in matters of faith, ethics, good conduct.

In contrast to the Hebrew element in the Judeo-Christian heritage, Christians hold to the basic belief that Christ is the Messiah and that historic Christianity as revealed in the New Testament and in the lives of believers is a vital and necessary basis for a good education. In contrast to so-called 'modernism' in the Protestant churches the heirs of Historic Christianity part company with it, particularly when it comes to limiting basic truths to the findings of science in the field of human relations, psychology, sociology, epistemology, and indeed theology. In contrast to contemporary deviations from the basic conception of Truth as indicated here, conservative Christians hold to their confessional statements as relevant expressions of, and applications of, Scriptural Truth in a contemporary world. They allow Scripture to interpret Scripture and they attach great importance to the purposeful application of the two major streams of revealed truth, Law and Gospel, as these reveal both the holiness and the mercy of the God whom they worship, and whose part in the education of youth Christians consider indispensable.

VALUES: What is man's chief good? Is it freedom? Immortality? God? What is the one thing needful? What gives persons, and what should give them, most pleasure? What has greatest survival value for man? Intelligence? Faith? Hope? Charity? Or is it money and the things that money can buy? Savings for a rainy day? Honor? Power? Is there anything that man takes 'with him'? Are spiritual values real? Moral values? How does education develop an appreciation of these values? How important is it to have many good friends? To have God as a Friend? To have been 'born again'? A good education surely includes an appreciation of the best things in life.

ETHIC: An *ethic* and a code of conduct which has evolved in the evolutionary process, as a result of the working out of the law of survival of the fittest, is wholly inadequate in a good program of education as Christians see it. The idea that might makes right, that the strongest survive, has in recent decades led to tragic deviations and has had devastating results in the history of mankind. To limit ethics to the science of ethics, to the exclusion of the ethics of revelation, is wholly inadequate. This has even now resulted in an immoral chaos in a generation which has been educated largely on the basis of such a fragmentary conception of ethics. When it comes to defining sin and virtue, Christians believe that historic Christianity has a very important and indispensable part to play in the education of man. As a protest, and as a safeguard for their heritage, even from the viewpoint of good citizenship, sincere Christians regard as a fatal deficiency in education the process of deciding questions of morality and ethics by counting noses. Christians believe in the democratic process. They value the ballot very highly, when used to determine questions of temporal, political and economic wisdom. But their educational program is based on the belief that chaos and social decay, moral irresponsibility, and immaturity into adulthood results from a fragmentary conception of ethics. They believe that a good education must be undergirded with an ethic that is inclusive enough to embrace the ethics of God and eternity. "Thus saith the Lord." Here Christians stand. They cannot do otherwise. And, incidentally, they believe this stand contributes much toward the attainment of good citizenship. Not only moral maturity but freedom itself finds its strongest bulwark in a complete and whole conception of ethics. Conscience, as the inner policeman, is more effective than multitudes of laws, officers of the law, and jails.

THE GOOD LIFE: The Christian conception of *the good life* assuredly includes a good standard of living. Creature comforts are important. Vocational and professional efficiency are important. A good education should keep this in mind and in its curriculum. In contrast to a surviving emphasis among Catholic colleagues, in our common battle for completeness as against exclusivism in education, Protestants have rejected ideals of poverty, of celibacy, and unquestioning obedience. Protestant education is based on the belief that the good life can be lived outside rather than within the walls of the convent and the monastery. The Reformation has given the religious people in our culture the new conception that the good life is found in doing one's very best in whatever station and role in life which one chooses to follow. The idea of the greatest happiness for the greatest number has its vulnerable facets. True joy, real purpose and fulfillment is found in a life of service well rendered. To live and to work creatively in a socially significant enterprise so as to reflect the glory of God and so as to express actively the love of God in service to the neighbor — both at home and abroad — that still comes very close to the Good Life, as visualized by Protestant educators. The learners' own maximum self-development in such a way as not to hinder but rather to help others in their maximum self-development, to the glory of God, is a basic element in the conception of the Good Life as Christian theologians and educators see it.

A GOOD EDUCATION: This we summarize briefly, by way of introduction to a philosophy of good education. The ideals of a Christian education, an education which is based not on a fragmentary but on a whole, complete and inclusive conception of Reality, of Man, of Truth, of Ethics, of Values, of the Good Life, and, by *implication,* of a Good Education.

NB. Those who wish to use this volume as a textbook in a College, or Seminary, level course on Educational Philosophy may order a Syllabus from the author. It contains a statement on Objectives, Basic Units, course details, and a graphic (blackboard) sketch to outline the major divisions and sub-divisions of the course.

1. Definition of terms: "Christian" in this study is synonymous with "heirs of historic Christianity." Protestants and Catholics are included in this concept. Christians and Jews have the Old but not the New Testament in common. Both are included in "God-centered" education. "Idea-centered" education corresponds to idealism. In this system of thought, "mind" is the original constituent of the universe. Matter has come from Mind, even as minds have come from that source. "Matter-centered" philosophy of education is based on the assumption that atoms, matter and energy, physical entities, space-time configurations, be they ever so minute, are the original and the only constituents of existents or phenomena. Materialism, secularism, naturalism, are synonymous terms. Pragmatism, instrumentalism, operationalism, experimentalism, even though they are primarily epistemological concepts, belong to matter-centered category. They all exclude the spiritual, non-natural, elements.

Chapter I

REALITY

A: THE PROBLEM

What is real? Do some existents only appear to be real? Are there two kinds of realities, material and spiritual? Is it dualistic? Or is existence monistic? If monistic, that is of one kind only, is it essentially physical or is it non-physical? If it is in the first place, physical, how did the physical come to take on the appearance of nature, how did it come to manifest itself in a material way? Is the material universe simply a materialization in time? Or, is the mental and spiritual world simply a refinement in time of the physical universe?

Assuming that at this time existence is both material and spiritual, which of the two was pre-existent? And which of the two kinds of existences is abiding, and indestructible? Which came first in time and which will continue forever? The ideas, the mind, the logos, or matter and motion, or God?

Can these ultimate questions about the ultimate nature of reality ever be answered logically? Or scientifically? Or do the answers to these questions remain what they are now, a matter of *faith?* Can logic and reason attain to certainty? Can the scientific method ever get beyond degrees of probability? Beyond hunches and hypotheses?

Theology and the theologians have ever said: I believe. And I base my program of action, including my program of education, on that faith. Science and logic deny that *faith* is a valid means of getting at the truth. Yet, they operate on basic assumptions.

What is the universe made of? Does the analysis of matter into infinitesimally small particles, with names like pion, lambda, hyperon, pi zero meson, all said to be measurable but only with fermi, one of which measures 4/10 trillionth of an inch, does this supersede the concept of 'spirituality'? Does the existence of a 'coercive order' which permeates all nature, supply us with a satisfactory answer to the questions about the nature of existence? Does the supposed discovery that every unit of existence, including the very smallest of units, is 'autodynamic' bring us any closer to the ultimate reality of existence? Does Hegel's 'dialectical idealism' bring us closer to the answer than Marx's 'dialectical materialism'? Does God, and do souls, and does eternity, cease to exist when man ceases to believe in them, as Nietzsche suggested? Are God and immortality only 'Wunschwesen,' creations of man's hopes and fears, as Folk phychologists have suggested. Or are they real existences?

Material objects, like a chair, a table, appear to be real. Are they? Or do they only appear to be real? It has been seriously contended, by idealists, that all such objects are merely appearances, and that they hide as behind a veil, a universal reality which is only a series of universals.

Let's admit that there is no design in nature. But, there is order. Nature behaves in a predictable manner. Whence is that order?

Whatever else philosophy may be, it is and it always has been, from the days of the ancient Greek Milesians to the present nuclear physicists, a serious and an honest quest for reality.

Is existence possibly after all dual in nature? Is it partly material and partly spiritual? That was the historic conception. But philosophers have tended to reject dualism. They have made out their case either for monistic materialism or monistic mentalism, or spiritualism.

Must we reconcile ourselves to the fact that the ultimate nature of reality is beyond reach? That neither logic nor science can apprehend the ultimate nature of existence and that therefore this is in the realm of *faith*? That leads to the question: Is it important? Does it make any practical difference what one believes concerning the ultimate nature of existence? Perhaps we should forget about this problem and direct our efforts toward more practical problems?

Here we must emphatically disagree. Our contention is that it makes a world of difference what a person believes, or what his basic assumptions are concerning the ultimate nature of existence. And certainly, it makes a world of difference in the development of valid ultimate objectives in education. That in turn makes a crucial difference in the content of the curriculum. That is to say, one's belief, or in case the reader has a morbid anti-feeling against beliefs and creeds, one's basic assumptions, concerning the nature of reality, is a first necessary step toward the development of a coherent and internally consistent philosophy of education. One's conception of truth, of the nature of man, of ethics, of values, of the good life, will be radically different, depending on the philosopher's basic assumption concerning the nature of reality. Since this issue is of such crucial significance, we ought to look carefully at the reason why some educators build a philosophy of education on the assumptions of materialism and materialistically oriented beliefs; why others feel that idealism and idea-oriented philosophies offer a more valid basis on which to build an educational philosophy; and why others again base their educational philosophy on foundations which include the Scriptures and faith in God and eternity.

B: REALITY AS SEEN BY THE HEIRS OF HISTORIC CHRISTIANITY

"This I believe," say the heirs of historic Christianity. "In the beginning God created heaven and earth."[1] This very first sentence in the Bible states clearly the basic assumption, or belief, of the heirs of the Judeo-Christian heritage concerning the nature of reality. The eternal, pre-existent, spiritual, non-physical God created in time, ex nihilo, by divine fiat, heaven and earth, both invisible and visible, spiritual and material, existences.

The existence of a non-material, non-created, eternal God is practically everywhere in Scriptures taken for granted. The Scriptures never go out of their way to prove the existence of God. Scriptures also go on the assumption that faith in the existence of an eternal God cannot be logically arrived at. Neither can scientific evidence produce faith even though it is true: "the heavens declare the glory of God." The development of faith in the eternal God is a function of God himself as he has revealed himself in

3

His great acts in Creation, in Redemption, and in Sanctification as these are recorded and revealed in Holy Writ. The Holy Spirit operates on the minds and hearts of man through the means of Grace, through Word and Sacrament. Certain it is, that while reason and observation may make it seem very probable that God does exist, this in itself is not yet saving faith and that understanding of God as holy and as merciful comes not through logic nor through natural science but through the Word. This knowledge of God is indeed the very core and purpose of Scriptures, to lead to a saving faith in God. Its purpose is to "make men wise unto salvation through faith in Christ."[2]

Luther believed not in a deus fictus, not in a deus absconditus, but in a deus vivens. Though God in Christ was crucified, died, yet He was alive. In Luke, chapter 24, we have a significant record of how that faith in the deus vivens was brought into existence. "Beginning at Moses and the prophets he expounded unto them all the scriptures the things concerning himself. — And their eyes were opened and they knew him."[3]

The resurrection of Christ and the incarnation of God in Christ[4] as recorded in John provide a basis and original stimulus for the Christian's faith in the invisible yet living, personal God. Christians believe that Jesus is the Christ, the long awaited Messiah, Son of God and Savior of the world. This need not presuppose a spatial concept as if God came down from out there, as Robinson frequently and ironically asserts.

Furthermore, in the person of Christ, the New Testament believer sees the union of the spiritual and the material, the eternal and the temporal, the unchanging and the changing, the unseen and the seen, God and man. The two worlds are so closely united in the person of Christ that whatever can ordinarily be said only of the one nature but not of the other, can, since that union, be said of the other. Thus the believer can believe and confess that in Christ God was born, God suffered, God died. Similarly it can be believed and said that man, in Christ, is pre-existent, eternal, unchanging, living, everywhere, at the same time; even as Jesus said, "Before Abraham was, I am."

When man comes to know, accept and believe in Christ as his

4

Savior and Lord, he partakes of and shares in the very nature of God, even as St. Peter said to the Christians of his day: "Through faith in the Gospel promises of God in Christ you have been made partakers of the divine nature."[5] Paul expresses the same conviction when he states of himself: "Not I, but Christ liveth in me; and the life which I now live in the flesh I live by the faith of the Son of God, who loved me and gave himself for me."[6]

This, incidentally, states in a few incisive words the basic aim and purpose of Christian education: Through Sacrament and Word, to bring individuals to a faith in Christ, the living and ever present God, and thus to be forgiven, accepted, justified, and united with the deus vivens, the living God. It is thus that the individual is 'born again'; he is a new creature, he partakes of the very nature of God, he is made a saint, and he is truly a godly, and a God-like, character; thus he shares in the freedom of God and also in the immortality of God.

While the philosophy of the heirs of historic Christianity seems to maintain a duality of reality, it is monistic in its interpretation of reality. For purposes of discussion and communication we still speak of Creator and creation, of body and soul, yet they are fused into one. The intellectual separation of matter and mind, body and soul, God and creation, is necessary lest we get lost in a vapory pantheism. This in turn would open the door to an equally vapory emergent evolution. It is only in the realm of faith, personal faith in the deus vivens, the living Christ, that this fusion and thorough integration of matter and spirit can be realized.

Thus we have very briefly, though succinctly, indicated that in the personality of Christ, and in the personality of the Christian believer, the deplored dichotomy of subject vs object, of matter and spirit, appearance and reality, have become resolved and inseparably united. Thus for God-in-Christ, for the Christian believer, space and time, have been superseded by a spaceless and timeless existence; the distinction between Creator and creation tends to disappear, since the believer, sharing the life of God, becomes spiritual, non-secular, immortal, free, creative.

Through faith, not through science, not through reason, not

through public opinion, but through faith, a person is united with Christ, and thus he is united with God and the eternal. He shares in eternal life. Even as Christ to the Christian believer is by faith "the same yesterday, today, and forever."[7] "He that believeth on the Son hath everlasting life."[8] Again, "He that hath the Son hath life."[9] Here we have racial integration in depth.

The theology of the Roman Catholic church and its philosophy of education has drawn rather heavily on idealism to support, for example, the existence of God.

> Catholic philosophy holds that there is a reality outside of and beyond material things, as the soul, the freedom of the will, the operation of the intellect, and that there are ways of investigating these realities and their activities that are not included in the methods of natural science.[10]

Thomas Aquinas sought to harmonize Scriptures with an Aristotelian philosophy. Thus the idealistic conception of reality, and its arguments for the existence of God came to be a prominent element in the philosophizing of the heirs of historic Christianity. By following reason the Thomists, and with them the scholastic tradition, argue that there must be a 'first mover' to set things in motion. Thus their conception of God took on the form of identifying God as the Uncaused First Cause. Aquinas also based the existence of God on the existence of beings whose non-existence is possible. He reasoned that the scale of perfection implied a perfect being. That being is God.

Asked by pollster George Gallup whether they believed in the existence of God, 96% of the college students are reported to have answered that they did. Asked on what they based their belief they answered in different ways, among the answers being idealist arguments as the order and majesty of the world around us; there must be a Creator to explain the origin of man and the world. They also gave purely pragmatic answers such as: "Believing in God gives me great comfort." "Past experience in life gives me faith that there is God."

The beliefs of the heirs of historic Christianity have been widely attacked as untenable. It has long ago become necessary

6

to answer the critics; not to apologize for their belief but to enter on a whole disipline called apologetics in the study of theology. We must briefly, at least, refer to these attempts to 'justify faith' over against the idealistic and the materialistic interpretation of reality. This all the more so, since the materialistically oriented philosophers of education have gradually, in the Western world, become so sure of themselves that they have come to claim a monopoly of education, an education which is wholly within the orbit of the concept that everything that cannot be explained in terms of matter and motion is wholly obsolete, out of date, and a hindrance to progress.

C: REALITY AS SEEN BY IDEALISM AND IDEALISTICALLY ORIENTED PHILOSOPHY

Two names that stand out in the attempts to apply the idealistic philosophy of reality to the educational program are Horne and Greene. Horne presented the idealistic viewpoint in an article entitled "An Idealistic Philosophy of Education" in the *Forty-First Yearbook of the National Society for the Study of Education*.[11] He wrote:

> The conception of God as herein reached is that of one absolute mind, complete and self-moving. Being absolute, there are no other gods. Being mind he is not less than personal; being complete in himself, there is no change of time, neither increase nor decrease; time exists in him as a part but he does not exist in time and grow old with centuries.

Horne seems to feel that if materialism continues to refine the concept of matter and motion it will eventually end up in some form of 'idealism'. He insists that God is not co-extensive with time or place. His God is all-inclusive.

> From the standpoint of the (materialistic) physicist matter eventually disappears into some form of energy, like electricity; from the point of view of the speculative philosopher energy disappears into some form of consciousness,

7

like attention. — The energy of the whole world thus in the last analysis may be held to be the attentive aspect of the consciousness of God.[12]

We are tempted to ask whether this is a restatement of Spinoza's deus sive natura philosophy or of Judaism's transcendent Jehovah. But Horne says No.

"Our conception is neither a transcendent dualism nor an immanent pantheism, but an idealistic theism. God is the self-conscious unity of all reality. Within his life falls the life of nature and of man."[13]

Plato is quite generally regarded as the father of idealism. The universe as he conceived it was spiritual monism. Things are only shadows. Existence is dual in nature. The universals and the "forms" are pre-existent, eternal, indestructible, unchanging. Educational philosophy in his conception had the function of discovering these 'forms' and accepting them as fundamental. For that reason he contended that the heads of governments ought to be philosophers. In "The Republic", this education of future philosopher kings was well spelled out.[14]

George Santayana[15] might be classified as a materialist. However, he remained strongly attached to both the Platonic tradition and to Catholic theology. Of Plato and idealism he had this to say:

Platonism would be entirely stultified and eviscerated if it were not suffered to be all that modern criticism most thoroughly dislikes: I mean supernaturalistic, realistic, dualistic. This is only another way of saying that according to the Platonic doctrine God and the unseen world really exist in themselves so that they precede, create, attract, and survive their earthly emanations.

Descartes was among those who undergirded the idealistic interpretation of reality in a philosophical manner so incisively that he, with Plato, is regarded as the one who in later years divided reality into two separate component parts and, incidentally, made the spiritual element to stand out as the one most abiding element in reality. His most widely quoted phrase is "Cogito ergo sum";

8

thus he asserts that we come closest to reality in the realm of thought.

> What of thinking? I find here that thought is an attribute that belongs to me. I am, I exist. That is certain. But how often? Just when I think? For it might possibly be the case if I ceased entirely to think that I should likewise cease altogether to exist. — To speak accurately, I am not more than a thing which thinks; that is to say, a mind, a soul, or an understanding, or a reason.[16]

Thus Descartes began a long controversy in philosophy about the nature of reality. Descartes has also been referred to as the father of rationalism. His analogy of wax is characteristic of his defense of idealism. Wax has odor, color, figure, size, texture, temperature. But place the wax near a fire and what happens? All the sense stimuli disappear. Only the impressions left on the mind remain. Hence, the reality of wax is but a mental entity. "I do not admit in myself anything but mind," he stated.[17]

George Berkeley elaborated this approach to reality as he sought to defend the tenet of the Church concerning the reality of God. He sought to defend the basic beliefs of historic Christianity with the weapons of idealism.

Sir James Jeans is a more recent apologeticist for a faith in God, also on idealist grounds. "The universe can best be pictured, although still very imperfectly and inadequately, as consisting of pure thought, the thought of what, for want of a better term, we must describe as a mathematical thinker."[18]

The religions of the East do not consistently presuppose the existence of a spiritual, eternal, pre-existent God. The pantheon of Shintoism includes nature gods, but it concentrates on the worship of ancestors, nature and heroes. Animism enters in. Buddhism can be conceived of as a system of ethics without the existence of a God. While re-incarnation in another life played a prominent role in their philosophy or life, they considered nirvana, or complete extinction of the individual, as the ideal.

A recent spokesman for Buddhism appears to have been influenced by Western idealism. "There is purpose in each thing, purpose in the totality of things, purpose in the universal process."[19]

While he does not hold to the conception of reality as seen by the heirs of historic Christianity, he does come to the defense of idealism in its battle against materialism and Western-related philosophies. He does continue the traditional Buddhistic emphasis on ethics and conduct.

> Wisdom lies less in what we learn and more in our reaction to that learning; less in the quantity, more in the quality of our knowledge; less in the accumulation of facts and more in the knowledge of principles; less in the possession of ideas, more in right employment of them.[20]

It is in the area of origins, of creation, of evolution, that idealism holds out for basic assumptions of historic Christianity. Idealists see purpose in nature and conclude this purpose and design, and consequent order and fitness in nature, must compel us to reject the materialistic conception of reality and to believe in an eternal mind at work in the emerging phenomena of nature.

The arguments advanced by scripturally and idealistically oriented writers can be summarized as follows:

Whenever we look into the question of origins, we find that at some stages events must have taken place to which science and biology cannot give satisfactory answers. Chemical elements came into existence endowed from the start with astonishingly ordered potentialities. Was it chance that gave hydrogen, carbon, nitrogen their remarkable properties? Our planet came to be placed at the right distance from the sun, with oceans to keep the temperature balanced, with tilted axis to give the seasons, with its weight correct to allow escape of hydrogen but the retention of oxygen. Then life came. Then three-dimensional structures of atoms, arranged in shapes of bewildering complexity, blue-printed with instructions for self-reproductions; we can understand how a new type or order, once established can multiply by degrading compounds and quanta of light, but how do thousands of new kinds of order arise?

Chance variations do not seem to satisfy the conditions. Has

Darwin's theory of natural selection gone deep enough? What were the criteria by which this selection took place, or takes place? Particularly since some biological structures must be there at once or they can not serve the purpose which presumably they were to serve.

Leibniz denied the physical interaction between monads. Their coexistence and intercourse are regulated by "the pre-established harmony" which is the work of God.[21]

Is the question of the nature of reality important? "The usual problems of philosophy lie just beneath the surface of educational terms. The nature of the world must be met before a satisfactory conclusion can be formed as to what to do next in our present predicament."[22]

The position of idealism with reference to the problem of reality is simply that of Plato's original concept of the real and the shadow. The essence of existence lies in the area of ideas, of forms. These are pre-existent, eternal, absolute, unchanging, non-material. Hence, a good education must, above all, help the learner to discover and to accept these universal forms of thought. In the Middle Ages, philosophers tended to settle for the *ante res* in the problem whether universals existed *before* particulars, or *in* particulars, or only post (*after*) particulars. More recently a historian of philosophy summarized the faith of the idealist thus:

> Thought is one of those principles of things, one of those primary conditions of reality for which philosophy has been seeking, the principal of which is divined in the logos of Heraclitus, the One of the Pythagorians, the nous of Anaxagora. Thought is the unifying principle, that which unifies and measures reality; it is indeed, the measure of all things.[23]

If that still leaves the reader in some doubt as to the conception of reality held by idealism, and whether this has any bearing on educational philosophy, its objectives and its curricula, we shall grant Horne, the most valid exponent of idealism and its implications for education, the floor once again:

Mind is not matter. Matter occupies space, mind does not. Mind has no weight. Matter has. Mind has no dimensions, matter has. The soul (Augustine: De Quantitatae Animae) is not corporal. The mind that thinks cannot itself be matter, and matter cannot think itself. The mind has meanings. The mind has a remembered past and an anticipated future. The mind has conscience. Matter is indifferent to right and wrong. The language of ethics is inapplicable to the reactions of matter. — Mind comes from mind. Like comes from like. Mind is too unlike matter to be a derivate of matter. — Emergent evolution itself is the outcome of an immanent design or intention. That implies an *eternal* and *universal purpose.* — In its cruder materialistic form in the 18th Century, the view was held that *the brain secretes* thought as the liver secretes bile. But *bile is material. Mind is non-material.*[24]

A more recent exponent of the idealistic conception of reality became articulate in the *Fifty-Fourth Yearbook of the National Society of Education.* His point is largely that variant philosophies of education merely reflect different emphases rather than radically different interpretations of reality. "More significant than any specificable type of philosophy is the larger pattern of partly contrasting, partly overlapping, emphases and trends of contemporary belief on ultimate matter."[25]

Idealism as a philosophy of life and education was evidently uppermost in the minds of those who wrote the Constitution and its Preamble. Idealism has lived on in various types of non-Christian religious groups such as Unitarianism, Universalism, Christian Science, and more recently, in the emergence of so-called 'modern' groups who claim to belong within the family of the heirs of historical Christianity but who are more properly classified as heirs of idealism. Ethical societies, theosophical societies and variant types of humanistic groups similarly spell out the implication of an idealistic, if not actually a materialistic, interpretation of an existence that is limited to the purely natural and this wordly. Deism of the 17th and 18th Century and theism are other expressions of idealism.

12

The quest of philosophers for a realistic description of reality has been as honest and persistent as their quest for a valid description of truth. Yet, the latter is still dependent on the former. Even as the nature of man, of ethics, of values, of the good life and therefore, of the good education, hinge finally upon the starting point, the nature of reality. We have looked at the conception of reality as it is believed in by the heirs of historic Christianity; we have noted the basic assumption of idealist philosophers concerning the nature of ultimate reality. It remains to present a picture of reality as believed in by the materialists and by that large family of satellite educational philosophies which orbit around the concept that reality is purely monistically and exclusively physical, merely matter and motion.

To begin with a comprehensive statement of the case of modern materialism:

> Modern materialism asserts that with the advent of organic life, new biological laws began to operate. The principles of *physics* and *chemistry* necessarily *apply,* but are not by themselves sufficient to the biological level. Thus mechanism is emphatically *rejected.* The higher levels (of integration) are more highly organized and more complex, exhibiting new behavior traits. Within the organic level we have cell, tissue, organ, organ system, organism and population. Each level, except the first, contains all lower levels within it. Each is characterized by distinctive laws. . . . There is no evidence that with security and basic needs supplied, man will not make use of his additional abundance, realizing indefinite potentialities.[26]

Materialistic conceptions of reality differ radically from idealistic world views. The method of natural science has not uncovered either the God of the Christian nor the universals of the idealist. Crass, mechanistic materialism has tended to go under cover in current culture. Yet, with the emergence of the evolutionary principle of some 100 years ago, materialism has become the most widely accepted view of reality. The unchanging element in historic Christianity as well as in idealism has all but disappeared in current culture. In current culture, reality is fluid, ever changing.

Materialism is a philosophical theory which regards matter as the original cause of all phenomena, even psychic phenomena. It asserts that all psychic processes are due to changes of the material molecules. It denies the existence of the soul. It reached its greatest development in the 18th Century writings of French Encyclopedists. It is commonly associated with the names of Holbach, Diderot, and subsequently Feuerbach, Haeckel and others.

Materialism as a philosophy of reality found its most recent consistent exponents in Marx and Engels and under the name of *Dialectical Materialism.*

This method of defining existence followed to some extent that of Hegel and his thesis of dialectical idealism. Both operated with dialectic. Only, with this radical difference, as Marx himself pointed out:

> My own dialective method is not only different from the Hegelian but it is direct opposite. For Hegel, the thinking process is the demiurge (creator) of the real world, and the real world is only the outward manifestation of the Idea. With me on the other hand, the ideal is nothing else than the material world reflected by the human mind and translated into terms of thought.[27]

As Sidney Hook puts it, "Marx turned Hegel right side up. As Hegel had turned things wrong side down."[28]

Marx became elated when he discovered the concept of the 'auto-dynamic' element in all constituent elements of nature. This is the basic assumption, or faith, which underlies the theory of evolution.

14

This theory to account for the origin and development of organism, from amoeba to man, is also known as Darwinism. Some 100 years ago, in 1859, Charles Darwin set forth this theory.[29]

What later was termed the 'auto-dynamic' nature was spelled out in Darwin's evolutionary theory. Granted that nature is purely physical monism and that auto-dynamism or spontaneous development of life is based on facts it explains reality without a supernatural factor, i.e., without God. Biological evolution is a process of continuous change from a lower, simpler or worse condition to a higher, more complex or better state; change from the heterogeneous to the homogeneous and a concomitant change from the homogeneous to the heterogeneous; the biological development of a race, species or group; the theory that the various types of animals and plants, including mankind, had their origin in other pre-existing types. Creative evolution and emergent evolution are further theories which seek to explain why nature and its various forms have emerged as they have. The latter assumes that an 'elan vital', a vital force is extant in all nature and that explains why there has been an evolution. Darwinism has also been defined as the theory of the origin and perpetuation of a new species of animals and plants, holding that an organism tends to produce offspring which vary slightly from the parent; that the process of natural selection tends to favor the survival of individuals whose peculiarities render them best adapted to their environment and that chiefly by the continued operation of these factors new species not only have been and may still be produced but organisms of widely different groups may have arisen from widely different ancestors. This process is known as biological evolution, a process which accounts for the origin and survival of man, in contrast to the Genesis story of creation.

By this same process of increasing complexity and refinement of organism and their specialized function as evidenced in the organs of sense, and more especially in the ability to act intelligently in any given situation, also the mind of man, his higher-

15

than-animal-I.Q., has been the most important factor in his development and that this same ability to act intelligently is even now the most important factor in his survival in a highly competitive and increasingly destructible environment. That makes the 'ability to think' a prime objective in education.

> No mental process occurs without its appropriate neural pattern. There are not two processes that satisfy basic needs one mental and the other physical, but rather one psychobiological process. — The study of behavior is the only scientific approach to the understanding of the minds. — Obviously excluded by our position are dualism, parallelism and simple reductionist identity views of mental and bodily processes.[30]

Behaviorism in educational psychology is an attempt to spell out the implications of materialistic philosophy of life in the area of mental and emotional experiences.

Currently the most radical and the most consistent spelling out of the materialistic philosophy of existence has taken place in communism. There is no room for Christianity's most central goal of education, namely the cultivation of love. God and love are out.

> We hate Christianity and Christians. Even the best of them must be considered our worst enemies. Christian love is an obstacle to the development of the revolution. Down with love of one's neighbors. What we want is hate! Only then can we conquer the universe.[31]

But is not the radical application of the materialistic philosophy of existence a temporary and passing phenomenon in the history of culture? Radical revolutions of thought and social organization tend to taper off after a period of time and come back to a general level of balance and toleration. There is some evidence that scientism, and also dialectical materialism is tapering off and moderating. But even granting that cultural changes come in waves and tend to recede, yet, there appears to be a persistent assumption and belief that historical Christianity and with it also Idealism haven't a ghost of a chance to survive on our planet; that religion is doomed; that the natural sciences are in the saddle; that the nature of existence is increasingly accepted as being physical monism, or monistic physicalism; that only those truths which have been arrived at by the method of the physical sciences are really true; that valid ethical codes of conduct can be only those which have originated in the social matrices and are therefore man-made, relative and changing; that man is continuous with nature, differing from the vertebrates only in degree. Now, if that is realistic, then the Church and all proponents of supernatural realities, including the idealists, had better prepare to evacuate and close down church-sponsored schools, including their seminaries, as was done behind the iron curtain. Or, as an alternative, do what the surviving Orthodox church in communist countries has done, adjust their objectives and their curricula to fit into the philosophy of existence which has been ruthlessly insisted upon in Soviet-controlled countries. That means making peace with physical monism.

We have referred to philosophies of education which move within the orbit of materialism. Unless the origin and character of these philosophies are honestly identified they can readily mislead. They tend then to put educators and theologians to sleep, prompt them to feel and say: It can't happen here. By identifying the following 'philosophies', as oriented to the materialistic interpretation of reality, we mean to alert God-centered and American educators to the fact that it can happen here and that in fact it is happening here.

Secularism

American tax-supported education is admittedly secular. It has been said that this is the secret weapon of communism — which is to say that America will destroy itself through its secularism. The assumption here is that a nation such as America which had its roots in historic Christianity and the willingness to suffer and migrate and fight for the heritage of God and freedom, is doomed to desintegration, moral and political, because it has, in its philosophy of tax-supported education, cut itself off completely from the roots which gave it birth and virility. Secularism

17

is a view of life based on the premise that religion, God, the sacred, the religious, should be ignored or purposely excluded. It has far-reaching implications for education, both as to the objectives of education, the curriculum and instructional materials. Ethics should become situation ethics with reference to the present life and social welfare, without reference to Revelation or religion. What Webster has to say about 'materialism' might with equal validity be said of 'secularism'; "A doctrine or theory or principle according to which the only or highest values, or objectives of living, lie in material well being and pleasure and in the furtherance of material progress. Also, a pre-occupation with or tendency to seek material things rather than intellectual or spiritual."[32]

Let the reader page through the objectives, the curriculum, and the instructional material, as well as the daily classroom schedule, of any tax-supported school in America and he will find the reason for Lin Yutang's evaluation of American culture:

> The world is shifting; scientific materialism has cut Christian faith from under; Christianity has nothing to do with modern politics or business and it is politics and business that are shaping our lives.[33]

An education based on secularism and which is therefore secular in its ends and its means to attain those ends is moving our citizens of tomorrow toward a thoroughgoing materialism, in most respects the same as that which is now promoted behind the iron curtain except of course that individuals are still very important.

> We don't need the hypotheses of an immaterial soul or spirit which in turn controls our brain activities. All we need is the philosophically monistic assumption according to which certain processes in the cerebral cortex are empirically identical with the directly experienced qualities of willing, thinking, scrutinizing, deliberating, choosing, deciding, etc. — The dualistic hypothesis of an immaterial but causally efficacious spirit may be rejected as factually meaningless.[34]

18

Tax-supported schools, attended by 90% of the youth of A-merica, are secular in their purposes and in the means of attaining their immediate and their ultimate goals in terms of personalities. The Supreme Court has recently ruled that public schools are and must be secular, even to the extent of eliminating all and every type of prayer. This was quite a shock for large segments of the American public, and the declaration was followed by an outburst of indignant reactions, frequently centering on what they called mistaken interpretation of the First Amendment to the Constitution. The critics held that this phrase in the Constitution was designed only to prevent a recurrence of a traditional European practice of recognizing and supporting, also financially, a particular denomination. They held that the phrase "Congress shall make no law respecting an establishment of religion, or prohibiting the free exercise thereof" was designed purely to prevent any preference to be shown anyone or other of the many religious groups or denominations, but was never intended to support only secular schools.

The ruling of the Supreme Court against prayers in tax-supported schools is simply an honest and valid way of spelling out the implications of a philosophy of education to which Americans have quite generally subscribed, namely, that it should be secular. And secularism is rooted, both cognitively and attitudinally in the contemporary conception of a physical monistic universe.

The educational implications of secularism have been pointed up by Lehman.[35]

> Unacceptable behavior, laziness, failure to work up to capacity, indifference, inattentiveness, delinquency, etc., all ultimately have their foundation in securalism. It will be the task of the teacher in a God-centered school to subject his pupils to divine attention and enlightenment that they may learn to walk in the freedom of the reality of God.

The escape from the deadening bondage of secularism is possible only when those who are secular by nature, are born again into a spiritual level of existence.

19

Naturalism

Naturalism, according to Webster, is a "theory that expands conceptions drawn from the natural sciences into a world view, and that denies that anything has a supernatural or more than natural significance; especially, the doctrine that cause and effect laws (as in physics and chemistry) are adequate to account for all phenomena and that teleological conceptions of nature are invalid; a denial of the miraculous or supernatural in religion."

Lin Yutang asks: "How did we come to be naturalistic, deterministic, and materialistic? The dead hand of science is upon the West. The objective study of matter has colored man's thinking and brought us all three: naturalism, materialism, determinism. Science has therefore destroyed human values. Materialism has destroyed subtlety, insight and faith in things unseen. Determinism has destroyed the capacity for hope."[36] There is a naturalistic view of the struggle of nations for survival; there is the fundamental materialistic background and there is the determinism of human affairs which we have unconscionably borrowed from a deterministic view of the physical universe, as governed by mechanistic laws. With it freedom of the will has disappeared.

Naturalism as a philosophy of education was effectively popularized by Rousseau in his *Émile*. Herbert Spencer made his contribution through his widely-used book *What Education is of Most Worth?* His answer was an unequivocal: Science. Study of Nature.

This is not to say that naturalism in education has made no worthwhile contributions to the teaching-learning process in any and all classrooms of America. It has. Even as some elements in progressive education have been accepted and widely applied for example to methods in Christian education.

But, naturalism, like its progenitor materialism, is but a fragment of the total reality. It tends to exclude too much. This criticism of naturalism has been voiced persistently by Catholic educational philosophies. It speaks of the 'exclusivism' of naturalism and of an education that is based on the philosophy of naturalism.

Exclusivism may be said to be the main defect in every modern system of education. They have, each in turn, arisen from a one-sided concern of reality, of man, and of life.[37]

Humanism

There are those philosophers of education which have hesitated to go it all the way with the materialistic 'Weltanschauung'. At least they want to salvage a semblance of what the heirs of historic Christianity cherish as the One Thing Needful. Thus Dewey, second to none among influential educational philosophers in America writes:

> I shall develop another conception of the nature of the religious phase of experience, one that separates it from the supernatural, the things that have grown up around it. I shall try to show that these deviations are encumbrances and that what is genuinely religious will undergo an emancipation when it is relieved from them. — This view goes contrary to traditional religion, including those that have the greatest hold upon the religious minded today.[38]

Again,

> I am not proposing a religion but rather the emancipation of elements and outlooks that may be called religious. For the moment we have a religion, whether it be that of the Sioux Indians, or of Judaism, or of Christianity, that moment the ideal factors in experience that may be called religious take on a load that is not inherent in them, a load of current beliefs and of institutional practices that are irrelevant to them. — The historic increase of the ethical and ideal content of religions suggests that the process of purification may be carried further.[39]

Pragmatism

William James[40] continued the emphasis on epistemology inaugurated by Peirce[41] that the practical workability and fruitfulness of an idea give it the stamp of valid truth. This is quite evidently an application of the method of the natural science, and

21

therefore of the materialistic philosophy of education. It has given prominence to giving attention to the practical difference that one idea or method makes over against another. This theory of truth has virtues and it has great weaknesses. Particularly when it comes to establishing morals, ethics, and codes of conduct, it has wrought chaos among the teen-agers of America. The prevalent idea that promiscuous, pre-marital, sexual intercourse is perfectly good, provided only that there be no social consequences, in the form of an illegitimate child, evidently has its origin in a pragmatic theory of ethics.

Instrumentalism

Among educational philosophers and philosophies which move and have their being within the orbit of materialism, we find 'instrumentalism', usually associated with the name of Dewey.

This is a further development of the pragmatic method of establishing the validity of truth, of ethics, of values. It represents the characteristic Dewey emphasis on 'thinking' as a function or instrument of the organism.[42] In this process mind and the 'thinking' of an organism, has played a very important role in the survival of a species. The world in which expediency has been an only guide to action and the only deterrent to evildoing, whether in the family circle or in international relations, is without a compass and without a fixed North Star to guide mankind. The point we are interested in here is that neither pragmatism nor instrumentalism could have developed in a universe as seen by idealism, and certainly not in a world as seen by the heirs of historic Christianity.

Evolutionism

Out of the basic assumption that all existence is nothing more than physical, came also the relatively new answer to the question of origins. How valid is the Genesis account of the origin of the material universe? Though others before and after Darwin have contributed to the concept of origins, origin of the sun, the moon, the stars, our planet, its plants, its animals, man himself, Darwin's Origin of Species,[43] has undoubtedly done more than any other single concept to re-shape man's thinking about himself and his environment; his origin, his nature, his purpose, his education, his destiny. Here is a concept that has really radically changed the immediate and the ultimate objectives, as well as the curriculum, of a good education. Darwin suggested that there is no need for a belief in God in order to account for creation and the great variations in creation, from amoeba to man. There is no God and no metaphysics in Darwin's theory of the Descent of Man. Natural selection, as the explanatory thesis for the development of species was kept free from any kind of idealistic conception of God, and certainly it contained the dynamite that blasted the foundation of Genesis, many of the Psalms, and of John 1.

> At the present day an unusual argument for the existence of an intelligent God is drawn from the deep inward conviction and feelings which are experienced by most men. — Formerly I was led by feelings such as these to the firm conviction of the existence of God and of the immortality of the soul. — But now, (after his visit to the Brazilian forest) the grandest scenes would not cause any such feelings to rise in my mind. — I cannot see that such inward convictions and feelings are of any weight as evidence of what really exists.[44]

There are, as we have hinted before, those tenderhearted philosophers who do not have the courage of stating plainly that they accept the materialistic philosophy of life and of education. So they talk about theistic evolution, theistic humanism, theistic existentialism, theistic realism; but such theistic versions of philosophies which have their origin and their axis of orientation in materialism are a mere front. In reality, these and other versions, such as pragmatism, instrumentalism, operationalism, are transmitters of a materialistic philosophy of life and of education.

Experimentalism

The principal spokesman for this Dewey-related philosophy of existence and of education is Childs.

Like pragmatism and instrumentalism, experimentalism is primarily concerned with method. It tries to shy away from metaphysical problems. But, any philosophy of education, if it wants to be taken seriously, as a philosophy, must come to grips with basic assumptions and beliefs concerning reality, the nature of man, of truth, of ethics, of values and of the good life. Experimentalism does begin and continue with the basic assumption of materialism that all is but matter in motion, that every real existence is an event. Nature, and reality, is a series of beginnings and endings. "The task of education within the school and in society at large is viewed from the perspective of a world order in which the mixture of the stable and the precarious makes 'creative intelligence' the supreme essential."[45]

Progressivism

This represents a continuation and further elaboration of the Peirce-James-Dewey-Childs stream of educational philosophy. A philosopher of educational theory and practice whose name is frequently associated with progressive education, even Progressivism, spelled with a capital "P", may be helpfully quoted.

> We get closer to reality when we are in the thick of things, when we are tilling the soil, running machines; when we participate wholeheartedly in the events of our community, when we become immersed in the empirical stream. Human experience, with its terrible sufferings and its delights, sorrows, joys, beauties, uglinesses, hatred, and loves, this is the reality into which, for better or worse, all men are born, and in which they perform their role until they die. Ontological beliefs that are thus formed on experience may be said to possess a strong evolutionary quality. Experience is struggle. Life is action and change. — Man's unique function is mind. Man's mind exists within the flow of experience, not at all outside of it.— Mind

24

exists only in terms of its activities. Mind is a way of experiencing. Experience is spatial, spreading fanwise. It is limitless.[46]

E: SUMMARY AND CONCLUSION

Now What? What's the answer? What can be done about the problem that tax-supported education in America is dedicated to a purely materialistic and secularistic program of educational objectives, curriculum content, learning experiences?

The court ruling against prayer in public schools has been justified on the ground that the prayer in question was developed and recommended by the Board of Regents of the State of New York. Is anyone so naive as to think that the ruling would have been less exclusive if a parent-teacher group had written and introduced the prayer?

Is the solution in an intensified program of education by the churches and the homes as the late President Kennedy suggested? The churches have only the crumbs of desirable school time left to them: Sundays, Saturdays, summer vacations, evening classes. Intensified parent education? Parents are even now the products of an education which trained them to shrug their shoulders at any training of their youth in which God has a central place.

We have no quarrel with the Supreme Court ruling, designed to confirm the out-lawing of God from tax-supported classrooms. The Supreme Court spelled out what they considered to be the American law, written into the First Amendment of the Constitution.[47]

Our quarrel is with a philosophy of government and of its education which apparently has committed itself to a strict separation of church and state, to the extent of an educational system which excludes God from the classrooms, their objectives, their curricula, and their learning experiences. And one which, in addition, claims an absolute monopoly of the educational tax dollar.

Should all the serious heirs of historic Christianity join Bishop Pike's crusade and "demand action, by constitutional amendment, aimed at erasing the court's decision"?[48]

What's your recommendation? — you say. Do you want to rob the American public school of support? No. Do you want a pluralistic system of schools, patterned after our pluralistic culture? No, even though that appears not altogether inconsistent.

Do you want teacher qualifications to include a test in religion? No. Do you want teachers to teach religious truths that they themselves do not believe? No.

What then do you suggest?

For one thing, I believe that those who are seriously interested in helping to develop the best possible kind of education for Americans should give serious attention to, and come up with some helpful reactions to the concerns expressed by Brubacher:

> There is a current anxiety that the public schools, over-anxious to avoid sectarianism, are neglecting religion and becoming too secular. Is there a religious dimension to education which is being neglected? Would more attention to such a dimension give current education a much-needed stability and sense of direction? Will more attention to religion in the public school confuse the proper spheres of God and Caesar? Should we re-examine the 19th Century tradition of the divorce of church and state in the field of public education?[49]

I also believe that the heirs of the Judeo-Christian heritage would fail if they did not in some constructive way respond to Wild when he states:

> There are the historical facts which seem to show that the most sacrificial generosity, the deepest humility, the most intensive aspiration, and, in short, the highest quality of human life has been elicited by religious faith. This seems true the world over. The maintenance of human culture requires the commitment of millions of individuals to common purposes which elicit real devotion. Many experienced observers with some knowledge of human history doubt if anything short of religious faith is capable of exerting such a widespread and intensive appeal to the minds and hearts of men.[50]

It seems that most sensible tax payers and parents should and do feel that an appreciation of our highest values in American culture should be cultivated somehow in an otherwise exemplary school system, which costs American tax payers some 40 billion dollars annually.

Part-Time Agencies?

Every intelligent and trained educator must agree that so-called part-time agencies are not the answer to the deficiency in tax-supported schools: Sunday periods of 45 minutes or less of what goes by the name of instruction; Saturday morning classes; here and there released-time classes; vacation period classes for two weeks each summer. These make-shifts in education have no special classroom facilities, the teachers are untrained, attendance is voluntary and therefore only about 57% of the enrollment — all of which leads us to conclude that they are not the answer.

Is Change Possible?

We are set in our ways. It's too late to make any radical changes. We cannot back-track. Let good enough alone. That is a common response to suggestions that the present arrangement of having the finest of public school buildings, well equipped, with highly trained teachers, and yet lacking the one thing needful and which is therefore deficient; that somehow, in some way something should be done about it. Apparently, they'd rather be red than dead.

But we did change. During the first 170 years of education in our country, God and prayer, Bible teaching and worship, *did* have a central place in the schools of that America which was the mecca of immigrants. That means that for seven generations God and prayers did have a part in the education of those sturdy, freedom-loving, stand-on-their-own feet, American pioneers. When and why was God excluded from the objectives, the curriculum and the daily schedule of American tax-supported schools?

Institutions of higher learning were practically all planted, nurtured and supported by churches and church-related groups. How did we ever arrive at the point where we spend freely for college and university education but suddenly become very sensitive and

27

conscientious to make sure that no tax dollars are spent on colleges and universities when they are, and because they are, church-related or privately sponsored. Has the state become the only god and helper for worthy causes who must be implored and cajoled into giving a helping hand to research and learning that America needs today as never before?

Was the inauguration of this policy of withholding support from such institutions necessary? Ah, but they are not state-controlled. As though church-sponsored elementary and secondary schools are not controlled. The state directly, or indirectly, through accrediting agencies exerts supervisory control to make sure not only that the physical safety of the students is safe-guarded, but curriculum content, teacher training, and certification, attendance records, counselling provisions, all of these and other factors insure adequately that a good program of education is provided. Tests and testing are multitudinous, so that students themselves and their parents would soon discover if the educational program were below standard.

Why then have parents and churches sold out so completely to the Leviathan, the State?

It is said: We did not want to repeat the European history, with its religious wars. But could we not have retained God in the classroom and at the same time eliminated so-called religious wars? Was it necessary to throw out the baby with the bath? The fact is that countries in Europe to this day have eliminated religious wars and yet have retained God in their educational systems. Excepting of course for those countries which are being squeezed to death behind the iron curtain.

I have before me a recent government publication, official in character, bearing on education in their country. The Department of Public Instruction in nine of the countries responded to my request for literature of this kind. In all and in each of them, it was reported that religion, Scripture, Bible study had a definite assignment in the curriculum and also in the daily schedule: in West Germany, Denmark, Norway, Sweden, Finland, Iceland, England, Wales, and Scotland, and the Netherlands. In the elementary schools there were daily periods of instruction during the week; at the secondary level either daily, biweekly, or three times a week. With these periods allotted to religion they self-evidently have prayers and other forms of worship. Why must the U.S.A. alone, of all freedom-loving countries, line up with the U.S.S.R. in excluding God from their schools?

Then there is the Canadian system of education in which parents are by law permitted to choose between 'separate' schools and public schools, and where subsequently the parents pay their school taxes to support the schools of their choice. Are Canadian and European schools and their living products inferior to those of American schools? In mental alertness the American might excel slightly. But academically, professionally, and vocationally, they are probably superior to the American product.

Here we cannot but recall an incident related in *The Christian Century*[51] a few years ago in which a Syrian mother, having immigrated with her boy from Syria to America and having enrolled her son in an American tax-supported school, discovered to her great dismay that God and prayer received no attention whatsoever in the new school. She cried bitterly and in keen disappointment said: "They have taken away my Lord." Yes, they have, mother, they have taken him out of the instructional materials; too bad, but true.

We feel the time has come, is in fact long overdue, that American mothers and fathers wake up to the fact that they have taken not only the picture of God-in-Christ, but also, the frame for that picture out of our tax-supported schools, and to cry with a swelling resounding through all the land: They have taken away our Lord! We MUST find a way in which believing parents can obtain a schooling for their children and teen-agers in which God has a central place.

Naturalism in Theology

Education and the common school, elementary and secondary, is not the only area of our culture in which the assumption is that reality is made entirely and exclusively by physical entities in motion. Particularly since the Darwinian idea of origins through natural selection and accidental variations has come to be widely accepted, as in fact it has even though in some details the evolutionary theory has gaps and unexplainable factors in it, the theory has had a corroding and eroding influence on many if not all facets of our culture. All natural sciences, all social sciences including psychology, psychiatry, and theology itself have undergone radical changes as a result of the unwarranted assumption that all reality is material, all is in a state of flux, all is therefore relative, all is the result of change and of reconstruction of experience; always with the clear understanding that reality is purely physical.

With theology there is usually linked a cosmology, a sociology, and psychology — psychology literally means a study of the soul — and these disciplines have undergone radical changes. These changes involve primarily the method of research and study and then changes also in content and end results, of course. Thus the concepts of sin, of grace, of guilt, and of forgiveness, of holiness, and the educational process of sanctification, have felt the impact of a naturalistic concept of the ultimate nature of nature.

The sweeping elimination of the supernatural, the wide acceptance of naturalism, the secular or somatic treatment of illness including the illness of the soul, the study of the Scriptures, their origin, their interpretation, their meaning then and today, have come under the kind of world view which we have been discussing in this chapter: Materialism, secularism, naturalism, etc.

Within the Protestant theology of historic Christianity particularly scholarship has been eagerly re-studying the sources of faith with a view to fit them to the naturalistic, evolutionary system of thought. The 'Bauersche Schule' in Tuebingen, produced David Strauss. Strauss in turn wrote Das Leben Jesu, in 1835, in which he advanced the 'Mythical theory' of the Gospel. Adolph Harnack continued the trend in Protestant theology toward realism and naturalism. In his "Das Wesen des Christentums" he identified the Gospel largely with a new ethic. Karl Barth was his student. Barth transmitted the Kierkegaardian existentialism into the arena of theology. The non-theistic branch of existentialism spells out the implication of secularism and materialism in the realm of theology. More recently Rudolph Bultman in his desire to make the Gospel message, the kerygma, more palatable to modern naturalistic and scientific man, has exerted a profound influence on theologians and thus on the heirs of the historic Christianity. Through his Form-Geschichte and Demythologisierung of the Christian heritage Bultman is but reflecting the Western emphasis on science with its tendency to develop a scientism which in turn paves the way for a naturalism which is tantamount to another faith, or a basic, unprovable assumption about the ultimate nature of nature, holding as it does that reality is entirely and exclusively physical and monistically physical.

So it is not only the philosophers in American education who are 'anxious and concerned', but it is in both the protestant and the catholic segments of Christianity, as well as the 'orthodox' segment of Judaism which is fighting a life and death struggle for the retention of God within our Western Culture.

But "We are not ready to embalm the Infinite. Accept Barth and the transcendant God is on his way out," stated Montgomery in a recent lecture on "Is God Dead?" Montgomery's critique of the theothanasia writing included such authors as Vahanian, *The Death of God;* Cox, *The Secular City,* 1965; Althizer, *The Gospel of Christian Atheism;* Hamilton, *The New Essence of Christianity;* Van Buren, *The Secular Meaning of the Gospel;* Stokes, *The Nontheistic Temper of the Modern Mind.*

Despite the trend of such eccentric theological experts, many theologians of scholarly repute, and certainly a large percentage of the 80 million Americans who still worship the Living God, not only on Easter Day but throughout the year, are "not ready to be God's pallbearers." (*Time,* 1/7/66. p. 70)

"We are no ready to embalm the Infinite. As a coroner, for the moment, I have become convinced there is some foul play involved in this particular death. We shall discover that the death-of-God theology represents a case of what mystery writers call the wrong corpse."[52] In other words, not the death of God but the spiritual death of one-time believers, is here finding expression.

The emptiness and the aloneness of many a universe from which

God has been eliminated is touchingly described by Samuel Beckett in *Waiting for Godot.* "No wonder then that life is lonesomely long when one lives it out wandering from meaninglessness to meaninglessness, from idol to idol, and not a hope in sight," says Vahanian, "The Empty Cradle," in *Theology Today.*

"Reputable theologians still believe in a transcendant God, wholly other God, and also of course in an indwelling God", states Eric Erickson in *Young Man Luther.*

Says Montgomery, "We finite cannot comprehend the Infinite. Check your ticket before you board the train of contemporary thought."

The latest attempt to provide for the survival of the God-concept in education is explored by Melzer, in *Functionalism, An Outline of Philosophy Today.* In effect he says that mere man-made, relative, and pragmatic morality is not the answer. For all who are willing to look at this problem objectively, it should be enough to study the moral monstrosity of a Hitler regime and of Marxian morality which declares that whatever helps the spread of Naziism or Communism is good and whatever hinders it is bad. On the American scene the increase of crime, being reported by Hoover as five times as rapid as the population increase, should prompt every thoughtful educator to read with an open mind the nature and results of such pragmatic philosophy. And then to take sides in these crucial issues of education. This volume provides a foundation for hoping against hope that God, the power of the Gospel, and the rejuvenating power of hope in God can be helpful in salvaging our spiritual heritage for coming generations.

The educational philosophies which we have briefly identified have one thing in common. They are based on a belief, on an unproven assumption, that reality and existence is limited to matter in motion, which is a monistic materialism. Another thing, they provide the basic 'faith' and unproven assumption which is the starting point, procedure, and end of tax-supported education in America. The question arises: Are Americans willing to discard into the waste basket, the faith of their fathers, the faith once delivered unto the saints, which has proven its worth in the history of Western culture of yesteryears, even though it is but a faith, for another faith which has nothing in it of 'the faith once delivered unto the saints, nothing of God, of eternal values, of eternal life, of immortality, and, by implication, nothing of freedom? As for this writer, and if he may be permitted to speak for the serious heirs of historic Christianity, including in many respects the heirs of the Judeo-Christian heritage, their answer is, NO. They are not ready to accept the summary conclusion of Reissner:

> With Darwin's theory the Aristotelian concept of changeless genera, species, and forms eternally setting the limits for the reproduction of individual organisms, was no longer tenable. The universe of changeless order had become a universe of endless change in the Western World.[53]

The heirs of historic Christianity choose to stay with "The unchanging Christ in a Changing World." They are seriously interested in an education for their children in which the objectives, the curriculum, the daily experiences and the daily schedule reflect their sincere, and we think, commendable desire to include "the fruit of the Spirit which is love, joy, peace, long-suffering, gentleness, goodness, faith, meekness, and temperance."[54] And they are equally serious about an education which in its objectives, curricula, instructional materials, experiences, reflects the earnest desire to eliminate, as far as possible, the natural tendency of men to indulge in "the works of the flesh, such as: adultery, fornication, uncleanness, lasciviousness, idolatry, witchcraft, hatred, variance, emulations, wrath, strife, seditions, heresies, envyings, murder, drunkenness, revellings and such like."[55]

CHAPTER II

MAN — ANTHROPOLOGY

A. THE PROBLEM

What then is man? In education, as indeed in government and the study of history, there is only one question that is greater: What is the nature of nature? Is there a God who created and who preserves the universe and man? Man is admittedly dust and he will again turn to dust as even devout believers admit when they say on the cemetery: Dust to dust. Ashes to ashes. Is there a valid basis for continuing that service in the words: It is sown in corruption; it is raised in incorruption. . . . It is sown a natural body; it is raised a spiritual body?[1]

What is the origin, the nature and the destiny of man? Has the study of anthropology made the Genesis story untenable?[2] Did God create man in His own image, or did man evolve from an ape-like ancestor? What has research in biology uncovered regarding man?

> What is the question now placed before society? This: Is man an ape? I repudiate this view with indignation and abhorrence. The church teaches us that man is made in the image of his Creator, a source of inspiration, a solace, a source from which only can flow every principle of morals and every divine truth. It is between these two contending interpretations of the nature of man and their consequences that society will have to decide. This rivalry is at the bottom of all human affairs. Upon our acceptance of that divine interpretation all sound and salutary legislation depends. That truth is the only security for civilization and the only guarantee for real progress.[3]

Again, "The struggle which centers in Berlin is seen by Eisenhower as a struggle between the *spiritual and the material interpretation* of man and his destiny."[4]

Henry Luce goes on to interpret Eisenhower as saying: On the two sides of the barbed wire and masonry wall raised by communists, two powerful philosophies which hold precise but opposite conceptions of man, find expression. On the East stands a complete philosophy of materialism, which defines man as a mere machine, soulless, and therefore fit only to be used as a slave for the glorification of the state. On the West stands the belief that man is a creature made in the image of his Creator. "What an enigma! What a monster! What a worm! Judge of all things, yet the sink of iniquity and error."[5]

What is the origin, the nature and the destiny of man? Is he by inheritance morally corrupt and bad? What of original sin? What about the possibility of changing human nature? "Can the leopard change his spots?" What about man's real potentials? Who am I? Whence have I come? What am I here for? Where do I end up? These are questions which confused young people are asking. This points up the importance of these questions.

Statesmen, social planners, educators, theologians, they all must regard the questions raised above as of primary importance. Long ago it was said, the most important study of man is man. Purposeful educational programs must and do invariably begin with basic assumptions and beliefs concerning man: his nature and his potentials. It is self-evident that educational objectives and programs vary in keeping with the answer given to the questions raised here. If man is different from the amoeba, the snail, the anthropoid apes, only in degree, but not in nature, it is obvious that educators must identify the factor by which man has become differentiated in degree from the lower forms of life; and education must then concentrate on the further development of those factors so that men, as a group and as individual persons, may reach their full potential as a species, and as individuals. If on the other hand man was created in the image of God but became alienated from God because of sin, education must concentrate on these facts, and it must bend all its efforts on fostering God-likeness and inseparable union with God as the ongoing and ultimate goal of education.

> A Christian doctrine of *man* is basic to any program of Christian education. A program that operates with something less or other than a Christian understanding of persons is likely to produce something less than or other than Christian persons.[6]

An educator who operates on a materialistic philosophy of education is in the position of one who is "riding a tiger." He can't get off.[7]

It makes a world of difference in the statement of objectives, of curriculum writers, of classroom teachers whether they have little animals, different only because they are more intelligent, in the classroom; or whether they have the off-spring of persons whose original forbears were created, created to be like God; alienated from God through sin; redeemed by the love of God in Christ; sanctified by the Holy Spirit operating through the Word and Sacrament; destined for a life of service to fellowman and to the glory of God, in time and hereafter forever and ever. An education based on these basic assumptions or beliefs, is bound to be radically different from a merely secular and purely naturalistic education. Informed parents will not say: What's the difference, public or parochial school?

B. MAN FROM THE VIEWPOINT OF THE
    JUDEO-CHRISTIAN HERITAGE

> And God said, Let us make man in our image, after our own likeness. And let them have dominion over the fish of the sea, and over the fowl of the air, and over the cattle, and over all the earth. So God created man in His own image, in the image of God created He him, male and female created He them.[8]

Racial discrimination and racial pride have no place in the history of man as seen by the heirs of historic Christianity. "And hath made of *one blood* all nations of men for to dwell on the face of the earth."[9]

The darkest chapter in the history of man is the story of sin and disobedience. Because of it "The Lord God sent him forth from the garden of Eden, to till the ground from which he was taken."[10] To understand man aright it is necessary to view him in the light that shone over Bethlehem about 1965 years ago, and in the light that shines from Calvary's cross. "In the beginning was the Word, and the Word was with God, and the Word was God."[11] "And the Word was made flesh and dwelt among us, and we beheld his glory, the glory as of the only begotten of the Father, full of grace and truth."[12]

The brightest chapter in the history of an individual person comes at a time when he is again united with God, through faith in Christ and through the forgiveness of sins. "As many as received Him to them gave He power to become the sons of God."[13] And there we remember that "Baptism doth also now save us."

At this point a person is born again. He is a new creature. He shares in the very nature of God. He begins to live not only secularly, not only naturally, but spiritually; he lives henceforth the eternal life. He has a foretaste of the joys of heaven. "And this is life eternal that they might know Thee, the only true God, and Jesus Christ whom Thou has sent."[14]

Man redeemed from sin by the sacrificial love of God, called by the Gospel, enlightened and sanctified is henceforth free and immortal. His status, his nature, his destiny, has taken on a new turn for something higher, greater, better. He is no more dust and dust only. He is no more merely secular. No more merely natural. The unbelievable has become a reality. Death is no longer the end of the trail. A regenerated Christian is a person who lives and works to the honor and glory of God, his Creator and Preserver, his Redeemer, and his Sanctifier; and he continues to glorify God. Was there ever a song of victory more exultant and more grand in its significance than that of the inspired writer Paul who wrote to the heirs of historic Christianity in Corinth. "O death, where is thy sting? O grave, where is thy victory? But thanks be to God which giveth us the victory through our Lord Jesus Christ."[15] Can the last evil be really and radically overcome?

In the very face of experiences in the natural world, the heirs of historic Christianity can say with confidence and conviction, at the very side of a 6-foot hole in the ground, ready to receive the earthly remains of a departed one: "It is sown a natural body; it is raised a spiritual body. There *is* a natural body and there *is* a spiritual body."[16]

As for the soul of the believer, Jesus, the Truth and the Life itself, said to the penitent malefactor on the Cross "Verily I say unto thee, To day thou shalt be with me in Paradise."[17] And let it be noted that the writer who made a record of these words was not originally a theologian. He was an M.D., one trained scientifically to deal with the body and its ills. Thoughtful man's highest goals have always centered in God and freedom and immortality. The believing heirs of historic Christianity have found all three: God, freedom and immortality. They have found it in the Messiah, Son of God and Savior of sinners. "If the Son therefore shall make you free, ye shall be free indeed."[18]

Man is no longer a slave to himself, to his passions and his natural appetites; he is no longer a means to another man's end in life; he is self-subsistent; he really exists. Yes, he still obeys the laws of God and of man, provided the latter do not conflict and run contrary to laws of God; i.e., the law of love. But he obeys because he finds joy in doing it; he wants to live that way; it is his privilege as a free man to live creatively and joyfully, in blessed union and cooperation with God. There man finds his real fulfillment, in the life that is hidden with Christ in God. Man is restless until he finds rest in God.

Must the "giving of an account" after death be taken seriously? All are agreed "it is appointed unto man once to die." Taxes and death, it has been said are inescapable. But "after this judgment." How many are agreed on that? And what comes after judgment? Is it a continuation of inseparable union with God? Or is it eternal alienation from God, in outer darkness? Or has the Catholic concept of purgatory, of progressive purification, a basis in reality? Is Easter based on fact or fancy? The answers to these and similar questions are beyond the realm of reason and experimentation. They are matters of faith. The heirs of Christianity trust the promise of Him: "Who is the same, yesterday, today and forever," and who said: "I will never leave thee nor forsake thee."[19] Christian education orbits around the Cross and the Living Christ. Any education which by-passes such issues as death and immortality and claims to be all inclusive has no claim on validity. And so the objectives of Lutheran education, as in fact the education sponsored by any and all serious heirs of historic Christianity, stand in rather sharp contrast to objectives in all educational efforts and systems which exclude or do not include, this conception of man. The objectives of God-centered education are the most important factors in education, radically different from both matter-centered and idea-centered or man-centered education.

While all honest and serious heirs of historic Christianity have the basic ideas concerning man in common this does not mean that they agree one hundred percent in all facets of this matter. Take the theology and educational philosophy of Catholicism, for example: while Catholic and Protestant education have common ground to stand on, they do not agree in all respects.

> The fall of man means simply the rejection and loss of the supernatural life. . . . For the restoration of man to this supernatural life of grace, God chose His own Son, the Second Adam, who took upon himself our own human nature. Through His Incarnation, Life, Passion, Death and Resurrection He gloriously atoned for Adam's sin. God's plan was with the Second Adam and thus, united with the very source of supernatural life, since He is God, be in a state better even than before the Fall. . . . In the mass, the priest pours water into the wine, thus symbolizing the union of our human nature with the divine nature of Christ.[20]

The image of man and consequent goals of Catholic education were stated similarly by Pope Pius XI:

> The supernatural completes the natural. Gratia percifit naturam, Grace perfects nature. A Catholic is neither Maniche nor Puritan: The true Christian product of Christian

39

education is the supernatural man who thinks, judges and acts consistently in accordance with right reason illumed by the supernatural light of the example and teaching of Christ.[21]

A spokesman for Protestant education indicates by the following quote that the Protestant concept of man has in it the elements of New Testament theology, but it also shows the influence of secular image of man. "Original sin" is one of those facets of the image of man which reveals variant modifications of that image.

The doctrine of original sin has sometimes been interpreted as an assertion that man in his original nature was sinful. It means rather that we are born into a humanity whose alienation from God influences our development long before we are ever conscious of it. There is in us a propensity toward self-centeredness. We are part of sinful humanity the depth of whose involvement in sin is revealed in the cross. It is in the heart of humanity even the most virtuous and religious humanity, to crucify the Son of God, and not by accident, but because as the revealer of the will of God, he is an affront to the proud will of man.[22]

Even a leading secularist in educational philosophy, makes some concessions to the historic Biblical concept of man when he states: "We all know that civilized man has a background of bestiality and superstition and that these elements are still with us."[23] Yet it is obvious that he is speaking of the nature of man in terms of biological evolution, according to which the progenitors of the human family were beasts in the field and in the trees. In keeping with this concept of man, his past and his future, Dewey could not possibly get beyond the goal of education as being the development of man's ability to think, to solve his problems and to progress toward higher, though purely natural, levels of living, for the individual and for society.

Liberal Protestant theology and education has been strongly influenced by the concept of man as held by idealistic philosophers. Hegel helped to make that transition from the Christian concept of man to the image held by idealism: "All that is real is rational. And all that is rational is real. Thinking and its thought product, the idea, is the primary; nature is the derived element."[24]

One finds these idealistic thoughts sprinkled in the spoken and printed words of Protestant and quasi-Protestant exponents of the concept of God and of man all about us. Man invariably is then presented as his own savior, in no need of a God who saves from sin. "Our minds, all our faculties are of God, like cells in the great universal plan. Man is a manifestation of God. Anyone can help himself by having the right thoughts."[25] Thus we see that the "sacred" or Biblical image of man has been considerably modified by the influence of idealism and secularism today as we shall note in the next section.

C. THE IMAGE OF MAN AMONG
IDEALISTICALLY ORIENTED PHILOSOPHERS

Man must be seen in his larger frame of reference. Idealism holds that the larger frame of reference is essentially spiritual in nature.

Idealism was and is essentially an attempt to hold the line against the upsurge of materialistically oriented philosophies. Hence idealism, also in its concept of man has major elements of historic Christianity in its description of man. It uses much of the vocabulary of the heirs of Judeo-Christian heritage. Thus Horne, probably the most widely accepted exponent of idealism in philosophy of education states: "Summing up the conception of the learner, our philosophy (idealism) dares to suggest that the learner is a finite person, that his real origin is deity, that his nature is freedom, and that his destiny is immortality."[26]

The fact that the universe is rational, orderly and predictable provides the idealist with a basis for concluding that man has essentially the marks of the universe and that he is in the first place a rational creature. The evidence of man's immortality lies in the rationality of the universe. The belief in man's immortality is a logical consequence of believing in the reality, universality, the pre-existence and the eternity of mind in the world. Education has the task of stimulating and guiding learners into the likeness of an infinite, eternal, idea, ideal or personality.

In 1957 the Religious Education Association sponsored a National Convention in Chicago. The entire conference program was centered in "Images of Man in Current Culture." On their programs they presented "images" of man as these were conceived by the three principal categories of philosophies of education. Following is the concept of man as presented by the idealistically oriented philosophy of education.

> Man is a product of nature and society. He is not definable wholly or chiefly by his biological needs, but also by ideals and values, through which his impulses are transformed. The distinctive characteristics of man are his freedom, his use of symbols, and his intelligence, which underlie his power to envisage and actualize his ideal possibilities. The goals of life are personal integration, a democratic society, and a maximum fulfillment of moral and spiritual capacities, such as the ability to love, to create and appreciate beauty, seek the truth and make intelligent ethical choices. These values are founded in a faith in progress and in the ultimacy of the process of creative emergence, in which existing structures undergo continuous reconstruction in the light of developing needs.[27]

The Religious Education Association which sponsored this conference and initiated this free for all discussion of the nature of man acted on the assumption that our culture is pluralistic; that it provides a diversity of images of man; that our political systems, our economic and social life, our literature, our arts and sciences and our religious traditions all assume and portray varying images of man; that mass media, as the press, radio, television, movies and advertising, make these images vivid for millions of viewers and listeners; that every educational and religious institution, assumes and fosters its own version of images of man. They suggest that children and teen-agers get their self-image from various sources; and that in the end these images will make a real difference in the kind of personalities and characters that grow out of these images. Hence the need for examining and appraising some of these prevailing images of man and considering the tasks of education and religion with respect to them. Here lies also the need for and the purpose of this unit on MAN in a philosophy of education. Following a presentation of the secular, or materialistic and evolutionary, concept of man we shall take note of current trends in literature which have tried to spell out the influence and further development of a culture which is increasingly materialistic, secular, natural and pragmatic. Such a culture moves from an attitude of complacency, i.e., apathetic indifference to God and godly values, to a state of mind that is increasingly rebellious against God and fellowman and ends up in an attitude of bombastic, house-wrecking nihilism. If true, it behooves us both as church people and as citizens to do what Brubacher bids educational philosophers do, examine the ship of our culture to see whether our compass and our rudder are properly set.

Without finalizing with too great finality, it might be noted here that if, as we are told, there is not a ghost of a chance for God and prayer and the vessel of our spiritual heritage, the Bible, to re-enter the one million, give or take a few, classrooms supported by taxes, in America, we of that historic Christianity heritage, ought possibly to explore the potentials of an idealistically-oriented tax-supported public educational system in America. Idealism would, at least, bring into the educational scene a sort of north star point of fixation, from which our rudder and compass in educational philosophy can be adjusted. The absolutes of idealism could conceivably alert teachers and learners once again to the absolute fact that fixed, unchanging, eternal, pre-existent, and eternally existent, truths do exist and that it is the teachers' and learners' task to re-discover these eternal truths of reality and truth, and of ethics and morality; that man IS responsible for what he does or fails to do; that man must give an account, that he cannot finally blame his ancestors nor his environment. This might help to stem the flood of licentious behavior with regard to the 4th, the 5th, the 6th and the 7th Commandments, in fact all of the Decalogue.

Let us now take a brief but critical look at the image of man as conceived and promoted by materialistically-oriented philosophies of education.

D. MATERIALISTICALLY ORIENTED CONCEPTS OF MAN

There are those who have held that no dictionary definition of man is possible. Man must be observed in action to gain a valid image of him. Similarly it is said that God cannot be pictured in propositions. God, it is said, has revealed Himself through a series of actions, such as creation, redemption, sanctification. God has revealed Himself in the birth, life, teaching, death and resurrection of His son, Jesus. Scriptures, it is also said, are not a static picture of God and man. They are rather the result of events, of things that have been done, things that have happened. So also with man. There appears to be a reluctance to say more about the nature of man than that he has behaved in certain ways. His mind also, largely assessed by Dewey, has ceased to be regarded as a static entity. It is rather thought of as a function of the total organism. It leads the organism to intelligent and appropriate action in given situations, actions that make for survival.

Materialistically-oriented philosophers have turned thumbs down on conceptions of man which are idealistically oriented as well as on concepts of man which are found in Genesis and in all parts of the Old and the New Testament. Elliot, an eminent spokesman for the materialistic conception of man, protests against the continued belief in those entities which are vaguely described as "spiritual."

> To this category belong not only ghosts, gods, souls ad hoc genus omne, for these have long been rejected from the beliefs of most advanced thinkers. The time has now come to include also in the condemned list that further imaginary entity which we call "mind," consciousness, together with its various sub-species of intellect, will, feeling, in so far as they are supposed to be independent of or different from material existences. . . . I will not deny that it (mind) is a direct datum of experience. But, there is no direct datum of experience to the effect that it is anything different from cerebral processes.[28]

As the Copernican system radically changed man's concept of the universe, and earth's place in the solar system, so similarly a book published in 1859, and written by Charles Darwin,[29] did bring about a revolutionary concept of man, his origin, his nature, and his place in the inorganic and organic world. Most of the learned dissertations about man, prior to 1859 in both theology and philosophy, have become relatively small issues, in the light of the overwhelming new assertion that man is continuous with nature, that he is different from animals only in degree, that his intelligence

44

is the most distinctive characteristic of man, that it alone helped man to emerge and to survive, in the ongoing battle for existence and sustenance. While biological evolution is vulnerable, from chemists, physicists, anthropologists, sociologists, it is nevertheless a theory of the origin of species, including man, which is almost taken as something that comes near to being a self-evident truth, also in educational philosophy.

> "The great antiquity of mankind upon earth has been conclusively established," writes Lewis H. Morgan, in *Ancient Society*. "The latest investigations respecting the early conditions of the human race are tending to the conclusion that mankind commenced their career at the bottom of the scale and worked their way up from savagery to civilization through the slow accumulation of experimental knowledge."[30]

The one most important factor in the evolutionary process by which man evolved as man was his ability and his willingness to think. It was his higher than animal IQ that helped him to become differentiated and to survive. For his thinking led to inventions, discoveries; to social organizations, from simple families, to phratries, to tribes, to nations, to international organizations. Intelligence helped man to evolve tools. Tools helped him to produce creature comforts in ever greater quantities. And, if we are to follow Marx and the philosophy of Lenin, Stalin, and Khrushchev, Utopia for man will have arrived when the instruments of productive labor will have been communized, and man will then have become a contented, non-competitive, unselfish organism in a classless society. The economic environment will be such as to have brought about the regeneration and transformation of man into a new creature and into a more abundant life. Of course, that optimistic faith needs yet to be verified. At this stage of man's development history seems plainly to say: Never. The weaknesses of man that made him horribly inhuman to fellowman in the past will, alas, continue despite of living in a land in which creature comforts are available in abundance as never before in the history of man. As civilized man approaches the phantom of a fearless life, new enemies emerge that cause man to live in dread fear of

45

things to come. The condition of human existence which John foresaw for those human beings which would die in the faith of the Lamb of God and described as being a state in which, "They shall hunger no more, neither thirst anymore; neither shall the sun light on them nor any heat. For the Lamb which is in the midst of the throne shall feed them, and shall lead them unto living fountains of water: and God shall wipe away all tears from their eyes."[31]

It is this state of Utopia which has been envisaged by many social philosophers, from Plato to Marx. For living here and now, Man has successfully provided himself with creature comforts in an ever increasing measure, reaching its highest pinnacle of perfection in the U.S.A. And the USSR hopes to forge ahead in this enterprise and surpass the capitalistic man within a foreseeable time.

Unfortunately history does not seem to support the corollary thesis that if man is once supplied with creature comforts he will be peace-loving, congenial and contented. Nor does history support the belief that man's egocentric tendencies will be arrested and that he will be transformed into a theocentric organism, or that, since God will long have been dead, into an altero-centric being.

Current trends in the fine arts, especially in literature, seem to say that in a culture in which man has become indifferent to God, man moves on into a state of mind in which he is totally bewildered, confused; to a state in which he is increasingly on the warpath against all authority; in which he sees no meaning; and in which he shows signs of becoming utterly disgusted with existence; inclines to be nihilistic and would end humanity and his abode, the earth. The following are illustrations of what we mean. The literature of complacency and indifference to an unchangeable fate is reminiscent of the "apatheia" and the "ataraxeia" philosophy of the Greeks. The despair of those who are caught in the maelstrom of atheism is illustrated by those who wait hopelessly for Godot. The spirit of defiance breathes in Caitlin Thomas' *Leftover Life*.[32] a somewhat similar character is pictured in John Osborne's *Look Back in Anger*. "He rants at her like a wounded adolescent, shrieking until the world shall listen to his story of pain, anger and unfocussed frustration."[33] Osborne's characters are

46

in desperate flight out of the pain of being human into an animal anesthesia. Tennessee Williams' main character ends up as a carcass, picked up by the street cleaners from an alley. His *Camino Real* is even surpassed by his *Cat On The Hot Tin Roof*.[34] This is a drama of defiance which conveys the idea that man is a beast and that he will die. Sex and money are the only honest goals in his life. It reads like a medley of lechery, alcoholism, homosexuality, blasphemy, greed, brutality, hatred, obscenity. If this is realistic realism in America of the second half of the twentieth century, as it pretends to be, it is very much like that of Rome in the days preceding its fall, as described by Paul in his letter to the Romans.

> Behind a facade of "wisdom" they became just fools, fools who would exchange the glory of the eternal God for an imitation image of a mortal man, or of creatures that run or fly or crawl. They gave up God: and therefore God gave them up — to be the playthings of their own foul desires in dishonoring their own bodies.

> These men deliberately forfeited the Truth of God and accepted a lie, paying homage and giving service to the creature instead of to the Creator, who alone is worthy to be worshipped for ever and ever, Amen. God therefore handed them over to disgraceful passions. Their women exchanged the normal practices of sexual intercourse for something which is abnormal and unnatural. Similarly the men, turning from natural intercourse with women, were swept into lustful passions for one another. Men with men performed these shameful horrors, receiving, of course, in their own personalities the consequences of sexual perversity.

> Moreover, since they considered themselves too high and mighty to acknowledge God, He allowed them to become the slaves of their degenerate minds, and to perform unmentionable deeds. They became filled with wickedness, rottenness, greed and malice: their minds became steeped in envy, murder, quarrelsomeness, deceitfulness and spite. They became whisperers-behind-doors, stabbers-in-the-back, God-haters; they overflowed with insolent pride and boastfulness, and their minds teemed with diabolical invention.

They scoffed at duty to parents; they mocked at learning, recognized no obligations of honor, lost all natural affection, and had no use for mercy. More than this — being well aware of God's pronouncement that all who do these things deserve to die, they not only continued their own practices, but did not hesitate to give their thorough approval to others who did the same.[35]

In the light of this quote from Paul we can understand why he was determined to bring a new element into the curriculum of education to the people of the ancient decaying world. This urge was prompted in part by the grace of God to Paul and partly by an awareness of the unmet needs of the people of Rome, as he expressed this desire for reformation of the education of these peoples of his day:

I feel myself under a sort of universal obligation, I owe something to all men, from cultured Greek to ignorant savage. That is why I want, as far as my ability will carry me, to preach the Gospel to you who live in Rome as well. For I am not ashamed of the Gospel. I see it as the very power of God working for the salvation of everyone who believes it, both Jew and Greek. I see in it God's plan for imparting righteousness to men, a process begun and continued by their faith. For, as the scripture says: The righteous shall live by faith.[36]

The long-range effects of a materialistic conception of man, of naturalism and secularism in sixteen years of education, are in the process of becoming evident even now. And we have not even resorted to the statistical analyses of FBI reports on the increase in crime and juvenile delinquency. We share fully, as the reader may have concluded by this time, John Brubacher's six-fold "current anxieties" among philosophers of education, reaching into the concerns of parents, classroom educators, law makers, judges and prison wardens. At this point we refer particularly to his first-named anxiety: "There is a current anxiety that *modern education is adrift without rudder, chart or compass.*"[37] Is there a way of regaining our sense of direction? he asks. Are there no enduring structures in culture? Is culture altogether relativistic? The heirs of historic Christianity believe there are enduring structures in culture. There is a basis for absolute truth and morality in education.

E. SUMMARY AND CONCLUSION

Christians regard themselves as citizens in two countries. They are citizens of the country in which they were born, live and have their earthly sustenance. They regard themselves also as citizens in the kingdom of God. They are anxious to be good citizens in both kingdoms. They want to "render unto Caesar the things that are Caesar's and unto God the things that are God's."[38] Living in a free and democratic country, they desire to participate in the affairs of the community. They are anxious to help in improving what appears to be in need of improvement. Even though segments of Christianity — particularly such as the Roman Catholic, Lutheran, Episcopalian, Seventh Day Adventist and Christian Reformed — maintain their own church-sponsored schools, they nevertheless have a real and a sustained interest in making tax-supported education, in America, and in Western Culture, the very best possible under the circumstances. The principle of separation of Church and State has been a large step away from a state-supported church and a church-supported state. Hence our interest in improving the public schools so that they meet more nearly the real needs of America's children and teen-agers. But, what *are* the real needs of man?

We admit that much has been learned through the scientific study of man, as individual and as a group. Through observation, history, psychology, psycho-analysis, sociology, anthropology, even chemistry, physics and biology, much information about man has been accumulated which helps the theologians to be better informed educators, pastors and counsellors; also legislators, judges and prison administrators. But we also hold that much of the wisdom of the ages, of God's self-revelation in the Holy Scriptures, has been pushed aside as obsolete and non-relevant in the 20th century, not understandable and not applicable to modern man. We believe that particularly the theory of man's biological evolution through self-initiated solutions to his problems of survival, has

49

been prematurely accepted and acted on as valid for a good program of educating the young.

The theory that all existences including man are dust and dust only is not well established. Our misgivings stem from many sources. Two of these have already been briefly indicated: The hypothetical character of the basic assumption concerning the origin, nature, purpose and destiny of man; and the disturbing social and moral trends in those countries in which this, or these, hypotheses have been assumed to be valid and adequate for a good education of man.

First, we should hear a few more witness for the retention of God in the classrooms of America. Particularly at this time in relation to the concept of man, and the nature of the educand and his basic needs. We note that even realists agree with the heirs of historic Christianity that man is not the measure of truth. Which is to say that "becoming known is an event that happens to things assumed to exist prior to and independently of the act of knowing. . . . Theory of knowledge is the birthplace of contentions."[39] For that reason educational philosophers ought to learn and remember also what God, who is the final measure of all things, has contributed to our knowledge of man, his origin, nature, purpose, his weaknesses and his potentials. God as Creator, Redeemer and Sanctifier of man has revealed much valid information about man.

Elimination of the Scriptures, i.e., the Bible, the Word of God, from the curriculum and instructional materials of tax-supported schools was an event of far-reaching consequences. To have the leaders of public schools feel that they can single-handedly meet the needs of growing children and teen-agers without the experiences that grow out of the use of the Bible; or for Christians to feel that they can tack on this vital part of our total culture with a brief one hour on Sunday morning, with non-professional teachers, in facilities where five to ten classes meet in one room at the same time, is to do several things: It is to say to the growing child and teen-ager: God and whatever His Word has to say is really not very important today. You can get a good education even though you ignore God and learn nothing about what the

Scriptures say concerning you and whence you are, why you are here and where you are going. Again, this is one way of impoverishing our culture. Take the spiritual element out of our culture and you have robbed it of something very rich, stimulating, refining, ennobling, and life-giving. "Gnothi se auton," said the Greeks. The boys and girls will neither know the universe nor will they know themselves unless they learn to see themselves in the light of the "'mystery, the tragedy and the salvation of man,"[40] which they contact in the sacred writings.

In a plea to retain the sacred image of man, in contrast to the mere secular image of man, Shinn continued to say:

> Behind the confusion of our times, the sacred image of man can point to the genuine mystery of selfhood. Behind frustration and despair it can point to the authentic tragedy in human life. Behind the schemes of manipulations, which have proved all to feeble to deal with the dark archangels of our day, it can point to the gift of salvation from a living God. The sacred image of Christian faith is the image of God in action in Jesus Christ. Through him we discover what it is to know God, and neighbor and self.[41]

Supporting this thesis that educators should by all means retain the sacred image of man is Gustav Weigel, S.J., who addressed the same National Conference of the Religious Education Association, "The notion of man in Christ is dynamic twenty-four hours of the day. No phase of human existence is left untouched by it, precisely because it elevates the whole man so that nothing human is left excluded."[42]

To some readers the support of an Encyclical on Christian education, coming from Pius XI will bear some weight, in defense of the theses here defended that despite all that anthropology, and materialistically-oriented psychology claims to have discovered about man, we still ought to continue to build on the basic assumption and belief that man is more than different in degree from the animal world: "The proper and immediate end of Christian education is to cooperate with divine grace in forming

51

the true and perfect Christian, that is to form Christ himself in those who are regenerated by baptism."[43]

All the arguments about man's collective strength to overcome all obstacles to progress, to overcome also the inherent weaknesses of man, including what theologians know as "original sin," to make man to be more perfect and unselfish, leaves the heirs of historic Christianity cold. For sure, man's collective strength cannot overcome time nor death. We cannot enter into this new "hymn of hope," nor do we believe that our youth should be taught that democracy does all and more than the Christian religion ever accomplished for man.

> A new articulateness, a new sense of collective strength, a newly wrathful but righteous indignation, a new hymn of hope for the fulfillment of a world-wide democratic humanity, all are mingled together in a vast, rumbling, infinitely powerful mass of hundreds of millions of men of many colors, levels of culture. . . . The imminent task before us is to harness the schools to this strength, to this giant of democratic power.[44]

Christians are quite agreed that in an age of plenty no one should need to starve in this wide world. As far as creature comforts are concerned and sharing this kind of wealth, they believe that a democratic world can achieve this kind of "greatest happiness for the greatest number" more effectively than any other kind of government including that of communism. Christians believe that, and they believe this is important for the welfare of man because their theology has laid the basic foundation for this kind of philosophy of government. But that is still a far way from agreeing that therefore we can now dispense with the faith of our fathers and substitute for it the faith of Dewey or Brameld.

We do not agree that Thorndike's conception of the original nature of man is watertight. On the assumption that man is different from a Chimpanzee only in degree, Thorndike advanced the thesis that biological urges, drives, desires, wants, are the original determiners of man's behavior. Supplied with the satisfiers of these wants man is on the way of becoming angelic in his attitudes and behavior. Man wants and needs more than those material things that satisfy his hunger, thirst, rest, sleep, warmth, coolness, action, sex, escape when frightened, riddance of pain. Nor are we willing to accept the thesis that these material things are the final determiners of values, the arbiters of that which is right and wrong, good or bad; good if they help man to obtain these satisfiers and bad if they hinder the acquisition of these things; beautiful if they bring the human being closer to these soothers of his appetites, ugly if they hinder or prevent the gratification of these biological appetites.[45]

"Arguments used to support biological evolution of man are assembled and used to rationalize a theory, a substitute for God," says Clark in his *Darwin: Before and After.*[46]

"Beyond similarity in biological needs, man has no similarity with animals at all, save so far as both came from the powers of the same Creator," says Karl W. Keller, in his article on *Basic Aims of Education.*[47]

"What makes man a 'homo sapiens'?" this author goes on to ask. "The setting up of distinctly human ways of carrying on animal activities, the setting up of values, the use of symbols to express ideas, the ability to think, the ability to change his environment to make it more suitable, the use of accumulated knowledge, the aspiring to an ideal."[48]

While we agree with this definition of "homo sapiens" it could be after all a matter of differing from the higher vertebrates only in degree. Something has been left unsaid or unemphasized here. We invariably come back to the truth well expressed by an eminent Presbyterian educator: "A Christian doctrine of man is basic to any program of Christian education, a program that operates with something less than or other than a Christian understanding of persons is likely to produce something less than or other than a Christian person. The starting point for a Christian in his definition of true humanity is Jesus Christ. He is for us, not only the revelation of the true God, but also of man."[49]

Historic Christianity and idealistically oriented philosophy are still agreed today that materialistically oriented interpretation of existence is inadequate and untenable. Paul E. Klopsteg is a professor of Physics at Northwestern University, Evanston, and a former President of the American Association for the Advancement of Science. In an address titled "This I Believe" given at the Sunday Evening Club in Orchestra Hall, Chicago, on April 7, 1963, he stated among other things:

> These (natural laws) in so far as they are known, were discovered by human intelligence. However, the operations of nature in accordance with natural laws are independent of human intelligence. All evidence indicates that these laws are immutable and unchanging. I find no alternative to the belief that when matter and energy were created, the natural laws came simultaneously into existence, and, I repeat, they are immutable and unchanging. Were this not true and were nature capricious instead of orderly, the universe were chaotic and unpredictable. The order and dependability of nature's laws are the common denominator of all research in science. The single satisfactory explanation for this remarkable fact is an infallible intelligence by which such order was ordained "in the beginning." From such considerations I have arrived at the strong conviction that laws of nature are the principles established through the infinite wisdom of God, supreme, omniscient, beyond the comprehension of man. . . . Man's appearance on this planet is but one manifestation of the orderly operation of the Laws of God. Accordingly, as a basis for my philosophy, I believe in God. . . . I accept Jesus' teaching as the time-tested means for establishing what He called the Kingdom of God, a workable philosophy by which we should strive to live.[50]

The trouble with current attempts to develop an adequate conception of man, says Portman, is that writers start invariably with the assumption that there is nothing distinctive and unique about man. "The most widely known and accepted conception of man as a biological development invariably refers to the most highly developed mammal as norm for man and they thus from the very beginning cancel out of the make-up of man that which is most distinctive and unique about man, and thus cancel out the incomparable, the spiritual, in man."[51]

Some modern Protestant theologians have accepted the secular and naturalistic image of man and have blasted unwittingly the foundations of their heritage. Bultmann, for example, is a great scholar. He had good intentions. He was intent on making the Gospel relevant to modern man in our day. But he started with a wrong criterion of truth. In *"Der Moderne Mensch,"* he started with man as the measure of all things. From there he proceeded to use the Christian community, the local congregation, the Church, as the source of truth. Thus he enclosed God in a finite community. He did in the Church what Dewey did in the community. Made it i.e., man, the source of truth, the arbiter of right and wrong.[52] This tendency to deify man leaves no room for the Living God, not even when that man, or group of men, is made up of regenerate, born again men.

This is not to say that only the Scriptures and the Confessions of the Church may be used in arriving at an image of man. That would mean to perpetuate an uninformed image of man. Psychology, psychiatry, sociology, anthropology, have a contribution to make to an informed concept of nature, including man. "What Then Is Man," a Graduate Study, III, written by men on the staff of Concordia Seminary, St. Louis, and of the Graduate School of the University of Minnesota, have made that point clear, in a plea to pastors, religious educators, psychologists and psychiatrists to get together, learn from each other and learn to speak and understand each other's vocabulary.[53] In the Foreword of this study we read:

> This study is of particular significance for our day. It seeks to grapple with one of the most crucial issues confronting theology, namely, what to make of the insights and concept of theology and psychiatry. Both have contributed too much to an understanding of human nature to be ignored. Yet both often proceed as though theology did not exist or as though it were a subject smacking of the superstition of a previous age.[54]

It is true, and all Christian educators need to remind themselves that we no longer live in a pre-Copernican nor in a pre-Darwinian age as Luther did. And yet, even though we now seem to know that light travels at the rate of 186,000 miles per second and that light from millions of other solar systems has been traveling earthward since creation and yet has not arrived on our planet; that our sun is but one of millions of other similar solar systems, and that our earth is the only one as far as we now know that has this strange creature called MAN on it, yet we can safely go on the assumption, and belief, that some characteristics of man identified by Luther are still there. "God formed man in His own image to be a participator of God and one designed to enjoy God's rest."[55] Speaking of the original nature of man Luther often declared that he is idolatrous by nature, self-centered, and in bondage. He quoted Jesus to the effect that natural man is spiritually dead and impotent, "Without me ye can do nothing."[56] The problem of the will of man, is it free or is it in bondage, was one of the major concerns of theologians and philosophers in the Middle Ages. Luther conceded a liberum arbitrium (free will) to natural man in matters "such as building a house, administering a public office, piloting a ship," but in making spiritual decisions natural man is impotent and his will is not free to choose rightly."[57] Emil Brunner asks a pertinent question regarding the freedom of man:

> Who are the people who are really free? Precisely those who do not claim to be their own masters, but who own a Master. This allegiance renders them trustworthy, responsible, and really free. If ye abide in my Word ye shall know the truth and the truth shall make you free. This freedom is the emerging greatness of man, predestined to be conformed to the image of God.[58]

In his notes on Zacharias 1:3, Luther stated that "Man's greatest honor is that God himself became a man," as related in the Christmas story. In dealing with the origin of man Luther's comment on Genesis 2:7 states:

> The difference which God made in the original creation of man and cattle shows man's immortality. And though all the other works of God fill us with wonder and are truly magnificent yet man is the most excellent creature. This is evident from the fact that in creating him God had

recourse to his deep counsel and proceeded in a new manner. For God does not leave it to the earth to bring forth man as it brought forth the beasts and the trees. But God formed man in his own image to be a participator of God and one designed to enjoy God's rest.[59]

While we admit, also among Christian educators, that Luther's ideas in many respects are obsolete; that Luther was indeed in many respects a product of his age, and that he spoke a language which seems anachronistic to many today, yet when it comes to identifying the origin and nature of man the heirs of historic Christianity cannot agree that Darwin's case for biological evolution, and man's continuity with animals, has been proven to a point that we should be satisfied with an education of man that is based on Darwin rather than on Genesis and on First Corinthians, chapter 15. We have more than serious misgivings. We don't buy.

If it is really true that man is merely the inevitable culmination of an improbable chemical reaction then the fact that he has been able to trace himself back to it is remarkable. That come to understand their own nature is a staggering supposition. It is also a preposterous one. Man is now as free as before to suppose that inside the whirling cosmos of the invisible atom as in the massive spirals of countless nebulae in endless space there is Order and Purpose, as was believed of all, only incredibly vaster.[60]

One cannot but marvel at the docility with which Americans, including many good Christian parents and pastors, have accepted as satisfactory a secular and naturalistic education. The naiveness of educational leaders in assuming that youth can be given a complete education for the whole person while at the same time bypassing and ignoring God and the Biblical and historic nature of the persons to be educated is an equally great marvel. The fact remains, of course, that while the theory of biological evolution has now in many school text books been placed as a theory in the last chapter of the text book in biology, or history of mankind, yet the theory is everywhere implicitly accepted as undoubtedly the real story of man. And of course, school, university and community museums with exhibits portending to give a valid history of the earth and of man are found everywhere, and they do their educational work. They most effectively convey ideas and foster concepts that are indelible, and have a far-reaching educational influence. Recently the new State of Illinois Museum was dedicated. One of the first exhibits that met the eyes of viewers was an exhibit of strata of rocks, with fossils of organisms from mollusks to man, portending to show that man is indeed the product of a million-year process of evolution. They of course say nothing about the fact that the age of the rocks is determined by the kind of fossils found there and that the age of the fossils is determined, in turn, by the age of the fossils!

Must not educators and education change as the data concerning the origin, nature and destiny of man keeps piling up? The answer is Yes and No. Maritain, a Thomist, has a quotable quote on this question.

> Man evolves in history. Yet his nature is such, his place and value in the cosmos, his dignity, rights and aspirations as a person, and his destiny, do not change. Consequently the secondary aims of education have to be adjusted to changing conditions in successsive historical periods; but as concerns the *primary,* as well as the intrinsic domination it exercises on the secondary aims, it is sheer illusion to speak of ceaseless reconstruction of the aims of education.[61]

The God-believing educator too holds to the ultimate aim of a good education as being "inseparable union with God." That calls for the elimination of that which separates man from the holy God: Sin.

God Himself has come to the rescue of sinful man, helplessly and hopelessly entangled in the mire of sin and selfishness. He sent "the Just for the unjust, to bring them to God."[62] He has also provided the means whereby the benefits of this sacrifice are brought to individual persons, and whereby faith is both created and sustained. Here lies the source of hope for humanity. The Christian philosophy of education does not agree that man will be radically changed, and "saved" as it were, by changing the economic order, as communists believed, or as secular sociologists believe; nor do the heirs of historic Christianity believe that an abundance of this world's goods, and a surplus of creature comforts, will really change for the better either man, or mankind. Rather a radical change within, a regeneration, a new birth, through faith in the Son of God, Savior from sin, and hope of the world, is a necessary prerequisite and aim of a good education.

Perhaps we shall have to arrive at the conclusion that since a good government cannot and should not have God and His man-changing power in its classroom, it was a mistake to turn over the task of educating the young to the government. Even an Oriental, though a Christian, Lin Yutang has indicated the source of our confusion and of our weaknesses in education.

> The natural scientist says: God, freedom and goodness of man are not exact knowledge, and do not lie in my field. But the professor of human studies says, God, freedom and goodness of man lie within my department. But they cannot be handled scientifically, and I wish to be a scientist. Therefore I am compelled to ignore them and look somewhere else for mechanical laws. Only in that way can I hope to be modern and keep my job. And since science cannot discover God, the soul, and the goodness of man, perhaps they do not exist at all. There the confusion begins.[63]

Of course, governments, too, are of God. The powers that be are of God. And governments have always had the right and the duty to educate their young in the interest of their own progress and survival. And no one should expect our government to pull out of the field of education. Possibly the confusion and our problems of "federal aid to education" grew out of the government's assumption that as far as the tax dollar is concerned, it and it alone has and must continue to have a monopoly of education. Possibly a beginning toward improvement of the total situation could be made with the recognition by philosophers of education that secularism represents only a fragment of reality and that all that a secular government can hope to offer in education is but a fragmentary education. Once that is recognized — which admittedly

calls for a large measure of humility, not likely to be found —
ways could be found to include God and His Word in the total
program of education as is done, without any qualms of conscience
either by the government or the church, or the taxpayer, in all
European countries on the fortunate side of the iron curtain. The
writer recently reassured himself of this arrangement by writing
to nine different state departments of public education and receiving copies of their laws regulating the support of education, the
curricula, the courses and daily schedules, all of which indicated
that Scripture study, Bible study, or Religion, has what appears to
be a self-evident place in the thinking of these educators and the
parents of the youth. In addition to having Scripture study in the
public schools' daily schedule, the governments in most of these
countries also make funds available for church-maintained schools,
up to 80% of capital costs and up to 70% of the operating costs.

Once there is a recognition of the importance of God in education and a degree of humility, ways can be found, it seems, to
keep God close to the next generation of the human family. And
we think they do belong together.

Perhaps we should at this point permit William Hocking in his
"What Man Can Make of Man" to make a pertinent remark: "It
is not strange that with the complete victory of scientific methods,
natural science overshot its mark. Instead of saying, we have no
place for purposes and values of things in our laboratories it said
in effect, we have now dismissed purposes and values from the
universe,"[64] and we add: from our schools.

To train baboons and the babies of baboons in your classroom
is one thing. But to educate a person created in the image of God
and to develop in him God-likeness is quite another thing. Who
then and what then is man? What's your answer?

CHAPTER III

EPISTEMOLOGY: THE NATURE
AND IMPORTANCE OF KNOWLEDGE AND OF TRUTH

A. THE PROBLEM

"Is it really true that we shall all rise again, as taught in our religion? And that we shall live and see each other again, all, Ilusha too?" This thoughtful question was asked by the sorrowing friends of little Ilusha. The question was addressed to the younger of the three Karamazov brothers by the friends of Ilusha at whose graveside they still lingered after the funeral. "Is it really *true?*" That is one of the persistent questions with which mankind has ever been concerned. At the graveside there, they probably heard the words "Dust to dust. Ashes to ashes," but there they also heard the words of hope "In the certain hope of the resurrection from the dead." The younger Karamazov would not, could not, rob the sad little boys of their wavering faith nor their flickering hope. The youngest of the three Karamazov brothers[1] assured them, "Certainly we shall all see each other again and tell each other with joy and gladness all that has happened." This revived their faith and made them glad. They said: "And now let us go to the funeral feast, to our eating of pancakes. And now we go hand in hand, and always so, all our lives, *hand in hand.* Hurrah for Karamazov!" We ponder, Would there have been gladness, and hope, and walking "hand in hand," if the answer had been given by a doubter, or a skeptic, or an atheist instead of by a believer?

Why are Catholics maintaining 10,000 parochial schools even though they all must support a free system of schools in America, open to all alike, Catholics, Lutherans, Jews, and others? Why do various Protestant groups maintain 2,500 church-sponsored schools? Why do Jews support 125 synagogue-related schools? And why are these schools growing in number in our country?

Catholics in Chicago maintain as many high schools as are maintained by the public school system. They support 335 elementary schools in that same metropolitan area. The Lutherans (Synodical Conference) maintain fifty elementary schools. True, many of these schools were started when linguistic and ethnic pride were very strong. But then we ask how come that in the 1956-57 period these same Lutherans built three high schools in the Chicago-land area, each costing about one million dollars? Why do the Christian Reformed people maintain elementary, high schools, and why have they built a Junior College at Worth, Illinois in that area in the last decade? One obvious reason lies in the field of *epistemology*. They are persuaded that the lives of their young ones would be impoverished if they were to grow up and be educated in a school in which Christian faith, Judeo-Christian hope and Gospel-motivated charity has no place. And they know that if these values are to be maintained and transmitted to the next generation, these children and young people must have an education in which there is a firm basis of truth other than that of science. They need the revelation and the eternal wisdom of God as it is found in the Scriptures, both Old and New Testament. It seems unfortunate that in our fine schools the next generation of Americans is being schooled without that Abiding Truth.

> "The founders of our country brought with them little wealth in money and goods but much in riches of a higher kind, a deep religious faith as well as a wholesome respect for learning."[2]

What can and what are tax-supported schools doing today to cultivate that "deep religious faith" in the thirty-five million children and teen-agers who daily attend these schools? The immigrants and their early descendants during the first 170 years of America's history were educated in the 4 R's, reading, 'riting, 'rithmetic, and religion. Their faith and their life were based on the truths of Scripture. God had a central place in every classroom. They were taught Bible truths, habits of prayer and worship on every school day. In all but communist-controlled schools the daily schedule in public elementary and high schools of Europe still calls for the teaching of Scriptures, and familiarity with forms of worship and church history. But not in free and democratic America. Whither America? Who will effectively condition our youth to those values which we all cherish highly, particularly also in contrast to communist countries?

The preservation, transmission, and refinement of culture has ever been the concern of statesmen and educators. We are presently confronted with a very crucial problem. We are standing at the crossroads. Socrates, in ancient Greece, was very much concerned. Truth and piety, certainty and goodness, what are they and how can they be transmitted?

"I am fated to be under the power of a daemonical nature who keeps me wondering continually in search of *truth* and still at a loss of where to find it."

So opined Socrates in discoursing on the nature of piety. "ti esti."[3] That is the question also when it comes to defining truth today. What is it? "ti esti?"

Truth is conformity with reality, you say. But then we are at once confronted with an even greater problem: What is the nature of reality? Is it monistic? Is it dualistic? If so, do we have two sources of truth? Is all of reality comprehended in physical monism, and does that mean that the method of the physical sciences has a monopoly on truth? If reality is essentially "idealistic," or spiritual, does that mean that idealism has a monopoly on truth?

What is the place of *reason* in establishing truth? Is the syllogism an authentic source of truth, as Aristotle and, later, the scholastics, held? Can the mind be relied upon to give us a true and complete picture of reality? Or, is it true that the mind is so constituted that all sense impressions are at once categorized and reproduced in the forms and categories which are inherent in the structure of the mind? Do universals come into existence *in* rebus, or *post* res, or are they extant *ante* res? Did white things exist in, after, or before, whiteness existed?

Is truth everywhere the same, at all times and under all circumstances, as Hutchins and Adler[4] held? Or do circumstances alter cases? Do we agree with Ralph Harper when he states:

Every truth is externally a chameleon but internally always the same. All ideas have a closet of costumes. Truth has its disguises which only the patient and learned mind can detect. Far too much emotion is wasted in public and private life on differences that are only verbally irreconcilable.[5]

Other epistemological questions appear on the horizon. Is truth arrived at by a majority vote? Do ballots establish authentic truth? What is the relationship between the knowing subject and the known object? Are these identical? Failure to identify them is the source of unending trouble, claimed both Marx[6] and Dewey.[7] Is it permissible to distinguish between different kinds of truth, such as self-evident truths, revealed truths, scientific truths? Are there varying degrees of truthfulness? Is all truth always only an approximation of the truth? Is it a mere hypothesis, with varying degrees of probability? Is truth always relative only? May we speak of absolute, necessary, eternal, and unchanging truths? Are truths discovered or are they made by man? May we speak of pre-existent truths? Is all truth internally consistent and must we insist, as Quenstedt and Pieper[8] do, that truth cannot have any contradictions? So that truths of science and truths of Scripture, for example, cannot ever be in conflict with each other? Is a fragmentary epistemology satisfactory? Can, for example, a scientist who has only one method of arriving at the truth, namely, the well established method of the physical sciences, validly exclude all judgments that are derived from the accumulated *wisdom of the ages,* or from specially *inspired writers,* or from *conventions* and church bodies which claim that when they speak "ex cathedra" they are speaking the "infallible" truth?

What is the nature of *"self-evident truths?"* The opening sentences of our Constitution, declare: "We hold these truths to be self evident that all men are created equal, that they are endowed by their Creator with certain unalienable rights, that among these are Life, Liberty, and the pursuit of Happiness."[9]

Are creeds of the churches true? For example the Apostolic Creed and the Nicene Creed? The various confessional statements of the Church, are they valid expressions of truth?

Is there any one authentic external criterion, a kind of polar star by which epistemologists can identify truths and also lies? What contribution, if any, has the study of "semantics" made to the establishment of true judgments?

How valid is the alleged current communist claim that whatever enhances the cause of communism is true and good? And whatever hinders the spread of communism throughout the world is not true and not good?[10] Does the end justify the means? Judgments and beliefs that have been arrived at through wishful thinking, how valid are they? How valid is the method of compromise between two contrary, or at least not fully agreeing, claims? Is the idealistic dialectic of Hegel[11] or the materialistic dialectic of Karl Marx[12] really a safe and sound way of arriving at the truth?

Just what lessons should we learn from Francis Bacon and his dissertations on various idols, as The Idols of the Tribe, the Idols of the Cave, Idols of the Market-place, and Idols of the Theatre?[13]

How valid is Hume's[14] claim that two or more series of data may correlate positively very highly and yet provide no basis for claiming any kind of cause and effect relationship? Lightning and thunder may frequently be closely associated with each other but can one ever conclude that one is cause and the other effect? Did Kant[15] ever successfully answer Hume's thesis of agnosticism?

What shall we say today, in 1966, in an age of science, of the claim made by an humble Nazarene: "I am the Way, the Truth, and the Life. No man cometh unto the Father but by me."[16] In matters of ultimate truths concerning God, Immortality and Freedom what shall we say to the claim that Unchanging Truth is found in Jesus Christ who is the same yesterday, today, and forever?[17]

Epistemology Is Important

The theory of knowledge and of truth is important for government, for sociologists, for all scholarly enterprises, and most assuredly it has important bearings on education. Obviously an educational system's philosophy of education will be different, radically different, depending on the basic assumptions and beliefs concerning what is true. The statement of objectives, of anticipated outcomes, the content, if not the organization of the curriculum, the training and qualification of teachers, the instructional materials, including text-books, audio-visual aids, library resources; the criteria for evaluating pupil progress, these all will be vitally affected and they will be different depending on the epistemology of a school and school system. Lest anyone suggest that surely a difference in epistemology cannot be a sufficient basis for establishing, with voluntary funds, a separate school system, let us take another look at the general importance of the subject and then let us look critically at the various types of epistemologies that underlie education in America and in Western culture.

An architect admittedly has a great responsibility in the development of plans and blueprints for a new structure. If his plans are based on miscalculations the results can be disastrous. For this reason epistemology has a very basic role in the development of what all Americans are seriously interested in, namely, the best possible education for the next generation.

"There is one unerring mark of a real lover of truth, viz., the not entertaining of any proposition with greater assurance than the proofs it is built on will warrant."[18]

Dewey was concerned about the improvement of education in America. He was very much concerned about epistemology.

> The problem of the relation of the actual and the ideal has always been the central problem of philosophy, in its metaphysical aspects, just as the relation between existence and idea has been the central theme of philosophy on the side of the theory of knowledge.[19]

Dewey was familiar with the old and the new in educational philosophies.

> History of philosophy shows that every main type of philosophic system has developed its own special interpretation of logical forms and relations. Indeed it is almost a convention to divide philosophy into ontology (reality) on the one side and a corresponding epistemology, (theory of

knowledge) on the other side. It is not accidental that spiritualistic and materialistic, monistic and dualistic, pluralistic, idealistic and realistic philosophies have evinced predilections for one or another type of logical doctrine. They have developed a logical theory (epistemology) consonant with their theory of nature and of man. It is to the credit of each main type of philosophy that it has attempted to make explicit its underlying logic.[20]

Obviously, the basic claims, beliefs, and assumptions concerning the nature, origin, and validity of truth are a fundamental starting point for any system and philosophy of education. This is doubly important in America today because of divided opinions about education, the threat of a dual, or multiple, system of education. The current issues in Washington concerning the reasonableness or unreasonableness of federal aid to education, public, private, and parochial, remind us that the problem is crucial. We are agreed that education, the best possible education, is a must. It is a matter of life and death, of survival and of possible extinction. But we are not agreed on some of the basic assumptions that are indispensable for a good education.

We would not under-estimate nor under-evaluate the importance and fruitfulness of the epistemology that underlies the physical science. In its field we have but to think of the modern miracles of communication and transportation. Admittedly the accepted method of science works. Predictions concerning the effects of drugs, of medical diagnoses and cures; predictions concerning the direction and distances of stellar bodies, of man-made moons and missiles, do come true. But, there are limitations. As Greene has stated it:

> I believe that man can know something, but not everything; that he can know many things with increasing clarity and assurance; but he can never, because he is incorrigibly finite, know anything with complete certainty and finality. Now we see darkly. But we do see. Ontology, epistemology, and axiology are complementary to one another and must be pursued in closest relation to one another.[21]

67

That is granted also by educators who are in the frame of reference of historic Christianity. It is Scriptural and true,

He died for all that they which live should not henceforth live unto themselves, but unto him which died for them and rose again.[22] [And again:] Faith without works is dead.[23]

Truth has been belittled, for various reasons, by some.

Radicals naturally belittle truth. Truth has a stabilizing influence that offers resistance to their revolutionary ambitions. The subjugated millions of Hitler and the nimble legions of Mussolini (and today we add that of Lenin, Stalin, Castro, Mao) are marshalled in a desperate conspiracy *against ancient citadels of truth*. The same iconoclastic zeal has flared up ominously in certain educational reformers. Having defined truth as relative they have jumped to the fantastic conclusion that it is of negligible educational importance. Finding certain traditions objectionable, and truth a component of tradition, they prepare to throw out the baby with the bath.[24]

No doubt this trend accounts for the tendency to minimize the importance of subject matter in American education.

The drift to which we refer finds its roots in the pragmatic emphasis on the dynamic rather than on the static aspects of life.[25]

When Dewey moves into the educational arena he often disparages the demands of subject matter in the schools and advocates more complete reliance on a training in methods of thinking.[26]

Thinking, it is said, can be developed in any problem situation without reference to significance of the content of the problem. If education continues to be based on an unsound epistemological basis, it will be adrift without compass or rudder. "It seems that American education finds itself at the crossroads."[27]

Education standing "at the crossroads!" This carries with it a down to earth challenge for educational leaders in America to ask themselves humbly and frankly some basic questions such as "education for what?" "Whence, wither and why?" One who has long been active in educational thinking, in a center from which much of the literature to promote and defend the pragmatic and instrumental approach to education, has this to say:

> After some years of wandering in the wilderness, educators are becoming more and more convinced that the individual interest, freedom, or liberty, furnishes no complete foundation for either the schools or the government of a democracy.[28]

Realist Breed made some criticisms of current educational thought.

> Forget his (Adler's) scholasticism, his supernaturalism and he still remains a prophet of the disaster that will overtake a decisive individualism, a flabby liberalism and an impotent skepticism. He appears to be saying: The *hour of decision has arrived*: One cannot build a program of education on the right to doubt. One must also believe. — The "unity-of-science" movement is a positivist's reaction on an international scale.[29]

Breed climaxes his criticism of anti-subject matter and anti-fixed truth educational program by citing an extreme case of a teacher who was asked in the classroom, first hour in the morning: "What is your program of teaching for today?" and she replied: "I don't know what it will be; the children haven't come in yet."[30]

This is an example of what happens when enthusiastic disciples run wild with a particular new idea for the improvement of education. A growing number of educators agree that epistemology is a good place to begin, if not a reformation in education, at least a re-emphasizing of fundamentals in education.

> There has been an increasing demand for light on fundamentals, on basic principles, on the essential meaning of education and the democratic way of life. This demand

69

for social clarification explains the revival of the philosophy of education as a subject of study for prospective educators.[31]

Western culture has a few key words in it which must not be overlooked. They include *"democracy"* and the implication that individual persons are of primary importance and that "We the People" must be consulted in any major program of government; furthermore *"science"* is of primary importance in the improvement of standards of living and in providing creature comforts for all the people; science is of inestimable importance in rendering citizens immune to the appeals of quackery whether in medicine or any other branch of study designed for the physical and mental welfare and improvement of our culture; ever since "Sputnik," Americans have redoubled their efforts in science education and they have gained an almost idolatrous faith in science as a means of competing successfully with communism.

"Tolerance" is a middle name for the public spirit in America. Americans are intolerant only of intolerance. The concept of *"change"* needs to have strong emphasis in the educational philosophy of tomorrow, even though the equation of change and "progress" has suffered some severe set-backs in recent decades. The concept of "pluralism" has been widely accepted and has resulted in the establishment of denominational ministries on the campuses of the majority of our colleges and universities. All of these cultural elements will need to be provided for in any revision of educational philosophy in America.

> It is accepted as axiomatic that the creed that permeates the state shall be the creed that permeates the school. No philosophy of education can therefore confidently aspire to general acceptance in the U. S. of America that does not square with democratic principles. We realists regard philosophy as continuous with science, not separate therefrom. Ours is a stubborn attempt to think our world consistently.[32]

From what has been said about a variety of elements in our American culture, we turn to the fact that America and American education, while united in some of its major objectives as these are comprehended in the concept of democracy, is undergirded by different epistemologies. We shall call attention to the probable implications of each of these but their final evaluation we shall leave to the reader.

B. EPISTEMOLOGY OF HISTORIC CHRISTIANITY

In the Judeo-Christian view of existence the abstractions of idealism become personalized. God, with a capital G, enters upon the epistemological scene. What is more natural than that the eternal and pre-existent One should make Himself known to that segment of His creation which He intended that it should be in His own image, i.e., mankind. What is more to be expected than that the Absolute Eternal One should reveal the Truth about Himself, about His efforts in creation, preservation, and sanctification to the apex of His creation: Man. In the sacred records and writings of the Judeo-Christian lineage, the heirs of the historic Christian heritage believe they have a reliable source of valid information about God and His works. In Scriptures, both Old and New Testament, they believe they have answers to man's most fundamental questions to which neither reason nor science can give adequate answers. What is the truth about man, his origin, his nature, his real purpose in life, his destiny? The Christian believes that God's efforts in behalf of man show themselves in his progressive self-revelation, with particular reference to His eternal Justice and His eternal Love. As these essential truths of the Law and Gospel are understood and accepted they tend to lead man first of all to a humbleness of mind and heart that is characteristic of those who seek truth as well as for those who seek holiness. The Good News of the Gospel leads the humble person to faith; to a joyful acceptance of God's free grace, as a gift of God. It is through such acceptance of God that man is born again, is justified and made acceptable before God, and is made to share in the very nature and life of God. It is thus, that man, in the view of historic Christianity finds the true God, and with Him he finds true freedom and a quality of life described as

71

godly, or eternal, here and now, and eventually to a blessed immortality.

In this chapter on epistemology we are not primarily concerned with the existence of God, but rather with the question whether the unseen God has revealed Himself in other than natural ways.

> The basic religious question is not: Is there a God and can man know him; rather, did God reveal Himself? If He did, the first question is answered in the affirmative. The answer to the second question does not come by weighing the pros and cons of revelation in general and the Biblical revelation in particular, but follows from listening to the Christian message such that hearing becomes believing, trusting, obeying. That this happens does not lie within the power of those who bring the message but within the power of the Holy Spirit.[33]

When the people of God say that their Scriptures are inspired they mean that

> the Holy Spirit exercised a special influence by which He guided His chosen instruments to speak the things He desired them to speak and to write the things He desired them to write, in the precise manner and in the very words in which He desired these things to be spoken and written.[34]

This conception and faith concerning the Scriptures is based on its own testimony concerning itself. It is a matter of faith. Neither reason nor the scientific method can either establish or dis-establish this belief. "Pasa graphe theopneustos" is an incisive quote on this point.[35] In its own words the Scriptures also define the central purpose of these inspired writings: "These things are written that ye might believe that Jesus is the Christ and that believing ye might have eternal life."[36]

This central purpose of Scriptures is clearly defined also in Paul's letter to a young pastor Timothy, when he wrote:

> From a child thou hast known the Holy Scriptures which are able to make thee wise unto salvation through faith

which is in Christ Jesus. All Scripture is given by inspiration of God and is profitable for doctrine, for reproof or correction for instruction in righteousness, that a man of God may be perfect, throughly furnished unto all good works.[37]

The centrality of Scriptures in the epistemology of historic Christianity is quite generally accepted by all branches of the visible church. Each one of them, from Roman Catholic to any of the more recent segments of Christianity, as the Church of God and the Pentecostal groups, would feel deeply hurt to have it suggested that the Scriptures were not the basis of the truth which they preach and teach. If the question is asked: If they all regard the Bible as valid truth, how come there are so many divisions within the church? Why can not the ecumenical movement, designed as it is to unite all Christendom, make more progress? The answer to that question is two-fold. In the first place, Scriptures were brought to a close with the solemn exhortation not to add to, nor to subtract from the Scriptures.[38]

Owing to current needs to emphasize certain of the Scriptural truths and owing also to the human frailty of adding to and subtracting from this treasure, some theologians have set aside some basic principles of interpretations, such as "sensus literalis unus est"[39] "Scriptura Scripturam interpretatur"[40] and the "analogia fidei"[41] and have at the same time been unable to resist the temptation to let reason play a role for which it is not qualified. The temptation to assimilate some elements in the culture in which the heirs of Christianity had to live, move, and have their being, was not successfully resisted and so "tradition" came to play an auxiliary role to Scripture. Also, to meet contemporary issues one segment of the visible church in particular has undertaken to solve matters of faith and life through the resolutions of councils and synods and thus to establish the voice of the church as an arbiter of divine truth. As the scientific method of research came to be accepted also by theologians, attempts were made to reconcile revealed truths with the findings of the physical sciences. Invariably these procedures tended to thwart the main purpose of the Scriptures, to paint a faint and sometimes a misleading picture of Him who is the Alpha and Omega, the beginning and the end, the first and the last in the Christian faith and life. That in turn invariably created confusion and opened up detours on the road to salvation, happiness, and heaven. Yet, when all has been said and conceded, it remains that the Scriptures are the source, even if not the "sola" source of truth, for all segments of Christendom.

The other part of the question: Why so many divisions in Christendom if the Scriptures are really a clear and valid source of truth, is answered by saying that the Church in its real sense IS one. All Christians confess each Sunday: I believe in the one holy catholic Church, the communion of saints. The "una sancta ecclesia"[42] is real. All, no matter of what color or on what side of the curtain, iron or bamboo, no matter in what denomination, Greek, Roman, Protestant; whosoever accepts Christ as the Messiah, as his personal Savior from sin, and as his personal hope for the future, is thereby a member of the body of Christ. He enjoys the "koinonia"[43] (fellowship) with God and with fellow believers. Effort to establish an outward, organic union among all segments of Christianity are not really urgent. The important thing is unity, unity in Christ. That is and always has been a spiritual reality. In Christ they are children of the same Father and they are therefore truly brothers and sisters. Here the brotherhood of man is more than an ideal; it is a present reality.

It stands to reason that the heirs of historic Christianity have a great interest in education. For them Christ makes the difference. The best in life, as individuals and as groups, is available for all. True freedom has its deepest foundation at this point.

"If ye continue in my word, then are ye my disciples indeed; and ye shall know the truth and the truth shall make you *free.*"[44]

A rich life, far beyond the enjoyment of creature comforts, is thus made available for all.

"I am come that ye might have life and that ye might have it more abundantly."[45]

Success in the pursuit of happiness is assured. Immortality is similarly assured, for "God so loved the world that He gave His only-begotten Son that whosoever believeth in Him shall not perish but shall have life everlasting."[46]

No more needs at this time to be said to make it obvious that the heirs of historic Christianity have an important contribution to make to the best possible kind of education of the children and teen-agers, in fact for all, from the cradle to the grave, in our free world.

Epistemology of the Old Testament

The Old Testament prophets, from Moses to Micah, recorded God's ongoing self-revelation as the God of power, of holiness, and of mercy. "In the beginning God created heaven and earth."[47] In the first chapter of Genesis God is recorded no less than thirty-two times as having done or said this and that. "Thus saith the Lord" appears again and again.

"Now these are commandments, the statutes and the judgments which the Lord your God has commanded."[48]

"Thus saith the Lord: Keep ye judgment and do justice, for my salvation is near to come and my righteousness to be revealed."[49]

> And the Lord spake unto Joshua: As I was with Moses so I will be with thee; I will not fail thee nor forsake thee. Be strong and of good courage. Only be thou strong and very courageous that thou mayest observe to do according to all the law which Moses my servant commanded thee: Turn not from it to the right hand or to the left, that thou mayest prosper whithersoever thou goest. This book of the law shall not depart out of thy mouth, but thou shalt meditate therein day and night that thou mayest observe to do according to all that is written therein; for then shalt thou make thy way prosperous and then shalt thou have good success. Have not I commanded thee? Be strong and of good courage; be not afraid, neither be thou dismayed, for the Lord thy God is with thee whithersoever thou goest.[50]

The prophets of the Old Testament never go out of their way to prove the reality of the personalized, non-physical One. They accept God as self-evident. Jehovah is the God most high. The inspired writers are concerned with recording what God said and what He did to guide and lead His people into a true and blessed life with Himself.

75

And they were persuaded that God and His Word must have a central place in the education of their youth.

> Abraham shall surely become a great and mighty nation
> and all the nations of the earth shall be blessed in him."
> Why? "For I know that he will command his children and
> his household after him, and they shall keep the way of
> the Lord, to do justice and judgement.[51]

Here, it is evident that God selected this people to be the carrier of His promises because they would place priority emphasis on education in which God and God's Words would have a central place. And where is the ancient nation that placed a greater emphasis on that kind of an education: Religious education. God-centered education. God and His Truth in the classroom and in the curriculum. And that emphasis was, of course, something that God had laid upon their consciences, especially on the consciences of the parents:

> And these words which I command thee this day shall be
> in thine heart and thou shalt teach them diligently to thy
> children and shalt talk of them when thou sittest in thine
> house, and when thou walkest in the way, and when thou
> liest down and when thou risest up. And thou shalt bind
> them for a sign upon thine hand, and they shall be as
> frontlets between thine eyes. And thou shalt write them
> upon the posts of thine house and on thy gates.[52]

And when prosperity comes to you, and you enjoy a great variety of creature comforts then

> Beware lest thou forget the Lord which brought thee forth
> out of the land of Egypt and from the house of bondage.[53]

The summary objective of Old Testament education centered in faith, in righteousness, in justice, in mercy.

> Hear O Israel, the Lord our God is one Lord. And thou
> shalt love the Lord thy God with all thine heart and with
> all thy soul and with all thy mind.[54]

The highest social values are embodied in the heritage of Old Testament Judaism:

> And now Israel what doth the Lord thy God require of thee, but to fear the Lord thy God, to walk in his ways, to love Him and to serve the Lord thy God with all thy heart and with all thy soul; to keep the commandments of the Lord and his statutes.[55]

While the Torah, the Law, appears to have a pre-eminent place in the total of truth as recorded in the Old Testament, it is also true that the promises of the Messiah and the grace and mercy of God, was ever before them. The liturgical services, the sacraments, the functions of the priest to intercede and most definitely the hymnology as recorded in the Psalms, show that the God of the Cross had a prominent place in the Old Testament section of the great Heritage. Messianic prophecies, like a red thread, run through the entire Old Testament from Moses to Micah.

This brief summary of Old Testament epistemology would be incomplete if there were not a reference to the fact that "truthfulness" in the Old Testament is an important element in the concept of truth. Truthfulness in God, and in His people, means that He can be absolutely depended upon to stand by His promises. He is willing, determined, and able to keep His promises. Thus Moses by inspiration declared: "God is the Rock, his work is perfect. For all his ways are judgment, a God of Truth and without iniquity, just and right is He."[56]

God can be depended upon to help the needy.

> Happy is he that hath the God of Jacob for his help; whose hope is in the Lord his God. Which made heaven, and earth, and sea, and all that is therein which *keepeth truth* forever. — The Lord shall reign forever.[57]

The writer to the Hebrew Christians, assured by inspiration that the Old Testament heritage had not come to an end for them now that they had accepted Christ as the Messiah, reminded them of the fact that God is *truthful,* that He and His promises of grace and mercy do not change.

> Wherein God, willing more abundantly to show unto the heirs of promise, the immutability of His counsel, confirmed it by an oath; that by two immutable things, in which it was impossible for refuge to lay hold upon the hope set before us: which hope we have as an anchor of the soul, both *sure and steadfast,* and which entered, even Jesus, made an high priest forever after the order of Melchisedec.[58]

This is a contribution to education where it is sorely needed. The God of His people in the Old Testament was to them a source of comfort, of courage, and of undaunted stubborn, Niemoeller-like, resistance to dictators' heels.

In addition we see a sharp difference in matters of righteous living between the then and there and the here and now.

We have quoted somewhat at length from the Old Testament so as to point up the difference between God-sanctioned behavior and what we have here in the United States of America, a democratic and permissive atmosphere. Obviously, we have gained something but we have also lost something of definiteness of truth and the nature of righteousness, or if you will, something of social and civic "competence."

Epistemology of the New Testament

Chinese converts to Christianity are said to speak of the New Testament as the Jesus Book. In sign language the Bible is signed by pointing a finger at the palm of each hand. Which means that the Scriptures tell of the crucified Savior.

When Paul addressed the philosophically oriented Greeks on Mars hill in Athens, he said to them:

> Ye men of Athens, I perceive that in all things ye are too superstitious. For as I passed by and beheld your devotions I found an altar with the inscription: To the Unknown God. Whom therefore ye ignorantly worshipped, Him declare I unto you.[59]

78

Passing up the truth held dear by Jews and Greeks, Paul devoted himself with unprecedented singleness of purpose to the preaching of the Gospel, the power of God unto salvation:

> The Jews require a sign and the Greeks seek after wisdom, but we preach Christ crucified, unto the Jews a stumbling block and unto the Greeks foolishness but unto them which are called, the power of God is wiser than men and the weakness of God is stronger than men.[60]

And so we see, in following through on the epistemology of Old and New Testament, that

> God, who at sundry times and in diverse manner spake in time past unto the fathers by the prophets, hath in these last days spoken to us by His Son, whom he hath appointed heir of all things, by whom also he made the world, who being the brightness of His glory and the express image of his person and upholds all things by the word of his power.[61]

Evidently then, God's self-revelation reached its culminating point in the incarnation[62] and finally in the Cross and in the open sepulchre.[63]

It is through faith in Him as the Messiah and the Savior of mankind that the individual persons find the highest and best in life. They find God. They possess eternal, unchanging Truth. They become mature. He is the same yesterday, today, and forever.[64]

He taught men to pray: Sanctify us through thy word. Thy word is truth. Holiness is the primary concern of the heirs of historic Christianity, but truth is still the means to that end. The intellectual aspect of the Christian heritage must not be underrated. It is important. And many Americans are deeply grieved that practically all of the money and wonderful educational effort spent on education of our youth systematically by-passes and ignores this vital element in our heritage.

"This is life eternal. That they might know Thee and whom thou hast sent."[65]

"If the Son shall make you free, ye shall be free indeed."[66]

What have the heirs of historic Christianity done with the Scriptures? Have they preserved it? Inwardly digested it? Lived it? Translated it into a way of life? What is considered the basis of truth among Christian churches?

We read in the early records about First-Century Christians:

> They continued steadfastly in the apostle's doctrine, and fellowship, and breaking of bread and prayer. And they had all things common and sold their possessions and goods, and parted them to all men as every man had need.[67]

It is obvious they sought to live and practice their newly obtained knowledge and truth. Lest anyone jump at a conclusion that here was communism and the dialectical truth of materialism in action, let it be noted that these Christians were intent on *giving*. This was a voluntary sharing of material things. This is quite in contrast to the doctrine of Soviet communism which is intent on *taking*. There is a world of difference.

Have the Catholic churches, East and West, retained Scriptures as a basis of truth? The answer is undoubtedly Yes, they have. But it must be admitted that this segment of Christianity has found it expedient to supplement Scripture by "tradition" and also by reason. Aristotle and the syllogism were studied and their influence led into "scholasticism." Also the councils and synods came to be regarded as having authority to give or withhold sanctions for truths relating to faith and life. Whether it was to meet the pressures of contemporary problems in the contemporary world we do not know, but the head of the Roman Catholic church is considered, since 1871, the spokesman for "infallible" truth, when he speaks "ex cathedra."

The Reformation movement represents a serious attempt to establish Scriptures and Scriptures alone, as the arbiter of truth in matters of faith and life. The followers of Luther followed through on his stand at the Diet of Worms, in 1521, on which occasion he stated:

Since your Imperial Majesty desires a clear, simple, and precise answer, I will give you one which has neither horns nor teeth. Unless I am convinced by the testimony of Holy Scriptures, or by clear reason, I cannot and will not recant for it is neither safe nor right to act against one's conscience. Here I stand. I cannot do otherwise.[68]

Not that reason, properly understood, has no place in Scriptural theology, but

"Who of us has ever denied reason in theology?" asked a widely quoted Lutheran theologian, Quenstedt. Without the use of a reason or intellect no one can occupy himself with theology. But reason must not be used in a "magisterial" role, but rather in a "ministerial" role.[69]

The heirs of Luther found if difficult to resist a common and persistent temptation to circumscribe "revelation" with reason. In the 16th and 17th century the Lutheran conception of "Scripture" was modified by the "usus magisterialis."[70] Attempts were made to show that Christianity is a "reasonable" faith.[71] Rationalism has been used to rationalize not only theology but also philosophy, scepticism, and more recently empiricism.[72] The relationship between Scripture and Reason, in matters epistemological in the Christian religion, have taken four different trends: Revelation is above reason; revelation and reason are in harmony; revelation and reason are in conflict, but may be held in compartments; and revelation is to be discarded in favor of reason.

Significant shifts of emphases are being noted among *modern theologians,* both in the Protestant and in the Catholic camp. Both tendencies point to a resurgence of the Scriptures as the one valid source of truth for the heirs of historic Christianity. In view, no doubt, of the growing threat of total atheism as represented by communism, there has become evident a trend toward rapprochement among the various segments of the Christian's epistemological heritage. Vatican Council II, the aggiornamento movement among Catholics, and ecumenism among all Christian groups bear this out.

Protestant theology has begun to listen to tradition as it has not since the Reformation. At the very same time Roman

Catholic theology has begun to listen to the Scriptures as it has not for many centuries.[73]

Although the gap between Protestants and Roman Catholics is much wider in New Testament studies than it is in Old Testament study, it is also much narrower than it used to be. In areas like textual studies the gap has been virtually closed, and in other areas it is becoming narrower all the time.[74]

The concept of *continuity* from the Old to the New Testament, from the First Century Church to the Church of the Middle Ages, from Catholicism to Protestantism appears to be increasingly recognized, so that the new is being increasingly understood in the light of the preceding period and in the light of the present emphases. A renewed study of the *Liturgy,* its nature and its role in the preservation and transmission of the historic Christian heritage, is tending in a similar direction of mutual appreciation and understanding:

Within the free churches there has arisen a new appreciation of the values in the tradition of the liturgy. Every major Protestant denomination has experienced a liturgical renaissance during the past generation. Although the varieties of Protestant worship still make the picture kaleidoscopic, there are more Catholic elements in it than there have been for centuries.[75]

Existentialism is a theological and philosophical term which owes its origin to Kierkegaard's quest for truth and for epistemological certainty.[76]

The *crisis theology* represents a strong tendency away from the Scriptural basis of truth, and makes the individual person's anxiety experiences a supplement for Scripture. The influence of Karl Barth, and his theological associate, Emil Brunner, represents an attempt to re-establish the Scripture alone principle.

His extreme Biblicism, as evidenced in his *Kirchliche Dog-matic*[77] caused him to deny all validity to natural theology and to ascribe not only pre-eminence but also absolute uniqueness to all parts of the Biblical revelation. — The theology of crisis has conceded too much to the modern temper. Yet no one can deny that by their work has also encouraged Lutherans of all lands to consider more carefully their own heritage. — Without too much fear of contradiction it can be stated that theirs has probably been the most important theological works since Schleiermacher.[78]

Neo-orthodoxy is not a complete return to the Scripture alone principle but it has done much as an antidote to a Scripture-corroding influence of liberalism and modernism. The principal reason for alerting the reader to the growing trends among all sections of historic Christianity lies in the growing need to gird more effectively for the present and growing threat of a wholly secularized, a completely non-theistic, and an aggressive atheistic threat to our spiritual heritage, in America and in all parts of the world. It is one thing to increase the effectiveness of our bullets, even if it costs up to 50 billion dollars a year. But the real battle must be fought not on the battle field, not in space, but in the field of epistemology. It behooves the heirs of historic Christianity to re-assess their epistemological assets, and to eliminate as far as possible their liabilities as these show up in the failure to accept and to live by the Truth as revealed to us in the Scriptures.

The much publicized conflict between *religion and science* needs a second close look in a chapter on epistemology. Western culture today is essentially scientific. It swears by the scientific method of arriving at valid truths. And yet, Americans and in fact the Western culture this side of the iron curtain, would like to consider themselves Christian. Is there room for both? Is the berth wide enough to provide for peaceful co-existence in our culture, and also in our chief agency for transmitting our culture to the next and coming generation, i.e., the educational program?

First of all it should be re-affirmed that the heirs of Judeo-Christian heritage are not enemies of science nor of the scientific method. They always have been intrigued by matter and the orderly and predictable behavior of matter. The Church is not an enemy of science. One of the major objectives of church-sponsored schools in America, elementary, secondary, and higher, is the study of both content and the method of science. Who would want to discourage that curiosity which gave birth to the natural sciences? Who would want to quench that thirst for knowledge which shows itself early in the lives of children and of which Anne Roe, eminent psychologist, wrote:

> A child can go for years living in his close family world. Then one day something happens. A bird or a crystal catches his mind and sets it wondering: Why is it the way it is? And why is it not like another bird or another crystal? He wonders how it is made. How it works. Then he begins to follow a line of thought, to ask questions and solitarily to hunt for answers. Suddenly knowledge has become interesting in itself. A whole new world has opened, the world of mysterious wonderful connections between things.[79]

The writer concludes that "this is the way in which great scientists have begun their careers."

It is not true that "believers" reject science and its valid findings, "not true," that is, as long as science operates in the sphere of reality in which its method of discovering the truth applies, i.e., physical nature. God's people are among the first to rejoice when progress is made toward "subduing the universe" and of having "dominion over it." Read Psalm 19. Read Paul's Letter to the Romans and see how he chides those who had nature with its persuasive arguments about the existence of God and yet refused to repent of their wickedness, or at least to adjust their morals to that natural knowledge of God. Page the names of scientists and see if not a proportionate share of them were of the Judeo-Christian cultural lineage. And if at times in the history of man it appeared as though they were intolerant of any new truths uncovered by science, we must charitably credit that to the weaknesses which persist even among the "believers" in the true God; but let us not debit the account of this cultural heritage for these aberrations.

What has been well said of the relationship between theology on one hand and reason and philosophy on the other hand needs to be said now of the relationship between religion and science. In the middle of the 17th century Quenstedt said:

> Reason and philosophy remaining in its boundaries, no truth of the sacred Scriptures conflicts with it. But, if reason leaves its boundaries all mysteries of faith, as the Trinity, the Incarnation, etc. conflict with it.[80]

The basic assumption is that theology and science operate in two different spheres of existence. Faith and revelation operate in the non-physical sphere of existence. While science operates in the sphere of the physical existence. In the army arrayed against freedom and faith, science and theology can coexist and fight a common enemy. But each must fight in its allocated segment of the line which each is particularly well equipped to defend. To claim a monopoly of the entire line of defense is presumptuous and fatal.

We may not agree in its entirety with Ramsey, but in the interest of mutual inderstanding and peaceful co-existence between science and theology we need to ponder also the following:

> It is a tremendous truth that religion spells mystery. And that mystery cannot be put into so many words. Oh, for theologians of the past who seem to have been present at the making of the world, or, instead of being on their knees with the Cross, are sitting on the throne of God asking him questions. When once theology loses that humility consign it to the refuse bin.[81]

> Without controversy great is the mystery of godliness: God was manifest in the flesh.[82]

It is interesting and instructive to listen to a scientist, a professor of electrical engineering, University of Minnesota, address himself pointedly to both scientists and theologians when he says:

> A theologian should not look with one eye on the Bible and with the other eye in a geology and biology text book. That will only lead to confusion. He should stick to his theological task and that is listening to the Bible and the Bible only. Harmonization links our thoughts to the wrong

problems. It creates the wrong impression that the Christian message is in some way subjected to science. Whereas in fact it is independent of it.[83]

He speaks with equal frankness to fellow scientists, reminding them they are "off base" when they attempt to improve on the distinctly spiritual heritage of Scriptural truths:

Science if often used in attacks against Christianity as well as its defense. Using it in an attack against Christianity indicates that one has not understood what the relationship between science and the Christian message is. Using it in defense of Christianity, as is often done in apologetic efforts, may suffer from the same defect.[84]

Many of these efforts to harmonize theology and science are attempts to defend something that does not need defense with means that cannot defend it.[85]

When science gradually broke out of the Biblical framework, this often meant a break with Biblical Christianity for the individual scientists. And this is not surprising, for it was generally admitted that science was a necessary support for Christian theology. Consequently, if this support gave way, there was nothing left. What was often not understood, was that the whole idea was wrong. The Christian message and its systematic presentation, theology, are independent of science and thus cannot be supported by it nor hampered by it.[86]

Heirs of the Biblical heritage protest against the idea that science has a monopoly on defining the ideological basis of our culture. Both the pre-Reformation and the post-Reformation heirs of historic Christianity protest against the idea that secular and materialistically-oriented education in America, or Europe, should have a monopoly on truth. They think that this claim to a monopoly of the truth represents a kind of educational totalitarianism that does not square with the pluralistic conception of culture which is characteristic of democracy.

In discussing the importance of a valid epistemology for the development of the best possible program of education for American youth, theologians are not unaware of the fact that great new discoveries in the field of the natural sciences have been made; that the scientific method of discovering new truths has been very fruitful and that therefore the educators and the theologians who are zealous to defend the ancient ways, and the ancient foundations of truth, should be willing to re-examine the validity of their beliefs in the light of confirmed new discoveries. Church people generally would not be willing to admit that they have not provided leadership in man's attempts to carry through on the Genesis injunction "to subdue the earth"[87] and to "have dominion over the creatures of the earth."[88] The natural sciences have a very proper and important place in any and every school system, particularly including those that are sponsored by groups which give to Scripture and Revelation an important place in their curriculum and daily schedule. The need for theologians and believers to give serious thought to any adjustment that needs to be made in relation to our changing world was recently well expressed by the President of America's largest theological seminary:

We are living in a restless turbulent age. Politics, economics, social relations, research, exploration, industry, architecture, art, music, and many other areas of endeavor are marked by revolutionary activity, startling discoveries, resultant dislocations and tensions, many frustrations and some fervent hopes for a better future. — It is not possible that so many and such varied and deep upheavals can take place around man and have profound effects upon him physically, intellectually, and emotionally, without spiritual repercussions. Theology must always concern itself with contemporary man and must endeavor to understand him and communicate to him the revelation of God in language, terminology, concepts that are intelligible, and meaningful to him. As their colleagues do in other fields of professional endeavor they (the theologians) must carefully evaluate what is new in method and content, and while rejecting everything that is subversive to the faith, they must adopt whatever can make an effective contribution toward an effective channel of communication between the revelation God has given us in the Sacred Scriptures and man in his present condition and environment. We cannot continue to coast on our theology. — I plead with all of our clergy to give serious thought to the recognition of theology as a vast and important frontier for our synod and to dedicate themselves to winning it.[89]

The same scholar and churchman notes very interesting parallels between developments in church and nation during the past one and one-quarter century and concludes that, as the nation, so the church needs to be concerned with the present and the future. The church dare not be satisfied with a mere "holding operation." It must look for "break-throughs into new phases of church work. They dare not bury their talents in the ground."[90]

Anent the same situation in the church and nation today the President of another institution, at Springfield, had this to say:

We cannot escape the conclusion that much of the difficulty in our church today is cultural and not doctrinal in origin. We are not minimizing the seriousness of the problem when we observe that the State of the Church Conference[91] is symptomatic of the difficulties arising from our church's passing from a cultural and social isolation into America's mainstream. In spite of two World Wars and the breakdown of the language barrier, the transition has not been completed. As a result, phenomena of the nature of the State of the Church Conference will be with us for a long time.[92]

Family quarrels have no place in this attempt to clarify issues in the area of a Philosophy of Education. However, it will serve to emphasize the importance of epistemology, in theology as in education and all other sciences, if we here refer to a current epistemological problem within the Synodical Conference of the Lutheran Churches. The issue which is disturbing the consciences of these representatives of historic Christianity is of course one that has appeared and has been resolved in practically all Protestant groups within recent decades. The meaning of inspiration and the status of Scriptures has been a live issue among Baptists,

88

Methodists, Presbyterians, Congregationalists, and others. It has usually been resolved by causing two fundamental new divisions among these church bodies, conservative and liberal, fundamental and non-fundamental or modern. *Modernism* in Protestant churches represents an adjustment to the claims of science that it has a monoply on truth and that revelation must be interpreted in the light of science and its findings. This has tended to make "modern" churches to have a sociology rather than a theology. They have ceased to "let God be God." This trend in the churches is concerned less with man's relation to God and more with man's relation to fellowman.

Concerning the "inerrancy" of the Scriptures, which is an issue among numerous Christian groups at this time, the latest authentic word appears to have been spoken by a spokesman of a group in Australia. Their latest document and pronouncement on this issue is quoted favorably in a review and an evaluation of the "State of Church Conference and the Documentation."[93]

Scharleman, high ranking chaplain in the U.S. Army and member of the Concordia Seminary Faculty, in St. Louis, is there reported to have stated:

"I cannot express my own concern for the use of the word 'inerrancy' in any better way than by quoting the statement devised by our Australian brethren; to wit:

This inerrancy of the Holy Scriptures cannot be seen with human eyes, nor can it be proved to human reason; it is an article of faith, a belief in something that is hidden and not obvious. We believe that the Scriptures are the Word of God and therefore inerrant. The term inerrancy has no reference to the variant reading found in the textual sources because of copyist errors or deliberate alterations; neither does it imply an absolute verbal accuracy in quotations and in parallel accounts, such absolute conformity evidently not having been a part of God's design. We believe that the Holy Writers whom God used, retained the distinctive features of their personalities (language and terminology, literary methods, conditions of life, knowledge of nature and history as apart from direct revelation and prophecy). God made use of them in such a manner that even that which human reason might call a deficiency in Holy Scripture must serve the divine purpose.[94]

The reference to "personality differences", including even "their knowledge of nature and history", is significant. Whether or not this affirmative statement by Lutherans in Australia will satisfy the concern and allay the fears of heresy among American members of the Synodical conference remains to be seen. Certain it is that at this time the epistemology of theology and of Christian education, in elementary and secondary school, colleges and seminaries, is the number one crucial issue in contemporary thinking of a significant section of historic Christianity.

The great concern about retaining the "Scripture alone" principle and to transmit it to the next generation is commendable. But it does not eliminate the need for making our heritage meaningful to the contemporary world and to work toward a modus vivendi for both types of epistemology: Revelation, science and reason. This concern to remain in touch with the contemporary and to make ourselves understood was recently voiced in the following language by the President of Valparaiso University:

> Lately I have been compelled by some assignment to thinking again of the basic problems confronting us in the church today. The more I thought about some of them the more I began to feel that now in the afternoon of the 20th Century *dialogue* between various elements in our life is essential. We are now firm as never before to the time and the hour of the dialogue all over the world and over the entire range of human thought and experience. There must be increasingly a dialogue between the church and the world, between culture and religion, between the Gospel and the non-Christian religions, between tradition and experiment, between Athens and Calvary between Geneva and Wittenberg, between God and Man.[95]

How this can be done effectively without losing the heritage of Scripture in the area of epistemology is one of the concerns of this chapter on Epistemology in Christian education. The current "existential" trend is toward interpreting the Scriptures in the light of the contemporary world. By way of contrast, the more typical and historical trend among other theologians is to interpret the contemporary world in the light of Scriptures.

How literally may and must Scriptures be interpreted? The principles of interpretation, the inerrancy problem, the relation of Old Testament prophecies to New Testament fulfillment, these and related problems are currently undergoing scholarly research. Also, Catholic and Protestant scholars are presently working on one text that will be agreeable to both Catholic and Protestant. That accomplished they hope to agree on one translation that is acceptable to both. Translations and new versions, of which there are many, must do justice to grammar, and to history. They must at the same time be meaningful to modern man. These criteria provided for, the churches should be moving one step toward true ecumenicity, and unity, while at the same time removing the divided churches' rock of offense to those outside of and also to those within the church. Hans Küng's dream so eloquently presented in his *That the World May Believe*[95a] will come closer toward realization. Milton S. Terry's *Biblical Hermeneutics* will probably appear in a somewhat revised edition.[95b]

C: THE EPISTEMOLOGY OF IDEALISM

In the world there is nothing greater than man. In man there is nothing greater than mind. Could mind have come from anything that is not mind? The answer of idealism is: No.

> Idealism is the conclusion that the universe is an expression of intelligence and will; that the enduring substance of the world is of the nature of mind; that the material is explained by the mental. Idealism as a philosophy stands in contrast with all those systems of thought that center in nature (naturalism) or in man (humanism).[96]

Idealism has a long history. In the chapter on Reality we noted that idealism represents the view that mind is not matter. The mind that thinks cannot itself be matter, and matter cannot think itself.

91

Thought is one of those principles of things, one of those primary conditions of reality for which philosophy has been seeking, a principle which was divined in the logos of Heraclitus, the One of the Pythagorians, the Nous of Anaxagoras. Thought is the unifying principle, that which unifies and measures reality. It is indeed, the measures of all things.[97]

Certainty man must have. Also in education. For that reason the best minds of our race have sought certainty. The ancients were much concerned about "becoming" and "being." Their quest for something permanent, pervading, and continuing was persistent. We say "ancients," though the quest continued and the end is not yet. Nor is this motivated exclusively by the felt need for something unchanging around which to organize our thinking, and our school curricula. The quest for certainty has always tended to center in the problem of values, and goodness, and morality, and ethics. But the trail seems inevitably to turn back into the intellectual aspect of existence, i.e., the nature of knowledge and of truth. Epistemology is not the only problem in a philosophy of education, but certainly it is one of the more crucial areas. And education will be different, principles or government, the conception of justice will differ and differ radically with the leader's conceptions of truth.

Few men stand higher in the history of idealism than Plato. In his dialogue with Theaetetus[98] his general concern is to develop, in a typically Socratic method, the concept of knowledge. He defined knowledge, as against opinion, the something based on the idealistic conception of reality. He advanced the doctrine of Ideas. He regarded ideas as entities that are real, eternal, pre-existent, unchanging, subsisting by themselves, even before they are discovered by the mind of man, continuing even after man, as individual, has vanished. Particulars are but representatives of a class. The class is of the nature of universals. Plato's arguments in defense of truths that are objective and not the result of man's subjective conceptions, were directed largely against another philosopher of his day, Protagoras. Protagoras had asserted that "man is the measure of all things," and that all judgments, principles, and laws are man-made. Learning is a matter of discovering aspects of reality. "The teacher's function is that of a mid-wife." His role is not to create but to bring to the surface something that already exists. "I myself practice midwifery," he stated, in defining his function as a teacher.

We can readily see that here is a conception of truth, and of education, which is radically different from that which we find in American education today, as so definitely spelled out in pragmatism and more especially in the instrumentalism of Dewey. There the function of a teacher is to create truth in close intelligent and purposeful co-operation with the class of learners. When the mind is alone, stated Plato, and engaged with "being," not with "becoming" it is in the process of discovering "ideas," i. e., universal truths. "The soul views some things by herself and others through bodily organs. The soul perceives the universals and all things by herself."[99] In the dialogue with Parmenides,[100] Plato further defended his doctrine of "ideas" as a unique species of existence. In Plato's well-known illustration of the cave in which man sees only *shadows* passing by, the transiency of observable phenomena and the reality and permanency of the immutable realities is further supported. It is evident that Plato's conception of "ideas" appears to have been embodied in the thinking of historic Christianity as this movement found it necessary to intellectuallize its emphasis on love and its unique "way of life." It is clear too that the world of Socrates (Plato, that is) is dual in nature, consisting of the transient phenomenal world, known to us through the medium of our senses, and the permanent, invisible world which we can know only through reason, or as the heirs of the Judeo-Christian heritage would say through faith. It is significant to note that when this type of epistemology is spelled out in terms of the State, it leads to a kind of totalitarian government as described in *The Republic*.[101] Censorship is introduced. Education is then rather completely slanted toward the needs of the state.

Descartes was one of those in quest for certainty. The dualistic conception of reality, and therefore of truth, was given further philosophic support through his efforts. In his own dedicated search for certainty he arrived at the conclusion that whatever we accept as true must above all be simple, clear, precise.

Descartes was a mathematician before he became a philosopher. In his *Meditations*[102] he brings the results of his cogitations. "Cogito ergo sum." I think and in thinking I exist. This was simple, clear, true. His illustration of wax, as something observable through the senses of sight, smell, touch, and after melting as something not thus observable through the senses, he sought to make clear to himself and others that the "sensible" world is less real than the world of ideas. "The mind alone perceives wax." The perception of wax is not an act of the senses, but of the mind, an act of intuition alone. He concluded that as wax really exists only in the mind, so all material things exist in the mind of God. And, "by the name God I understand a substance infinite." The extended world (as wax) is conceived by the non-extended mind. The Cartesian conception of reality and truth is a re-emphasis on reason, mind, as the source of all reliable truth.

The history of philosophic thought appears to have been largely a running battle in the field of epistemology. Epistemology is the story of the basic beliefs and assumptions of reality. These in turn are the basic foundation of education. Educational objectives, anticipated outcomes, curricula, instructional materials, are quite radically different, depending on the basic beliefs and assumptions. It is for this reason also that Kant has a permanent place in philosophy of education, and in the story of educational epistemology.

Kant[103] confessed that he had been awakened from his dogmatic slumber by David Hume[104] who contended in his *Treatise on Human Nature,* that neither through Reason nor through the scientific method could any valid truth be attained. In answering the question of scepticism, whether anything can be known, and scepticism's contention that nothing can be known, and in answer to his own question whether metaphysical knowledge is at all possible, Kant solved the problem, at least to his own satisfaction, by asserting that noumena, i.e., things in themselves, cannot be known by the experimental method.

Things in themselves we do not know. The soul is outside experience. Hence the soul and God and things in their higher realities are left free and unconfined by human laws. They are apprehended not by reason, but by faith.[105]

Metaphysics, therefore, is not a science [Prolegomena]. As concerns the sources of metaphysical cognition, its very concept implies that they cannot be empirical. Its principles must never be derived from experience. It must not be physical but metaphysical knowledge, lying beyond experience. It can, therefore, have for its basis neither external experience, which is the source of physics proper, nor internal which is the basis of empirical psychology. It is therefore *a priori* knowledge, coming from pure understanding and pure reason.[106]

In his attempts to firm up the foundation of science, which Hume had dynamited, and the foundation of religion, which had been equally disturbed, Kant conceived of existence as the experimentally approachable "phenomena" on the one hand and the "noumena," approachable and apprehensible through faith alone. "A priori" synthetic judgment cannot be attained through the methods of experimentalism. When the heirs of historic Christianity today organize intensive and extensive programs of education, from the cradle to the grave, when they even go to the trouble and expense of establishing and maintaining their own schools, it is largely because leadership in American education has, without adequate justification, accepted experimentalism as the one and only valid source of truth and guidance. God-centered education is an ongoing protest even though it is a minority protest, against naturalism to the exclusion of supernaturalism either in the form of idealism or of historic Judeo-Christian tradition. Kant's categorical imperative is something that should be given serious thought by those of us who are trying to improve public education and/or justify the existence of non-public education, in order that the American youth may be stabilized and helped to maturity of both thinking and acting.

Both Descartes and Kant go on the assumption of a duality of reality. But dualism has never satisfied the seekers of truth and certainty. The Cartesian answer is inadequate. Spinoza (1632-1677) attempted to harmonize and unify all existence and knowledge.

"Spinoza transformed the dualism of Descartes into a monism by making God the sole true substance and making mind and matter his manifestations."[107] Spinoza's pantheism exerted a great influence in German (Goethe) and British thought (the Romanticists). His ideas tended to develop into two directions, sometimes knows as "pancosmism", essentially atheistic or at least devoid of a personal God, or acosmism, which is closely allied with the theistic idealistic conception of existence.

The most pronounced type of idealism was developed by Berkeley,[108] a militant Anglican churchman of the first half of the 18th Century. He forthrightly stated his belief that "things have no existence outside of the mind."

> There is not other substance than spirit, and that which perceives. Matter is non-existent. The absolute existence of unthinking things are words without meaning. They include a contradiction. — There is no corporeal or material substance.[109]

What happens to science and the scientific method if we accept that extreme version of idealism? What becomes of scientifically established truth? How shall we account for the tremendous productivity, at least in terms of creature comforts, exploration, and control of inter-planetary space, and atomic power? Matter, and the method of studying and controlling matter and energy, is here to stay, at least for a long time to come. If there is a "lag" in the advancement of this science at present, in relation to progress in Soviet education, let American scientists and educators gird their loins and make up the lag at the earliest possible time. Americans of all shades of educational philosophies — materialist, idealist, or of the Judeo-Christian persuasion — will agree: science must be taught well, in elementary and high school, but we still contend that science is a fragmentary view of existence and therefore represents only a part of the whole truth. And a half-truth has often been called a lie. It tends to mislead. With even greater depth of conviction those of the historic Christianity school of thought are sure that Berkeleyan idealism is a fragmentary view of existence. It is unrealistic. It is untenable. Education based on such a view of life cannot but mislead.

Certainly it makes sense to question the materialistic claim of Locke particularly if it aspires, as it did, to *a monopoly of truth,* to wit:

> Whence has the mind, white and clean to begin with, all the materials of reason and knowledge? To this I answer in one word: experience. In that all our knowledge is founded; and from it ultimately derives itself. Our observation, employed either about external sensible objects or about the internal operations of our mind, is that which supplies our understanding with *all* the materials of our thinking. Those two are the fountains of knowledge, from whence *all* the ideas we have or can naturally have, do spring.[110]

But it makes equally good sense to rule out extreme idealism of the Berkeleyan type, as fragmentary, unrealistic, and, if really taken seriously, misleading.

A contributor to educational philosophy in the person of Herman Horne[111] has put in a good and a strong word for idealism in American education. Horne believes that there are good reasons for accepting idealism[112] because mind is the principle of explanation. Mind is not matter. Mind comes from mind. There can be no object without a subject. Personality is real. Man is a free moral agent. Idealism supports the belief in immortality. The intuition of the race suggests some form of idealism. Great minds in the history of the race have accepted idealism.

Matter is by itself purposeless. Materialism admits of no teleological tendency in nature. Yet there is order. There appears to be design. Matter cannot create order out of chaos. Yet, the behavior of nature is predictable, to the extent of nearly total elimination of error or doubt. Whence comes the order? How did the laws of nature come to be established? How are they maintained?

To what is the order of the world due? The order of the

97

world is the problem of cosmology. Idealism holds that the order of the world is due to the manifestation in space and time of an eternal and spiritual reality. Knowledge is the problem of epistemology. Idealism holds that knowledge is man thinking the thoughts and the purposes of this eternal spiritual reality as they are embodied in the world of fact.[113]

The origin, nature, and destiny of man is more fully dealt with in the chapter devoted to Man. However, when we come to appraise a philosophy of education and come to the question: So what? What difference does it make in the education of our children and young people? There must we take a brief look at man as he is pictured in the idealistic view of the universe. If our learners are groups of atoms that react to their environment in an atomistic, or mechanical way, then the learners are machines and educational efforts must be slanted toward that concept of man.

This view is inadequate because it omits consideration of the pupils as living, conscious beings who have intentions, desires, purposes, feelings, thoughts, and decisions of their own. It (naturalism, experimentalism) holds the pupil to be of the same essence as the earth upon which he treads. It omits the essential distinction that the earth does not know it is being trod upon, but the pupil does. A teacher who accepts naturalism as a philosophy may, while teaching, actually regard his pupils as non-mechanical and unpredictable in their responses but he will not be logically consistent.[114]

Personality is something unique. There are no two alike, each is different.

Personality has ultimate worth. We know nothing higher nor more valuable than self-hood and personality. Respect for personality in feeling and behavior is as lofty a virtue as we know. It is the virtue, which, if practiced, would solve our human problems.[115]

Echoes of support come from quarters who accept the historical Christian heritage. Man is dust indeed. But, he has a des-

98

tiny. Each child, bright or dull, white, black, or brown, is very important. What happens in culture patterns in which matter and motion have become the only basic considerations? Individuals become de-personalized robots. Not only that but the agony cries of suffering man come to us across the ocean, from out of the furnaces of Dachau. In materialistically oriented totalitarian countries the individual gets a number. It is the state that counts. Persons are expendable. Brainwashing and training in the goose-step may be an acceptable pattern of education but not in a country in which the basic values of historic Christianity, and shall we add here, of idealistically oriented educational program still persist.

> Education is the process whereby human kind is working out into fruitition its own inner nature; it is man's means of realizing his destination of reaching his goal of largest power, joy, and service.[116]

The individual is said to be largely a product of his environment, Admittedly, the genes still make their real contribution to the final product. The environment is largely social. Individuals composing the social environment are persons with purposes. The institutions surrounding learners have purposes. From this it is easy to infer, says Horne, that the cosmos, whose offspring man is, is purposeful too.

> For purposes to exist in part it is logical to suppose that purposes exist in the whole which explains the part. But as purpose in the part implies finite personality having purpose so may we posit purpose in the whole as infinite personality. From there we may pass to the conception of the pupil as a finite personality growing through our tutelage into the likeness of an infinite personality whose thought and purpose the world embodies. And thus the environment of the pupil may be sensed as spiritual.[117]

Education in and under idealistically oriented teachers and curricula tend to keep God in the picture. Of course, it is the God of theism or deism. But it is not a personal God. That being so schools ought to, if they are willing to spell out the implication of idealism, have God and self-revelations of God in their objectives and curricula.

> The conception of God, as herein reached is that of one absolute mind, complete and self-moving. Being absolute there are no other gods. Being mind he is not less than personal. Being complete in himself there is no change to time, neither increase nor decrease; time exists in him as a part but he does not exist in time nor grow old with centuries. — From the standpoint of the physicist, matter disappears into some form of energy, like electricity; from the viewpoint of the speculative (idealistic) philosopher energy disappears into some form of consciousness, like attention. The energy of the world thus in the last analysis may be held to be the attentive aspect of the consciousness of God. — Our conception is neither a transcendental dualism (Judaism's transcendant Jehovah) not an immanent pantheism (Spinoza's deus sive natura) but an *idealistic theism*. God is the self-conscious unity of all reality. Within his life falls the life of nature and of man.[118]

Obviously this definition of idealism is not far removed from Hegel's dialectic idealism. Idealism is critical of materialism because it (materialism) embraces only a fragment of the whole of reality, and by implication only a fragment of the whole truth. From the viewpoint of the heirs of Judeo-Christian heritage it is refreshing that a deeply rooted philosophy of truth joins in the protest against a monopoly of truth as claimed by experimental materialism. Prof. Fisher, from the staff of the University of Illinois, recently spoke on the Soviet Challenge, to the Alumni of Illinois University in Springfield. In it he made the point that the area *of truth,* of *epistemology presents a strategic battlefield for effectively combating the Soviet threat to "bury us."* Communism, he stated, is most attractive to those who know least. Education is the important factor in an aggressive offensive and defensive at this critical period of history. But, the idealists ask, education for what? *Secularism,* being a descendant and near relative of materialism, is *relatively impotent when it comes to stemming the tide of materialism.* We are not identifying materialistic epistemology with that of secularism but we are saying that both have but a fragment of the truth and therefore are in a very vulnerable position when it comes to defend the citadels of our real American way of life, and the real values that lie buried in historic Christianity, including that of God and freedom, the dignity of man, and finally the democratic way of life.

Marx was outspoken in his opposition to truth as that is visualized in an idealistic conception of the universe.

> My own dialectic method is not only different from the Hegelian, but it is its direct opposite. For Hegel — the thinking process is the demiurge (creator) of the real world and the real world is only the outward manifestation of "the Idea." With me on the other hand, the ideal is nothing else than the material world reflected by the human mind and translated into terms of thought.[119]

We are here concerned not only, and not primarily, with the basic assumptions which underlie our conception of reality; nor with only our conception of epistemology but, more specifically, with its implication for education. What contribution has idealism to suggest or to make to the education of our citizens for tomorrow?

> Education is the eternal process of superior adjustment of the physically and mentally developed, free, conscious human being, as manifested in the intellectual, emotional and volitional environment of man.[120]

It is helpful to the student of the epistemology of idealism to bear in mind a distinction that has been made by idealistically oriented educators between "subjective" idealism, as represented by Berkeley, and "objective" idealism of Plato and Kant. Greene, for example, identifies himself as not in agreement with the personal idealism of the former and associates himself with the latter. He joins the growing chorus of protest against the assumed

101

monopoly of materialistic experimentalism in the field of American education and proceeds to develop what might appear to be a defense even of historic Christianity but that turns out to be a dialectic compromise with materialistically oriented philosophy of education.

> What is needed, now and always, but especially now in these times of crisis, is a radical re-examination and reassessment of our entire educational structure, its ultimate objectives, its fundamental presuppositions, its basic procedures, all this in the existential context of our contemporary American society and of the total world situation, and no less urgently, in the still wider context of our best contemporary understanding of human nature and of the universe to which we belong.[121]

Idealist educators dissociate themselves, as do the heirs of historic Christianity, from current violent criticism of public education, such as "Why can't Johnnie read? Why are not the three 'R's taught anymore, as they used to be in the good old days?" These are not serious criticisms. They seldom get beyond the surface of things. They are found in evaluations of current public education as given for example in Buchanan's *Essay in Politics*:

> The truth is that neither our society nor its academic servants know what should be taught to the young. Less and less good teaching and learning are being done, and — the effects of bad teaching and learning are becoming evident. The general public has reasonable doubts that the academic institutions are providing the education the community needs for its survival. — There is no confidence that the members of the academic body can teach and learn what they ought to know or that there is any general will to find out what that might be. [122]

From direct contact with leaders in public education during the past twenty years, this writer agrees whole-heartedly with Greene in saying that the comment on teachers' unwillingness to grow professionally and to find out ways of improving their work of teaching is "too all-embracing to be fair." No other profession has crowded into the summer schools conducted by college and university departments of education, as have the members of the public and parochial school teaching profession, so as to continue their in-service professional growth. But, we must agree with Buchanan that the education provided today, to the tune of forty billion dollars a years in support of public education, to the exclusion of all others who provide good American education is not "the education that the community needs for survival." We rather agree with an idealistically oriented educator who states: "There is an urgent need for more basic thinking and planning to get back to fundamentals, with all the philosophical vigor we can muster."[123]

Idealism is severely critical of current educational thinking in American education, particularly because secularism is dominated by experimentalism to the rigid exclusion of either idealism or historic Christianity. And, except for the first one hundred and seventy years, when it was still saturated with idealistic morals and the epistemology of historic Chrstianity, the only tax-supported system of education in America is oriented to materialism, to the rigid exclusion of both idealism with its stabilizing principles, and of the power of historic Christianty. Today thoughtful people are beginning to see the long range results of education so conceived and practiced. Criticism comes from many quarters.

> Whenever materialism has found soil for its growth, limitarianism and the narrow bourns it imposes upon the world are in evidence. But this mutilation of reality, this cramping limitarianism, with its ideological strait jacket is nowhere more apparent than in human life. How poor and anemic it has become. It has dwindled to a drab existence, *guided solely by the impressions of the senses*, in the whirling stream of experiences it drifts along aimlessly, soul-lessly borne on by a tide that carries with it merely the *body and its appetites*. Modern man never plummets the depths of his own soul. This deeper stratum of his being is to him utterly unknown; for he deliberately has closed the shaft leading to it.[124]

The basic assumptions for a sound philosophy of epistemology on which to build a superstructure of the best possible kind of education is not identical with the beliefs of Judeo-Christian theology. Idealists are defending an important sector of the battle line in the all-out war against materialism and its epistemological implications. Educators of the historic Christianity school of educational philosophy hail their comrades in arms, salute them, and wish them more courage and more power, in strategic places, such as the National Society for the Study of Education.

> Education means that the origin of man is God, the nature of man is freedom and the destiny of man is immortality. Thus does philosophy still procure for us, not by scientific proofs but by plausible implications: God, Freedom, and Immortality.[125]

D: EPISTEMOLOGIES ORIENTED AROUND MATERIALISM

There are any number of so-called educational philosophies which are frequently treated as separate and independent philosophies of education. However, we recall an incident in the classroom of the University of Alberta in which the professor, British-educated Dr. McEachern, expressed disappointment with his class of graduate students in philosophy who had failed, as shown by their examination papers, to grasp an idea which the professor evidently considered basic and which he felt he had made explicit during the course of his presentation. It was the idea that basically there are two, and only two philosophies: Materialism and Spiritualism. He included idealism and faith in God in that one term. He was persuaded that there were only two philosophies. We could follow through on that idea and speak of only two philosophies, particularly if we would be willing to grant to Judeo-Christian religion a berth in the idealistic category. The basic belief and assumption which underly both idealism and Judeo-Christian beliefs are similar if not in some respects the same. Certainly both stand in bold contrast to the idea that there is nothing beyond matter and motion in all the universe. Our basic thesis is that secularly-oriented education is based on a fragmentary conception of reality, and its epistemology, as well as its ethic cannot, therefore, but be based on a partial, fragmentary philosophy of education. A similar severe criticism will have to be made of idealism. It too is but a fragmentary conception of reality and any epistemology, ethic, or ideal product of an education that is thus oriented, cannot but be fragmentary. Historic Christianity, by way of contrast to both materialism and idealism, is *all-inclusive*. Its basic assumption is that both matter and spirit are real entities and both must be given adequate consideration in any "realistic," true, valid, all-inclusive, and eternally good, philosophy of education.

We shall, therefore, identify three basically different educational ideologies in American philosophies of education: Materialism, idealism, and historic Christianity. Under materialism we shall deal with naturalism, secularism, positivism, pragmatism, instrumentalism, empiricism, experimentalism, logical empiricism, and also realism. We have hesitated to classify realism with the family of materialistically oriented philosophies of education for the simple reason that "realists," like Breed, have been strongly existential in their thinking and have therefore granted a hearing to other than typically materialistic theses. A similar thing might be said of "pragmatic" thinkers, because they too have shown a willingness to consider as true any approach to the problem of truth, provided only that it "works." They have ever conceded that faith provided it works, even if it is not based on experimental findings, is a valid method for apprehending certain truths.

Theology, a science revered in all times and countries by the greatest number of men; an object regarded by them as the most important, the most useful, and the most indispensible to the happiness of society. An examination on the principles upon which this pretended science is founded, forces us to acknowledge that these principles, formerly adjudged incontestable, are only hazardous suppositions, imagined ignorance, propagated by enthusiasm or knavery, adopted by timid credulity, preserved by cus-

105

tom which never reasons, and revered solely because not understood. — Instructors have long enough fixed men's minds upon heaven; let them now turn them upon the earth. An incomprehensible theology, ridiculous fables, impenetrable mysteries, puerile ceremonies, are too fatiguing to be longer endured. Let the human mind apply itself to what is natural, to intelligible objects, sensible truths, and useful knowledge.[126]

To understand what a consistent materialistic view of life means and what its implications are for epistemology one must read Hugh Elliot's *Modern Science and Materialism*. He will tolerate no theory of knowledge other than that which is oriented around matter and motion. His attitude over against sources of truth other than the physical sciences borders on the arrogant.

An age of science is necessarily an age of materialism. Ours is an age of science, and it may be said with truth that we are all materialists now. — The proposition which I here desire to advance is that every event occurring in the Universe, including those events known as mental, and all kinds of human action and conduct, are expressible purely in terms of matter and motion. The existing Universe and all other things and events occurring therein may be theoretically expressed in terms of matter and energy, undergoing continuous redistribution in accordance with the ordinary laws of physics and chemistry.[127]

Elliot also believes that a very moderate amount of analysis suffices altogether to dispel the contention of Mach and Karl Pearson that science must limit itself to the "how" of nature's behavior and that science can contribute nothing toward the "why" of nature's behavior patterns. He rejects any and all forms of teleology or purposiveness in nature.

Variations in the matter and motion are accounted for by accidental mutations. Survival of some forms of life rather than others is, of course, accounted for by Natural Selection.

Mind has no more real existence than fire. In each case we have to do exclusively with molecules undergoing disintegration or combination. This chemical activity suffices in itself for the whole of the phenomena flowing from the centre of activity, and the belief in any additional independent entity is a fallacy which itself can be expressed and explained in physico-chemical terms.[128]

It is this emphasis on the nature of reality and its implications for epistemology, together with the somewhat less than humble insistence on a monopoly of truth, that prompts the sponsors of God-centered education to stand rather firmly in building up their system and even to suggest that if the federal government wishes to support education in America they ought not to bypass their educational efforts and needs as if they had no real cause to maintain their own philosophy and system of education.

The principal objection to materialism and its concomitant method of establishing truth, and claiming a monopoly of truth, lies in the fact that it aspires to deal effectively with spiritual, moral, and social problems. It is not that psychology, sociology, and criminology have not contributed to the diagnosis and cure of emotional and social problems. It is the insistence of the scientific method of being the one and only source of truth, and the only approach to a cure of such problems that disturbs the idealist and the adherents of historic Christianity.

> The growth of science and technology, the advance of medicine, general education and general enlightenment have greatly increased the valid *authority of science*. Any number of social questions which were once the exclusive prerogative of religion and conventional morality, are now recognized as falling within the sphere of the *social sciences*. Sex and family relations are examples. Virtue and wickedness have largely given way to personality *adjustments* and maladjustments. *Crime* is traced in considerable measure to social causes. The school boy is no longer beaten because he neglects his studies. Nutritional, medical, personality factors instead are investigated. The home life, the associates of the boy are searched for contributing causes. This process has resulted in an increasingly *materialistic* outlook.[129]

Less outspoken critics of idealistic and Judeo-Christian thinking and more cautious advocates of the kind of materialistic thinking which we have quoted is usually referred to as "secularism."

Secularism

Secularism moves within the orbit of a materialistic philosophy of existence, but it is much less violent in its opposition to non-scientific epistemologies of education. It is far more tolerant, and permissive. But it is strictly concerned only with secular problems and projects. It concerns itself with problems of this world. It emphasizes a non-religious approach to the good of this life and to social welfare. American education is admittedly secular, in its educational philosophy, in its basic assumptions, in its objectives and in the curricular content designed to attain those objectives. The secular viewpoint by-passes matters of faith.

God and the Word of God are of no concern and of no consequence in a secular view of life. The question is raised sometimes whether tax-supported education is God-less. The fact is that God has no place in the classroom of the common schools of America. It would be quite unfair and unscholarly to refer to common schools of America as godless. But it is accurate to say that they are God-less. The former refers to behavior of students. No one should tolerate a statement or suspicion that in tax-supported schools students and teachers are necessarily godless. That may be true in specific instances. No representative member of a Christian group would dare to be so blind as to claim that students and teachers in parochial schools are never godless. On the other hand the designation of God-less is tenable and true. Tax-supported schools are secular, and it is widely held that they should continue to be. This is a too easy solution to the crucial problems confronting education in America today. At a time when God-less education in some nations of the world has come to be synonymous with unpredictable and godless national policies and programs, programs and ambitions which make it necessary currently to spend fifty billion dollars annually to protect the free world from being overrun and "buried" by anti-Christian and unpredictable, atheistic ideologies of the world, we in America should probably seriously ask ourselves whether a neutral-like secularism is a strong-enough bulwark to keep the threatening tide of communism in check and under control.

Naturalism

Closely related to an epistemology which passes under the name of secularism is that of naturalism. Naturalism as a theory of truth has been cultivated for a long period of time. Francis Bacon is properly regarded as the original sponsor of naturalism, Though Aristotle, in contrast to Plato, made initial thrusts into the realm of truth by closely observing and classifying nature and natural objects.

Really, there seems to be nothing more natural than "naturalism" in interpreting our environment. "Believers" cannot and do not object to that kind of an epistemology. Page the Scriptures and see if this be not so. The Psalmist began by observing his physical self, and his physical environment and from there proceeded to draw his conclusions: "I will praise thee for I am wonderfully made; marvelous are thy works. And that my soul knoweth right well."[130]

Another man of God, presumably David, quite obviously observed the stellar universe and exclaimed as a result: "The heavens declare the glory of God; and the firmament showeth his handiwork. Day unto day uttereth speech and night unto night showeth knowledge."[131]

The scientific method and the epistemology of science had its beginnings in close observation of nature and natural phenomena; in tabulating, mentally or otherwise, the things that were seen and heard and felt and smelt. Sense data are basic. By induction, generalizations are drawn. Thus man arrives at broad ideas, from hypotheses to theses, and sound beliefs. And why not? He may and he should.

There cannot possibly be any quarrel, by anybody, with anybody, for making the study of matter and energy, and the control of the same, the subject of special inquiry. An education and an educational philosophy which slights the physical sciences cannot and does not deserve anyone's enthusiastic support, in 1966, or ever. And certainly, the epistemology that has been developed for the fruitful pursuit of this phase of education, has proven its validity. The fruits are there: on the ground, under the ground, in the air, in inter-stellar space, in the research laboratories of commerce and industry, in the hospitals for ailing bodies, and, to a limited extent, in the hospitals for the mentally and emotionally sick, in the penal institutions, and assuredly on the battlefield, where those who have made science the last word in the determination of values make it necessary for us to fight. The trouble is that the epistemology underlying education, has been too strongly slanted in the direction of making familiarity with matter and motion the basic and *the only criterion of truth* and error, to the *exclusion of other tried and tested bases of truth.*

Aristotle's quest for truth and certainty, not exclusively but nevertheless very largely by observing nature, is proverbial. He was given the name "Ille Philosophus." He was the philosopher *catexochen.* He was a friend of Plato, the father of idealism, but he declared: Amicus Plato, sed magis amica veritas, meaning, Plato is dear to me but dearer to me is the truth.

Aristotle preached return to things, to the unwithered face of nature and reality. He had a lusty preference for the concrete particular, for the flesh and blood individual.

Despite his emphasis on "naturalism" Aristotle was so many sided that his epistemology did indeed give birth to a system of logic which has fallen somewhat into disrepute as a means of arriving at the truth but which nevertheless indicates that he had an open mind for other than those truths which were derived from observing and reflecting inductively on natural phenomena. The syllogistic method is usually associated with Aristotle; however, if the Organon of Aristotle pointed the way to a naturalistic interpretation of existence and of truth, it was the Novum Organum, by Francis Bacon, nearly two thousand years later, which gave to naturalism a strong lease on life. Said he:

110

I am of the opinion that if men had ready at hand a just history of nature and experience, and labored diligently thereon; and if they bind themselves to two rules, — the first to lay aside received opinions and notions; the second to refrain the mind for a time from the highest generalizations, and to those next to them, — they would be able, by the native and genuine force of the mind without any other art to fall into my form of interpretation. For interpretation is the true and natural work of the mind when freed from impediments.[132]

So wrote Bacon, the famed iconoclast of the early seventeenth century (1561-1626) and the originator of that thesis which states: Knowledge is power. Bacon was a thoroughgoing apostle of naturalism in education. As a current form of materialism, naturalism is probably the key word, also when it comes to identifying the epistemology undergirding education in America today.

At present time, materialism, or that vague form of materialism known as naturalism, is extremely influential in the Western world. Just as the idealist claims that all being is mind, so materialism claims that all being is quantitative and material. — Man is no exception. He is regarded merely as a highly complex physical organism, acting according to the same laws that holds of nature generally.[133]

During the last three centuries naturalism has dominated to a great extent the intellectual life of Western Europe and America. It has given rise to various theories of life, SUCH AS PRAGMATISM, INSTRUMENTALISM, POSITIVISM, SOCIALISM, COMMUNISM. Basically it has oriented all these by *making man continuous with nature,* by *confining his destiny to earth,* and by *eliminating the supernatural.*[134]

By the middle of the 19th Century the influence of naturalism was seen in the content of science, art, literature, and philosophy of education.[135]

The principal advocates of naturalism were men like Comte who stressed the positive approach to *knowledge* through the scientific method; Darwin, who in 1859 stirred the foundation of

111

philosophy and education by his *Origin of Species;* Spencer, who sought to explain the force and "The integration of matter and concomitant dissipation of movement." (At the end of his life Spencer expressed very pessimistic views about the future of *humanity.*) Huxley, Dewey, Thorndike, must be added to the list of those men who introduced and applied the naturalistic interpretation of existence to the problems of education.

It is difficult to apprehend the far-reaching influence which the epistemology of science, that is the scientific method of naturalism, has had on all phases of life, individuals, family, community, national and internation relations, during the last century.

> The outstanding contributions of the 19th and 20th Century in the human studies have concentrated on *physical* factors, of climate upon history (Huntington), of occupation on outlook (Marx), of heredity upon character (Lombrose), of environment upon ethics (Westermarck) and eyestrain upon genius; of origins by Renan, the social physics of Comte. — Hence arises the diligent fact-finding and fact-verification of Niebuhr and Ranke, of the economic interpretation of history of Charles Beard, the physiological psychology of Wundt, the behaviorist psychology of Watson, the experimental novel of Zola, the research materialistic dialectic of Marx. — The retreat from beauty by Picasso, the retreat from logic and sanity by Dali, the retreat from grammar by Gertrude Stein. In world politics it emerges as the cultural morphology of Spengler, the geopolitics of Haushofer and the economic panacea of Cordell Hull. — Everywhere an absence of spiritual principles, a cry for security and for meal tickets.[136]

Positivism

Positivism represents an epistemology which deals only with "positive" knowledge. It was developed by Auguste Comte, a French philosopher, in his *Cours de Philosophie Positive,* 1842. Positivism excludes all truth but those that have been developed by experience and observation. It is one of the large family of epistemologies that are oriented to the materialistic interpretation of existence. It assumes three stages through which human knowledge passes, the theological, the metaphysical, and the positivistic.

112

Now that the third stage has come, theology and metaphysics must be rejected. Comte sought to apply his theory of truth to sociological problems, and also to the development of a new religion. He endeavored to construct a religion of humanity in which a cult of the human race, and more especially of men of genius was to take place of the worship of God. Positivism denies the existence of God, of the soul and of course, of immortality. Positivism operates within the frame of reference of those epistemologies which "proceed as though theology did not exist or as though it were a subject smacking of the superstition of a previous age."[137]

Experimentalism

The three names which are most frequently associated with an epistemology which is characteristically American are those of Peirce,[138] James,[139] and Dewey.[140] The latter two are usually associated with divisions of materialistically oriented philosophies known as pragmatism and instrumentalism. Both of these however, are but illustrations of the experimental approach to the problem of truth and knowledge. The identification of values is frequently associated, especially among the experimentalist and related philosophies. In this section we are interested, however, chiefly in the nature and origin of truth and knowledge. Experimentalism is essentially a protest against the "spectator" theory of knowledge, as represented by traditional philosophies. It is therefore an equally virulent protest against any form of "dualism," against

> the tradition which divides fact from value, body from mind, matter from form, the world from the knower, and even the curriculum from the pupil. A sociology of dualism would seem indicated to account for the perverse divisiveness which men have continually introduced into their lives. — It is a little strange that epistemology has exercised the fascination that it has. — The scientist has consistently refused to be impressed by the problem of knowledge. — There are problems of knowledge, but they are not epistemological, that is not those of getting an already separated

subjective knower and objective world together again. —
Such knowledge (experimental) is in every case different
from what the spectator theory assumes, for it is knowledge which depends on actions and operations like those
of Wilson cloud chambers, Geiger counters, spectroscopes,
sphygmographs, statistical indices, documentary analysis, and
thousands of other entries to knowledge, entries which are
totally unlike the otiose contemplations basic to classic
theories of knowledge.[141]

Experimentalism goes on the basic assumption that existence
in its ultimate character is changing and uncertain; that life is
inherently experimental. And the aim of education is to enable
men and women to live more intelligently.

> In man, mind has appeared in nature. But that does not
> justify the conclusion that all nature is therefore mind. Man
> does live in a world, however, in which things are not all
> fixed, but in a world in which he can do something to make
> the goods of experience more secure and the evils less
> menacing. — Participate he must in the natural and social
> affairs. A basic aim of education therefore is to help him
> develop the attitudes and habits, and to gain the mastery of
> techniques which will serve to make that participation
> progressively more intelligent. — Creative intelligence in
> man is the supreme essential.[142]

Geiger goes on to explain that the "experimentalist interpretation of knowledge is a description of the way problems are
solved, above all by the scientific method." Geiger's conception
and defense of the experimental method is in part based on the
theory of evolution.

> If the implications of evolution are securely grasped the
> very foundations of dualism are cut away. To take evolution
> seriously is to accept biological continuity. And this means
> that the live creature (including man, of course) is not
> divided from its environment; that conscious experience and
> nature are not anti-thetical; that knowledge is a matter of
> vital participation in a world of which it is a part rather
> than the idle glances of a disinterested and outside watcher.

114

> To take evolution seriously, and how else can we take it, —
> is to be a naturalist; to be a naturalist is to see man, his
> works and his values as a great transaction going on within
> the world, and not outside it.[143]

The experimentalists are aware that the validity of their epistemological principles has been seriously called into question. Does experimentalism provide anything stable, any central North star-like point of orientation, both for knowledge, for ethics, and for education? Will the obvious relativity lead to epistemological and ethical chaos? Does experience and concomitant growth have any particular end, excepting more growth? Does this thesis of experimentalism encourage teen-agers and adults to go all out for experience, new and exciting experiences, never mind the social acceptance, ethical and moral standards, just so there are abundant experiences? What becomes of the experiences of living through Great Books? Was Mortimer Adler guilty of pedantry, of obscurantism? Is it safe to cut away from our spiritual and cultural heritage? The experimentalist is relentlessly on the warpath against indoctrination, against authoritarianism, against absolute and unchanging truths and standards.

Geiger quotes Thomas approvingly in the article to which reference has been made:

> The only lasting protection against the temptation to become
> authoritarian is to stake one's faith on the free process of
> experimental inquiry rather than on the existence of absolute
> truths and standards.[144]

The concept of experimentalism has undergone changes over a period of fifty years. This can be seen by comparing Peirce, rightly regarded as among the originators of experimentalism and Geiger whom we have quoted. In *Ways of Justifying Belief* Peirce states among other things:

> To satisfy our doubts, it is necessary that a method should
> be found by which our beliefs may be determined by noth-
> ing human, but by some external permanency — by some-
> thing upon which our thinking has no effects.[145]

In the experimentalism of John Dewey and of George Geiger, man through his creative intelligence has come to be regarded as participant creator, through his creative intelligence.

It is quite obvious on the one hand that while "experience" has come to play an increasingly important role in the transmission of our inheritance among those educators who are oriented to idealism as well as those who are still rooted in historic Christianity, their conception of experience is more limited than that of the present day representatives of "experimentalism." With them it is a means of assimilating the content of a given curriculum or selecting curriculum content. Experience, Yes. Experimentalism, No. Too much is at stake. The whole of the wisdom of the ages, the results of intuition and of inspiration is washed down the drain by applying the principles of experimentalism as a determiner or what is true and right and good. Consistent application of the experimental method in education would make ours an impoverished culture. Certainly we would cease to be a bulwark against the rising tide of a similarly oriented epistemology, that of communism. This must not be. They shall not pass. Give the experimentalists, the pragmatists, and the instrumentalists, time and they will taper off. They will come to their senses. They will discover that true wisdom was not born yesterday.

> Though experience be our only guide in reasoning concerning matters of fact, it must be acknowledged that this is not altogether infallible, but in some cases is apt to lead us into error.[146]

Pragmatism

As Peirce was intent on making ideas clear, as well as authentic and valid, so William James continued the effort to set up valid criteria for truth and for valid principles. Pragmatism proposed that the validity of an idea should be tested by the practical or pragmatic difference it would make if it were assumed to be true. If there were no practical difference two apparently different ideas would obviously be the same, or the difference would prove to be only verbal, not real. James proposed and applied the pragmatic test to truth itself. Ideas were to be accepted as true if they worked. (It is readily seen that Dewey's instrumentalism and experimentalism were essentially further refinements or reinterpretation of pragmatism.) It is clear that pragmatism is a continuing protest against the nature of truth as conceived by idealism or as thought of in the Judeo-Christian heritage. The shift of emphasis inaugurated, or strengthened, by pragmatism is away from a priori, deductive, revealed, or rationally-arrived-at truths. It represents a movement away from final, complete, absolute truths toward an emphasis on *processes*. Peirce had contended that any idea shall mean its consequences in experience. This leads eventually to the operational definition of truth. It limits inquiry to actual on-going experiences. Principles attain validity as they evidence observable distinctions within experience. Relations, too, are relations observed within experience. Ideas and moral precepts are to be tested in the social matrix. For this reason not only intellectually defensible maxims, but especially principles in morals and ethics afford a rich and crucial area of experimentation to determine the validity of such principles. If they work they are true. If they are unworkable they are not true and ought to be discarded or by-passed.

> Following James, men have increasingly accepted the idea of a "universe with the lid off", that the stream of affairs develops novelly, a mingling of the new with the old and familiar. And the actual event is precarious — we never know just how our efforts will turn out. It is on this basis that Dewey has said: All action is an invasion of the future; of the unknown. Conflict and uncertainty are ultimate traits.[147]

To understand the significance of pragmatism we must recall that historically it is associated with the emerging theory of evolution. Darwin's *Origin of Species* appeared in 1859; his *Descent of Man* appeared in 1871. The theory of evolution caused nothing short of a revolution in practically all branches of human concerns particularly also in the area of epistemology and education.

Out of the intensive thinking on the campus of both Chicago and Harvard Universities, Peirce's Metaphysical Club produced the thesis that there is an inseparable connection between cognition and purpose. That is pragmatism. Pragmatism stresses purposeful thinking, designed to improve some phase of the environment. Creative, purposeful thinking in the interest of intelligent action, that is a characteristic of pragmatism.[148] The theory of evolution would have been much less controversial and of less revolutionary consequences if it had not been applied to areas of thought that lay beyond the realm of biology and of science. However, early enthusiasm about the all-inclusive application of a theory as yet unproven, and applicable largely in the field of biology and of the physical sciences only, led to the use of explaining and attempting to improve morals, ethics, theory of government, and religious beliefs.

> Spencer read into evolution a dubious system of inevitable moral and theological interpretations.[149]

Spencer was the first to use biological standards for human ethics. He thought that the senses of man were molded in accordance with the all embracing law of evolution, from a less perfect to a more perfect state, from heterogeneity to homogeneity; from the simple to the complex; Spencer identified evolution with progress. Self-evidently, truth could henceforth be established only by the method of science. Hence the great emphasis on science studies in the schools. Evolution and science have essentially no concern with anything but the world of matter and motion. They are oriented to materialism. A trend toward a utilitarian definition of truth is self-evident with the emergence of the idea that only the useful organs survive and that the fittest specimen of any species are the ones to propagate and survive.

> From the moment that anyone posits evolutionism as the explanation of all life, including man, and substitutes a naturalistic cosmic setting for a supernatural one, it is only

logical that his education should ignore God, the supernatural, religion, the Ten Commandments, the eternal moral law, the soul, immortality, everything which in fact is above and beyond the purely empirical realm of existence.[150]

Did James feel that he had discovered something entirely new in the quest for truth and certainty? Not at all.

Pragmatism is nothing essentially new. It harmonizes with many ancient philosophic tendencies. It agrees with nominalism in always appealing to particulars; with utilitarianism in emphasizing practical aspects; with positivism in its disdain for verbal solutions, useless questions, and metaphysical abstractions. It has no doctrines, no dogmas, save its method.[151]

Pragmatism lies in the corridor of a hotel as it were. Off the corridor lead doorways into various rooms in which abide men who have widely divergent philosophies of truth and education: atheist, agnostic, idealist, men who believe in prayer to help solve their problems, radicals, revolutionaries. But all must pass through the corridor to come and to go. This means that everyone who has an idea, a plan, for social and economic betterment, or even a plan for personal salvation, a thesis to defend, an idea to sell, must pass inspection and pass the test: Does it work? Is it practically useful? What improvement in human welfare, improvement in social relations, yea, international relations, will it make? One feels that the ardent defenders of historic Christianity need not hesitate to apply the pragmatic test. Possibly they would render their cause a laudable service by showing a willingness to using the pragmatic net as a sieve to screen out those truths which our world is in special need of in this second half of the twentieth century. The purpose of this sifting would not be to eliminate any Scriptural truths merely because they do not have, or someone thinks they do not have, any immediately pressing use or application. Rather the purpose would be to focus attention on those revealed and historically proven truths which are particularly relevant to the solution of problem that are troubling institutions or individuals today. As a matter of fact this is being done every week, in the pulpit and in Christian classrooms. "Functional", "life-related", "related to the contemporary world", these are the key words in current literature and instructional materials, in homiletical classrooms within the realm of historic Christianity. Nor would this be anything new in the Protestant segment of Judeo-Christian heritage.

In this Preface to his *Small Catechism* Luther, for example, states:

> Dwell on each commandment, Petition and Part with its various works, uses, benefits, dangers, and harm. — Especially give most attention to the Commandment or Part which is most neglected among your people. For example, the Seventh Commandment which forbids stealing, you must particularly enforce among mechanics and merchants, also among farmers and servants; for among such people all kinds of unfaithfulness and thieving are frequent.[152]

In 1966 the pragmatic test of worthwhile teaching would self-evidently focus attention on the kinds of thievery which are current today, such as theft of cars, income tax evasion, embezzlement, robbery, fraud, etc.

One more example to illustrate that the pragmatic sieve has been used long before James came into the picture. Parental responsibility for bringing up their children "in the nurture and admonition of the Lord," to make them useful, educated, loyal and participating citizens; to develop maturity and a feeling of responsibility among the teen-agers. These are problems which need attention. The pragmatic test of the good curriculum would point up the indispensable elements which Luther pointed up in his Preface:

> Especially should you here urge civil rulers and parents to govern well and educate their children for service in schools, showing them their duty in this regard, and the greatness of their sin if they neglect it; for by such neglect they overthrow and destroy both the Kingdom of God and of this world, and show themselves to be the worst foes of God and man. Dwell on the great harm they do if they

will not help to educate their children for the ministry, for clerkships, and other offices, and on the terrible punishment God will visit upon them for it. It is necessary to preach of these things; for parents and rulers sin unspeakably in them, and the devil has a horrible object in view.[153]

Modern proponents of historic Christianity have a great variety of eternal truths to choose from and to propagate. Which shall they emphasize? Their central purpose, i.e., "making wise unto salvation through faith in Christ", should be their central criterion for the selection of instructional materials and emphases. And pragmatism agrees: If that is the reason for your existence, and if you can assure us that it works, by all means do well the task that you have set yourselves. And pragmatism would add: By all means let needs of individuals but also social needs today be your guide in selecting the truths that you teach and propagate especially today. Make your educational program functional, useful, life-related; let it be oriented to the contemporary world and its unsolved problems.

Pragmatism, then, need not be attacked broadside. Rather, it should be looked at again and again, by all who have an interest in developing the best possible education for the youth of America, or for all that, for the youth of all nations, on both sides of the iron curtain.

Having said such praiseworthy things about pragmatism and its influence in education, we must, however, remind ourselves that by its very nature pragmatism does open up the floodgates to novel faiths and strange ideas. It does give birth to new gods. It tends to give quackery, whether in medicine, in education, or in government, a strong lease on life, by putting these ideas on the same basis of respectability with old but proven, new but dependable, scientifically tested truths. This is true because pragmatism is oriented to the belief and assumption that matter and motion are the only real constituents of reality. Existence is matter is motion. "Panta rei" is an old idea. That makes everything in reality likewise fluid. Thus everything in nature and in culture enter the stream of the forever fluid. Nothing is stable. Nothing is constant. There is no North Star by which man can test and verify that he is going in the right direction. Going is not enough. Man must be concerned about going in the right direction. Education is good, very good. But education for what?

So pragmatism has two sides to it. On the one hand if we have today more functional, more life-related, more meaningful, more productive, more fruitful education, and we do have it, also in classroom of parish related schools, we should give Pierce and James and Dewey due credit. If on the other hand there is an alarming "current anxiety" as editor Brubacher contends then we must in all honesty and frankness lay much of this also at the door of those same men whom we have praised, among them Peirce, James, Dewey, together with those who have spelled out the implication of their epistemologies, as Kilpatrick, Rugg, and others.

The critics of pragmatism and perhaps even instrumentalism, should not be unmindful of the fact that

> William James in his own empirical way did what Kant tried to do in an a priori way, namely, to show the limits of science in order to make room for faith.[154]

> *The Will to Believe* was James' answer to agnostic evolutionism — the queerest idol ever manufactured in the philosophic cave.[155]

Pragmatism directs the attention of teacher and learner to what might be called the more significant elements in our heritage, and incidentally it thus directs attention away from those elements in our old and in our new cultural heritage that do not seem to be particularly relevant, or crucial, for these learners at this time.

> The pragmatic method means looking away from first things, principles, categories, supposed necessities and looking towards last things, fruits, consequences.[156]

> They are so many solving names. You can rest when you have them. You are at the end of your metaphysical quest. But if you follow the pragmatic method you cannot look on such words as closing your quest. You must bring

out of each word its *practical cash value,* set it at work within the stream of your experience — Such words provide no solution but a *program of action* designed at changes. Ideas become instruments.[157]

Not to bore the reader with James and pragmatism as bringing something new into the area of epistemologies, but, the ardent defender of the faith once delivered unto the saints will read with interest the following quote from James:

Pragmatism is completely genial. She will entertain any hypothesis, consider any evidence. It follows that in the religious field she is at a great advantage, both over positivistic empiricism, with its anti-theological bias, over religious rationalism, with its exclusive interest in the remote, the noble, the simple, and the abstract. Rationalism sticks to logic and the empyrean. Empiricism sticks to the external sense. Pragmatism is willing to *take anything,* to follow either logic or the senses. Her only test of probable truth is what works best in the way of leading us to do this, if the notions of God should prove to do it, how could pragmatism possibly deny God's existence? She could not declare as not true a notion that was pragmatically so successful. What other kind of truth could there be for her than all this agreement with concrete reality.[158]

It has been said with more than a grain of truth that pragmatism is thus willing to justify faith, even the faith that sinners are justified by faith, without the deeds of the law. So the core doctrine of historic Christianity is justified and acceptable to pragmatism, if it works!

Instrumentalism

A further development of the evolutionary and revolutionary thesis of pragmatism, experimentalism and utilitarianism brought educational thinking to the major thesis of John Dewey, generally referred to as "instrumentalism". Mind is a function of an organism. Homo sapiens has survived because "he used his head". Not faith, not God, not grace, not regeneration, not eternal truths of Scripture, not even logic or reason, is man's most prized possession. For all of them man might long ago have lost out in the battle for survival and he might have become as extinct as the dodo. Intelligence is the ladder by which he climbed out of the tree, and up again to higher levels of existence.

What is truth? That was Pilate's sceptical and rhetorical question. It was Dewey's very serious question. His *The Quest for Certainty* is evidence for that. The nature, origin, and criterion of valid knowledge and worthwhile truth, was Dewey's life-long concern, and he felt that he gradually discovered valid and worthwhile truths. Like his forbears, the naturalists, the empiricists, the positivists, and the pragmatists, Dewey declared frankly and unequivocally:

> There is but one sure road of access to truth, the road of patient, cooperative inquiry, operating by means of observation, experiment, record, and controlled reflection.[159]

Having frankly stated the positive side of truth, he was equally frank and outspoken in stating the negative side:

> Religious qualities and value, if they are real at all, are not bound up with any single item of intellectual asset, not even that of the existence of the God of theism. Under existing conditions the religious function in experience can be *emancipated* only through surrender of the whole notion of special truths that are religious by their own nature, together with the idea of peculiar avenues of access to such truths.[160]

This means of course that all cherished truths about the origin, dignity, purpose, and destiny of man, as found in Scripture, or as have been glimpsed in moments of intuition, ecstasy, prophecy, inspiration must be forthwith abandoned as obsolete.

The organic world consists of a great variety of organisms, from amoeba to man. An organism has needs, biological needs. It needs food, shelter, understanding, reproduction; man needs to learn to live peaceably with other persons. These things are necessary for survival. Needs irritate the organism. Irritation stimulates activities. Activities may be blind, instinctive, or they may be intelligent. Intelligent activity relates means to ends. It is purposeful. It foresees consequences. Ideas and the mind itself are instruments for adjustment. Adjustment is necessary for survival. The organism is surrounded by problems. Thinking is a means of solving problems, also the problem of survival. Ideas, the mind as a function, hunches, hypotheses are *instruments* of adjustment and of survival. At this point Dewey's *instrumentalism* appears on the scene, in the long evolutionary process.

Instrumentalism, like positivism, experimentalism, pragmatism, utilitarianism, is a protest against truths that are arrived at and maintained on the basis of logic, inspiration, tradition, or any other form of non-scientific procedure. Metaphysical and eternal truths are not valid. The validity of a proposition, of a judgment or principle must be determined pragmatically, instrumentally.

It has been said: "Alle Weisheit Liegt in Buechertiteln begraben." That is to say, examine the title of a book and you have a good idea what the author is trying to say. Applying that to Dewey we find such titles of his books as *Studies in Logical Theory* (1903), *The Quest for Certainty* (1907), *How We Think* (1910), *Democracy and Education* (1916), *Essays in Experimental Logic* (1917), *Reconstruction in Philosophy* (1920), *Human Nature and Conduct* (1922), *A Common Faith* (1934), *Logic, The Theory of Inquiry* (1938), *Experience and Education* (1938), *Interest and Effort in Education* (1940), *Problems of Men* (1946). Scattered throughout these volumes we find Dewey's epistemology. These writings are persistent attempts to wean educators, as well as political and social leaders, away from the idea that truths are static, finished, judgments, to be memorized. In *The Common Faith* the theory of instrumentalism is spelled out in religion. It is a protest against the dualistic conception of existence, and of truth. New truths are being evolved. There is no absolute abiding truth. There is, in fact, no such thing as truth. We cannot get beyond working hypotheses, with varying degrees of probability. The scientific method of arriving at useful, relatively valid truth is the one and only method of arriving at guesses with a high degree of probability.

In theology it is considered proper to interpret difficult portions of Scripture and confessional writings in the light of texts in which the meaning is very clear. The so-called "sedes doctrinae" (doctrinal texts) serve as fixed stars to guide the interpreter. The "analogy" of faith is another criterion of truth in interpreting Scriptural truths. It should be noted, however, that these criteria are objective. They do not change with the whims of individual persons. Nor do they change with whatever appears important at a certain place or time; or with whatever appears to be in the best interest of a movement, or an institution, a political party, or a religious denomination, or a nation.

Science and the experimental method frown upon the tendency to select data in order to prove a point; or to interpret data in support of preconceived notions. Neither Scripture nor natural phenomena ought to be approached with an axe to grind. And yet, the instrumental procedure does follow through with the "selection of data" from the total number of sense impressions available. It uses tentative hunches, or hypotheses as "directive ideas."

> Experimentation proceeds on the basis of a *directive idea.* But the difference between the role of the idea in determining a known object and the role assigned to it, e.g., in Kant's theory is as great as that between the Copernican and the Ptolemaic systems. For an idea in experiment is tentative, conditional, hypothetical, not fixed and rigorously determinative. It controls an action to be performed, but the *consequences* determine the worth of the directive idea. The latter does not fix the nature of the object. . . . Moreover in experiment everything takes place above board, in the open. Every step is overt and capable of being observed. Also, it can be repeated, step by step, by anyone. . . . . The whole process goes on where other existential processes go on in time.[161]

Since the scientific method of determining valid truth has become widely known and used, and since the writer has recently found it enlarged upon in each of some twenty textbooks, published for junior and senior high school classroom uses, by some twelve reputable publishers of classroom instructional materials (text-books) we shall briefly characterize the method under six specific steps:

First: State the problem. Identify it. Delimit and define it. Describe the unattained goal or objective, the source of irritation. Avoid research in any problem that cannot be approached by the scientific method. Choose a problem that is really relevant, crucial, socially significant. Why be troubled with problems that cannot be solved, as the ancients and the Mediaeval scholastics were.

Two: Read relevant literature to learn what others have observed and concluded. Read related research material critically to note whether scientific procedures have been followed; whether the sampling was really random; whether the results were quantified; whether the statistical data were analyzed according to well established formulae; whether the conclusions were too broad and general or too limited, usually the former; whether applications were made to a universe other than that which was involved in the experiment.

Three: Make a guess. Express your hunch. Set up a "directive idea". Express an hypothesis. State it as a null-hypothesis.

Four: Observe natural observable phenomena and record your sense impressions. Set up a rigorously controlled experiment. Identify the experimental factor. Limit the variable to one factor. As for example this writer did in carrying through an experiment to determine the relative effectiveness of "activities" in connection with the teaching and learning of the traditional course in religion for junior high students.[162] It was done to help teachers and pastors to improve their teaching of religion.

Five: Tabulate and analyze the data, i.e. the scores and the difference of the scores between pre-test and re-test. Compare the gains of the comparable control groups and the experimental groups. If the difference is not statistically significant the hypothesis remains unproven. The null-hypothesis is established. There is no difference. The hypothesis must be dropped as untenable. If the problem is really serious, another hypothesis must be set up and the experimental process of proving the null-hypothesis must be repeated, until the truth is found and a more fruitful method of teaching is discovered.

Six: Conclusions, within the limits of the experiment, are drawn. Applications to the method of teaching, writing, and publishing of instructional materials, etc. are drawn in harmony with the newly established hypothesis concerning improved methods of teaching. Nothing absolute and nothing final has been established. But, the hypothesis that has now been established as a thesis, as a safe guide of action, and the thesis has a degree of probability that is beyond the realm of reasonable doubt.

Possibly in this procedure a page has been taken from James' pragmatism and from Dewey's instrumentalism. But it should be noted that the validity of curriculum *content* was not on trial. The experiment had to do only with method. There is precisely the parting of the ways between the epistemology of experimentalism and that of historic Christianity.

An epistemological question is often raised in connection with the applicability of the scientific method to areas of existence other than the physical environment and the physical sciences. Is the method applicable to education? To curricular content? To morals and ethics? To establishing criteria for improving and refining religious truths? To standards of value? To test and prove political, economic, social, and governmental theories? Is the price mankind has paid, and is paying, not too great for experimenting with new theories of government, as observed in fascism, nazism, communism? Six million Jews exterminated! $46 billion in the U. S. annual budget to stem the tide of that type of experimentalism!

A significant change that would issue from carrying over experimental methods from physics to man concerns the import of standards, principles, rules. With transfer these and all tenets and creeds about good and goods would be recognized to be hypotheses. Instead of being rigidly fixed they would be treated as intellectual *instruments* to be tested and confirmed, and altered, through *consequences* effected by acting upon them. They would lose all pretense to finality, the ulterior source of dogmatism. It is both astonishing and depressing that so much of the energy of mankind has gone into fighting (with weapons of the flesh and of

128

the spirit) the truth of creeds, religious, moral, political, as distinct from what has gone into efforts to try creeds by putting them to the test of acting upon them. . . . Any belief is tentative, hypothetical; and, it is not just to be acted upon but it is to be *framed* with reference to its role as a guide for action.[163]

Let this for the present suffice to characterize the nature of Dewey's great contribution to American education, largely summarized in the name of "instrumentalism." We repeat that "instrumentalism" is but one of several streams of thought in which the implications of a materialistic interpretation of existence has been developed.

We have noted that positivism, secularism, experimentalism, pragmatism, instrumentalism, are closely related, tracing their origin and character to the common mother of materialism and naturalism. Further note must be taken of a philosophic movement which is less directly concerned with education and the transmission of our scientific and democratic heritage, but which may point a way toward some kind of a synthesis of divergent epistemologies. This refers to "logical empiricism."

Logical Empiricism

Dewey stressed the basic assumption that educational experience should not be limited by setting up specific aims or objectives. In the instrumental concept of education these objectives and aims are to emerge in the educational process. It is for the learner and the teacher to create these aims. The only definite objective in education is to stimulate and guide toward more educational experiences. In contrast to that emphasis, logical empiricism does bring ends, aims, and values back onto the educational scene.

In addition to knowledge there are presupposed ends, aims, purposes, valuations, preferences, which make up the very frame of the enterprise of applying knowledge. The distinction here drawn between knowledge and valuations is itself one of the main results of the logical empiricist reflections. — Primary attention will be given to the edu-

129

cational ideals as they appear in the light of the logical empiricist basic values. — Logical empiricism has often been hailed as the twentieth century sequel to the philosophy of the eighteenth century enlightenment. Just as the renaissance of science in the seventeenth century engendered the empiricist and naturalistic philosophies of the eighteenth century so the radical transformations of the scientific outlook at the beginning of our century produced a turning point. Owing to cultural lag the prevalent philosophies in each of these periods remained still largely in the bondage of traditional theological and metaphysical systems.[164]

This at first appears like a return to the ancient foundations of truth and goodness. However, the author goes on to explain the great need for bringing our current thinking and our epistemological bases of thinking and action up to date, and into harmony with our scientific age. We need to grow up. Tremendous changes have been wrought by science and changes need to be made in all other phases of our culture.

It has become imperative to abandon the dogmatic, otherworldly supernaturalistic, tender-minded, rationalistic, parochial conceptions and to replace them by critical, worldly, naturalistic, fact-minded, empirical, experimental, and universally applicable ways of thinking.[165]

Logical empiricism does however point to the fact that the mechanistic, pre-determined view of the universe has also become obsolete. Determinism once espoused by physicists and by the theory of natural selection in the evolutionary process is no longer adequate or tenable.

In connection with this development we have come to speak of the breakdown of the mechanistic world view. This seems to mean that the rigid determinism as well as certain other features of classical mechanism have to be relinquished. The world is no longer conceived along the lines of a machine or a clock work but rather in terms of the much more flexible concepts of fields, systems, waves, and probable functions. A few even think that modern quantum theory has provided the basis of free will.[166]

130

The principal exponent of logical empiricism is Vienna-trained Herbert Feigl. Because totalitarian governments followed through on the implications of science and the evolutionary theory as applied to the solution of human, ethnic problems, Feigl found it necessary to find a new home of freedom and human rights in America. America and the University of Minnesota gained by the transition. Philosopher Feigl is very confident that science can and eventually will be the one discipline through which man will reach higher levels of truth and a greater future for mankind.

> Significant discoveries of modern physics have left (even) the philosopher without a job. Philosophy is slowly learning that it is not the business of the philosopher but that of the scientist to discover the *truths* about matters of fact, even if it concerns the structure of the universe and man's place in it. — The metaphysical systems and cosmologies look pale and insignificant when compared with the account of the world given in modern science.[167]

Materialistic monism holds the future. Sociology, theology, government, education must all adjust themselves to the naturalistic and materialistic *Weltanschauung* or find themselves in a *cul de sac,* hopelessly living out their waning existence in a dead-end situation. Nor will any compromise with idealism, as tried in "emergent evolution" or a form of "vitalism" solve the dilemma.

> Most empiricists look with great suspicion upon the hypotheses of "vitalism" in biology, of mind-body dualism, of psychical research and of so-called empirical theologies which base their arguments on the observable facts of the world. They are inclined to reject hypotheses of this kind not necessarily as meaningless, but as superfluous in that it is likely that the observable facts in question can be more simply explained in terms of physical, biological, and psychological principles, i.e., within the frame of the naturalistic and the materialistic.[168]

Logical empiricism is seeking ever simpler and ever more inclusive principles of explaining all phenomena. It hopes eventually, to explain rather than merely to describe all observable phe-

131

nomena, to find just one concept which will explain all phenomena and thus arrive at a kind of all-inclusive god concept.

> There is a remarkable convergence of scientific theories. The two dominating theories of our time are the Einstein theory of relativity and the Heisenberg-Schroeder-Dirac theory of quanta, almost sufficient to deduce all the more specific disciplines and their laws. New and recalcitrant facts may require still higher levels of explanation. Science will probably never arrive at anything like theoretical completeness. Yet the surprising reductions of thermo-dynamics to molecular mechanics, of chemistry to the quanta, teach most clearly the following lessons: The aims of explanatory science consist in the comprehension of a maximum of observable data by means of a minimum of basic principles and concepts. Scientific explanation is however never ultimate or infallible, but always relative and always, so to speak "valid only until further notice."[169]

A little-known philosopher named Alexander[170] has evolved a somewhat similar theory of development. He posits three essentials; space, time, and deity. Space and time points show a trend toward increasing complexity and inclusiveness. Thus he arrives at configurations of space and time, all having the common element of activity at higher and ever higher levels, from the nucleus of the atom to solar systems, and finally the entire universe. Deity is always the next higher level of configuration toward which an existing level tends.

Peaceful coexistence of two opposing epistemologies is feasible provided both parties are sincerely intent on keeping the peace. An epistemology based on materialistically oriented systems of truth can coexist with systems of truth which are oriented to idealism or to historic Christianity. In the land of toleration and of pluralism, such as free America, such coexistence is thinkable, even though the historic foundations of truth and of ethics are being badly undermined. In a free country such a situation challenges each to leave no stone unturned to justify their efforts in building either the walls of Zion or the citadels of science. However, when a power-center, such as a political party, gains control of an entire nation, turns totalitarian, sets its mind on establishing a monopoly of truth, and ruthlessly proceeds to uproot all competitive epistemologies, the matter becomes serious, yes, a matter of national concern. It then comes to be a matter of survival, to be or not to be. The threat to bury the historic elements in a culture must be met with a determined resistance. And that leads us to comment finally on dialectical materialism.

Dialectical Materialism

The trend, growing out of scientific materialism, toward totalitarian monopolies of truth in recent decades had its day in fascism, then in naziism, and more recently in Marxian communism. Marxism is a dialectical philosophy borrowed from Hegel, but transformed into a dialectical materialism, whereas Hegel developed a system of dialectical idealism. According to Hegel the state is the divine Idea as it exists on earth. Marxism pictured reality as a "Bacchic dance in which there is not one of the constituents that is not drunk." The problem of being, not-being, and becoming were a great concern for Hegel, and subsequently for Marx. They proceeded with a thesis, antithesis, and synthesis, to arrive at a higher truth by compromise. Marx's emphasis and concern was largely with the status of the producer, with labor. Marx's *Das Kapital* is the Bible of communism.[171] Marx re-wrote history to conform with his epistemology.

> The form of economic production determines the formation of human society and the consciousness of its members, so that ideas, moral values, aesthetic standards, political and social concepts, educational and religious systems are to be conceived as produced by the economic situation. As long as the ideological superstructure remains in accordance with the conditions of economic production, civilization is healthy. Since today the conditions are changing more rapidly than the superstructure, cultural crises are unavoidable. Revolution becomes necessary.[172]

Marx conceived the dialectical materialism as a method of proceeding from the known to the unknown. That was his "working hypothesis." Dialectic method is possible because existence is in a state of constant fermentation. He agreed that at one stage of economic and social development the traditional system of civilization (capitalism) was useful, and very productive of the creature comforts. But today the traditional is outmoded.

> The challenge of Marxist thought is more profound than the challenge of Soviet armed force. Karl Marx and his many varied followers forged a new outlook on life, on man, on society, on history, and it was an outlook that arose entirely within our Western civilization. Original in conception, in sweep, and in application, it was yet the heir to the entire treasury of European and American experience.[173]

While it may be possible to trace the development through the entire history of Western culture, beginning with the Old Testament through the New Testament, through Greek, Roman, and Mediaeval theology and philosophy; through the Darwinian evolutionary revolution in thought; through the French Enlightenment; through the British and German thoughts on socialism, it is nevertheless true that Marx's thinking was essentially centered in the history, present status, and future greater possibilities of the class of laborers who produce the wealth of the world. Class conflict and the rule of the proletariat over against the long-privileged class of the bourgeoisie was his primary concern. Even his epistemology was largely shapened and colored by the class struggle. The end of dualism and the establishment of one matter-motion-oriented system of truth was his concern.

> The germs of the education of tomorrow are to be found in the factory system.[174]

Marx praised highly the progress made in Western capitalistic culture during the past hundred years, but expressed surprise that men should have been so slow to discover that these productive powers were given birth in "the womb of social labor." Our concern in this chapter on epistemology is primarily in communist definitions of truth. What were Marx and his followers for and what were they against?

> The doctrine of communism is orthodox Marxism. It is a comprehensive philosophy of life which includes an epistemology, a metaphysics, a philosophy of history, an applied theory of revolution, and a social ideal. The metaphysical foundation of Marxism is materialism. Matter and its motion is all that actually exist.[175]

The same author quotes Lenin directly as having declared it to be an absolute necessity to destroy any centers of truth not in agreement with materialism.

> All contemporary religions and churches, all and every kind of religious organizations, Marxism has always viewed as instruments of bourgeois reaction, serving as a defense of exploitation and the doping of the working class.[176]

There is no compromise. No peaceful co-existence between Marxism and historic Christianity when it comes to defining and defending truth. In fact, all citadels and all walls and all remnants of that part of Western culture must be ruthlessly destroyed before communism can be successfully established.

> It is impossible to build up communism in a society half of which believes in God and the other half fears the devil.[177]

Without going into details about the problem of knowledge that occupied the minds of Western philosophers, particularly since the days of Descartes, who is said to have originated the dualistic division of truth into idealism and materialism, on the basis of a division of society into workers and capitalists, we confirm the thesis that Marxism knows of no separation between knower and the known; they are one process.

> Whatever the other faults of Western thought may have been, none strikes deeper, in the eyes of Marx and Engels, than the artificial separation of the knowing subject from his known object.[178]

135

The violent and ruthless destruction of the Church, the closing of church buildings for worship purposes, the laws forbidding the assembling of youth for purposes of religious education, stem from a rigorous, consistent application of the epistemology of materialism.

> Religious misery is the expression of actual misery, and a protest against actual misery. Religion is the sigh of the oppressed creature, the heart of heartless world, the spirit of unspiritual conditions. It is the people's opium.[179]

The determined and deliberate destruction of all institutions or organizations that showed any signs of trying to salvage for themselves and for their children, an element in the culture and epistemology of either idealism or Judeo-Christian heritage has been summarized, step by step, year by year, by Prof. Timascheff,[180] Assistant Professor of Sociology at Fordham University.

The devices for religious persecution, according to Timascheff, have been through direct violence, such as imprisonment or execution of clergy and active laymen; closing of churches by force; use of former church buildings for anti-religious meetings; through various methods of interference in church life by depriving churches of legal and economic means; helping to launch schisms within the churches; prohibiting the churches from participation in charitable, cultural, and social activities; outright discriminations against clergy and active laymen; through eradication of religious education from schools and elsewhere; through anti-religious propaganda in schools and throughout the country. The printed page, such as "The Atheist," youth organizations such as "The Militant Atheist League"; the forbidding of replies to attack on religion; the program of strangulation of the churches was carried on through a period of now well nigh fifty years. There were periods of apparent let-up in the persecutions of churches and non-communist cultural groups, but that was for purposes of expediency so as not to lose the good will of too many Russians and believers outside of Russia and Russia-controlled satellites. The policies that grew out of "dialectical materialism" remain the same. We have in Russia, her enslaved satellites, and now in China, Cuba,

136

and Vietnam, a preview of what to expect in the free world, the tolerant and democratic world, when the time comes, for the communist world to "bury them" and their epistemology. Outside of stressing freedom, and tolerance, and a pluralistic culture, American schools are not well fortified nor equipped to stem the tide of materialism, because we ourselves are systematically "secular," strictly non-religious, materialistic in our philosophy of education. That places a doubly great responsibility on all who are in a position of influence not to ignore, not to by-pass, nor to be indifferent to all types of schools and educational ventures which have idealistic and Judeo-Christian ideals, with God, His worship and His word, but give them a definite place in our total program of education. We can see why the author of the lead article of the 54th Yearbook of the National Society for the Study of Education expressed concern about the state of education in America, and lists a series of reasons for the "current anxieties" that are felt among those who want to develop the best kind of education for American children and teen-agers. He expressed concern because American education is adrift, without rudder, chart, or compass; about educational aims that are vague, conflicting, and that lack the power to develop strong loyalties; about a serious let-down in standards of instruction; about our lack of certainty; about our democratic conception of education and our own fainthearted loyalty to it; about a social framework that allows the child too much freedom and does not subordinate him sufficiently to authority and control; and about public schools, over-anxious as they are to avoid sectarianism, are neglecting religion and becoming too secular; and he raises the possibility of "re-examining the nineteenth century tradition of the divorce of church and state in the field of public education."[181]

E. SUMMARY: IMPLICATIONS OF EPISTEMOLOGY FOR EDUCATION

As a transition from the relationship between science and theology we call attention to one area of conflict in particular as this bears on current educational problems. It is the tendency for some scientists to accept as valid and true one hypothesis which in itself

137

is very intriguing but which, when prematurely accepted as proven and true, tends to disturb and to irritate. We say "disturb" because curriculum and text-book writers tend to follow through on the theory and disparage every other truth, even if it comes from Scripture. The reference here is to the theory of evolution.

The origin of this conflict and irritation was pointed up many years ago, by Francis Bacon:

> There are found some minds given to extreme admiration for antiquity. Others to an extreme love and appetite for novelty. But few are so duly tempered that they can hold to the mean, neither carping at what has been well laid down by the ancients, nor despising what is well introduced by the moderns. This however turns to the great injury of science and of philosophy.[182]

Educators in the churches, both Catholic and Protestant, have expressed concern about this trend, well established by this time, in tax-supported schools, to develop a program of education that is based on an unproven theory about the origin and development of living organisms on our planet.

It appears that whenever a sociologist, a biologist, or a leader in a revolutionary movement in government seeks to justify his claim he begins by attacking and revamping the epistemology that undergirds the status quo. This was recognized long ago.

> When Protagoras wished to undermine the whole system of custom and use he attacked not moral knowledge only but knowledge in general.[183]

It is for this reason that a scientist educator in the Church recently expressed himself as follows on this point:

> Certainly in view of the many difficulties and problems for the evolutionist and in view of the fact that the problem is of such a nature that no final answer is possible, it would seem that a summary rejection of Scripture account is, to say the least, premature, even on the part of the scientists.[184]

Too much of what we have in our schools, in the statement of objectives and in the curricular provisions designed for the accomplishment of those objectives, is based on conjecture, on theory not yet proven, and therefore not generally accepted. Another basic contention of God's people is that hypothetical theories have without warrant and prematurely been accepted as true and these have therefore unwarrantly colored goals, instructional materials, curricular content. The elimination of eternal and unchanging truths in morals and ethics has tended to make America a lawless nation.[185] Discontent with the results of America's huge expenditure, about 40 billion dollars a year, has been growing.[186]

> There are still some among the biologists who feel that the fabric of theory accepted by the majority today is actually false and who say so. For the most part, the opinions of the dissenters have been given little credence. This group has formed a vocal but little heard minority. There exists as well a generally silent group of students engaged in biological pursuits who tend to disagree with much of the current thought but say or write little because they are not particularly interested, do not see that controversy over evolution is of any particular importance, or are so strongly in disagreement that it seems futile to undertake the monumental task of controverting the immense body of information and theory that exists in the formulation of modern thinking.[187]

What, then, is our response to Brubacher's concern about "current anxiety that the public schools, overanxious to avoid sectarianism, are neglecting religion and becoming too secular?"[188]

The effect of evolutionary theory on ethics is of particular concern to Christian educators. Ethical truths and standards are, in the evolutionary concept, man-made, flexible, utilitarian, instrumental. They have had far-reaching and devastating effects on morality and ethics. The much-decried lawlessness among American teen-agers, and their elders, can obviously to a large extent be traced to the corroding effect of the evolutionary hypothesis, and its relativism in morals. Once it is accepted that the fittest survive and that the strongest are the fittest, the gates are opened wide for the idea that "anything goes" as long as you can get away with it. When strong totalitarian nations accept this ethic, treaties become "scraps of paper," expediency is enthroned, the end justifies the mean, and truth is that which helps the nation to achieve its nationalist aspirations; whatever hinders or stands in the way of national socialism, or atheistic communism, is a lie. The heirs of God's eternal ethics of the true and the false, the bad and the good, believe that a large part of the world's troubles today are traceable to the corroding influence of a naked secularism, particularly because this is a part of the evolutionary theory.

We once again want to make clear that the scientific method has wrought miracles in the physical world. Some of these verified truths appear to reach into the area of existence and history once considered the exclusive realm of theology. Archaeological research is making an impact on theology.

> The carbon 14 method has been used for a great number of problems. The Dead Sea Scrolls turned out to have an age of 1917 years, as expected. The method has been used to date textiles, wood and charcoal from Egyptian tombs; to correlate the time scale between Babylonian and Christian calendars; to determine the end of the last ice age, etc. In general one can say that carbon dating has provided us with an interesting and generally reliable tool for determining the age of samples formed during the last 50,000 years.[189]

The scientific method, as a truth-finding procedure, shall have its rightful place and recognition in the natural sciences. It is only because the scientific method has been given a monopoly on all valid truths that it has fallen somewhat into disrepute. Our concern must be to safe-guard science in its unhampered pursuit of knowledge and truth in the infinitesimally microscopic behavior of the elements at the core of the atom as well as in its enthusiastic research into inter-stellar space. There must be no let-up in our emphasis on science even if it is only for the sake of survival in a fiercely competitive world.

On the other hand we must be equally concerned about preserving and communicating the Christian message. We are strongly committed in America to the principle of separation between church and state. So much so that many have well-nigh overlooked the truth which is well stated in the words "man is not made for the Sabbath but the Sabbath was made for man."[190]

Which is to say that even the laws of the Medes and Persians may be changed when it is obvious that the temporal and eternal welfare of millions of human beings is at stake. This is a partial response to editor Brubacher's suggestion "that the spheres of God and Caesar and the 19th Century tradition of the *divorce between church and state* in matters of public education *should once again be re-examined.*"[191]

Nor is this a solitary voice in the wilderness. A fellow-editor of the same NSSE Yearbook, Theodore Greene, expresses a supporting view:

> What is needed now, as always is a radical re-examination and reassessment of our entire educational structure, its ultimate objectives, its fundamental pre-suppositions, its basic procedure, — all this in the existential context of our contemporary American society and of the world situation and, no less urgently, in the still wider context of our best contemporary understanding of human nature and the universe to which we belong. — Different philosophical points of view are not mutually exclusive in all respects. All, of necessity, share some common presuppositions. Even more significant is the large pattern of partly contrasting and partly overlapping emphases and trends of contemporary belief on ultimate matters.[192]

Chapter IV

VALUES — AXIOLOGY

A. INTRODUCTION: THE PROBLEM

"Thou shalt have no other gods before me" (Ex. 20:3). What does it mean to have something, or someone, as god? Luther asks this question in his Large Catechism. In his comments on the First Commandment in the Decalogue, he asks:

> What is it to have a god?, or what is God? Answer: A god is that to which we look for all good and where we resort for help in every time of need; to have a god is simply to trust and believe in one with our whole heart. As I have often said, the confidence and faith of the heart alone make both God and an idol. If your faith and confidence are right. then likewise your God is the true God. On the other hand, if your confidence is false, it is wrong, then you have not the true God. For the two, faith and God, have inevitable connection. Now, I say, whatever your heart clings to and confides in, that is really your God.[1]

Many a person thinks he has God and entire sufficiency, i.e., he has money and riches; in them he trusts and proudly and securely boasts that he cares for no one. He surely has a god, called mammon. This is a universal idol on earth.[2] This desire for wealth cleaves to us until we are in our graves. In like manner, he who boasts great skill, wisdom, power and influence, and friends and honors, and trusts in them, has also a god, but not the one true God.[3]

So the basic question in this unit is: What do men value most, for themselves and for their country? What do they worship? What is the ultimate value for which they sacrifice their best effort, time and money?

142

What have philosophers in the past regarded as of ultimate value? Is it happiness? Happiness for the greatest number for the longest possible duration of time? Is it the pleasure of the pig or the pleasure of an artist, or a philosopher? What is the scope of the problem of this chapter? Was Francis Bacon wrestling with the same problem when he wrote about the four idols, the idols of the cave, the market place, the idols of the theatre and the idols of the tribe?[4]

What is the origin of difference in man's conception of values? Can values be arrived at objectively, scientifically, or is it always a matter of individual tastes and subjective judgments? What is meant by a "scale" of values? And a hierarchy of values? How important is the scale of values in a philosophy of education? Should parents, teachers and pastors, as well as administrators in education, be concerned about basic values which underlie all facets of education? Can an appreciation of values be taught or must educators rely upon them being caught?

Axiology, says Webster, is the theory or study of values, primarily of intrinsic values, as in ethics, aesthetics, and religion, but also of instrumental values, as those in economics, particularly with reference to the manner in which they can be known or experienced, their nature and kinds, and their ontological status.[5] An axiologist, states Webster, is a philosopher advocating an axiological theory of ethics contrasted with a demonologist.

Concerning the importance of this problem, especially in education, someone has recently written: "In a shipwreck the engineer sinks with the stoker. It is as much the scientists' business as the preachers'. The restitution of the values of life is the first job of modern man's intelligence."[6]

Leadership in Christian Education is well aware of the critical importance of a true concept of values in education.

> Two axiological questions which men have asked since the beginning of time are: What is the chief good in life? And, what is the nature of basic values? The teacher who believes that personal pleasure is the highest form of good operates differently from one who believes that anything which serves the welfare of society and the glory of God is good.[7]

143

Among Greek philosophers, as Aristotle, Plato, Socrates, and others, few, if any, problems received more attention than that of the summum bonum, i.e., the highest, the ultimate values.

> Some people say the highest good is pleasure; others that pleasure is something uttterly bad. — When theories disagree with the facts of perception, they fall into contempt and involve the truth itself in their destruction.[8]

The problem has become particularly crucial in American education for two reasons: The widely observable erosion of responsible behavior especially among the teen-agers and because the Supreme Court has recently reaffirmed that God, the supreme Good as historic Christianity conceives God, and the stable and stabilizing factor in moral behavior of the Word of God, are not to come into consideration in either the purposes, or the curriculum, or teacher selection and training, of tax-supported schools in America, the schools in which 90% of American youth receives its education.

Various attempts are being made to somehow keep moral and spiritual values in public education, even if God, for all practical purposes, must be considered as dead, says Raymond F. McBain, General Director of the Commission on Christian Higher Education, National Council of Churches of Christ in the U.S.A., in a Preface to a book dealing with this problem of conserving or rather re-introducing, moral and spiritual values in public education. He states:

> If life is to be more satisfying and less terrifying, moral and spiritual values must be given greater substance. — If modern man is not to perish as he finds his new place in a global society, his moral and spiritual values need to discipline and direct his scientific skills to that good and not evil may result from his creativity.[9]

The testimony of a man like Billy Graham might be suspect to some as alarmist. And yet he has become practically a national figure, closely associated with Presidents and other influential men in American public life. In a recent article appearing in *Decision*,[10]

144

he quotes an eminent Harvard sociologist, Pitirim O. Sorokin, as saying: "All values are unsettled: all norms are broken. Mental, moral, aesthetic and social anarchy reigns." He also quotes from the late President Kennedy's State of the Union Message to Congress:

> Each day the crises multiply. Each day the solution grows more difficult. Each day we are nearer the hour of maximum danger, as weapons spread and hostile weapons grow stronger. Our times are crucial. — Our improvements in transportation and communication (5,000 radio stations, 600 TV stations) have made us a world neighborhood without making us a brotherhood. Race is clashing against race, nationality against nationality, culture against culture. The decadence of the world is evident.

The disappearance of spirituality and the erosion of moral standards has become observable in the rapid, disproportionate rise in lawlessness, juvenile delinquency, the increase in broken homes, and particularly also in the presumably realistic picture of the state of morals in America and the world as depicted in the modern novel. What is the answer? What shall we do to be saved? Is there any hope of enthroning again the Living God, as true believers know Him, in the hearts and minds of the next generation? In a society that is increasingly secular, naturalistic, god-less, is it possible to salvage at least the basic eternal, unchanging values and with it the eternal standards of good behavior, social conduct? What can religious people do to stem the tide of moral disintegration? What contribution can historic Christianity make to restore spiritual and moral stability in a chaotic society?

In dealing with this problem of basic values and their survival in our culture, we propose to proceed as we have done in dealing with other equally great issues in American, Western, and world-wide situations. Even though these three bases are not always in clear and distinct isolation from each other, even though values as they originated in what we have called a matter-centered, idea-centered, and a God-centered philosophy of life, and of education, we shall nevertheless follow through on this threefold basis of diagnosing, evaluating the state of value concepts, and as far as possible, stemming the process of spiritual and moral decay, and of salvaging for individuals, families, nations and mankind, the ultimate and the intermediate values as we have always had them in God and in God's Word.

B. VALUES AMONG THE HEIRS OF HISTORIC CHRISTIANITY: GOD-CENTERED

The one word which best summarizes for the Christian believer the highest good and that which is of greatest value to himself and to others, is GOD. "God is love."[11] But God is far more than an abstract value such as love is. "God is a Spirit and they that value him highly, enough to worship him, must love and worship him in Spirit and thus in truth." "God is the Being who has made the world and man and to whom man is responsible," writes R. R. Kaemmerer, "The Nature and Attributes of God," in *The Abiding Word*.[12] God is apparent to man through the power and design in the natural world, through the pattern of the forces in history.[13] This natural knowledge is basic to every human system of religion and most of its philosophies. From behind the veil and mask of nature and history God speaks to man in an act of self-revelation through which his true nature and character are more completely made clear. This act is the incarnation of Jesus Christ, the Son of God (Deus Revelatus). The purpose of this revelation was to remove the cleavage between God and man and to meet the problem of man's sin and rebellion against God and to atone for that sin.[14] In this act God is revealed as being infinitely pained by man's deviation from holiness, yet infinitely desirous to repair the breach, to the point of himself assuming responsibility for this repair at the cost of His own sacrifice. Thus God is revealed as perfect and holy, as personal, and driven by love to bring man into (union and) conformity with himself. God is eternal, not subject to time or to change.[15] God is not confined to space. God is not limited as are creatures as to power, knowledge and wisdom. All the resources of the nature of God are at the disposal of the man in Christ and by him are recognized to be at work for his good.[16] The insight into God and the power to grasp

146

and to trust in God (faith) as the forgiving Father, is the work of God himself, the gift of the Spirit. The Christian Church has summarized the nature and the knowledge of God (and the possession of God) in the concept of the Trinity as one being expressing himself toward men in the (work of Creation, Redemption, and Sanctification) distinct personalities of Father, Son and Spirit.[17]

While God himself is the ultimate value, and while forgiveness and fellowship, yea, union with God, is the one supreme value which causes the believer to rejoice and to feel that he possesses all that matters in time and eternity, there are a number of intermediate values which are truly valuable because they represent steps and means through which a sinner comes into possession of God.

There is no fellowship, no communion and no union with God, no possession of the supreme value, except through the forgiveness of sins. Forgiveness means acceptance of God. It means justification. This, however, is possible only through Christ, who is the propitiation for our sins and not for ours only but for the sins of the whole world.[18] Christ and His blessings are appropriated by the individual alone by faith in Christ. For this reason Christians, and Christian education in particular, regard it as of paramount importance to sustain and strengthen a personal faith in Jesus as Savior. And since "faith cometh by hearing and hearing by the Word of God,"[19] the Scriptures assume a very important place in the scale of values within Christendom. And the use of Word and Sacrament as a means of creating and strengthening that faith is of primary importance. Here at this point it becomes obvious why Christian education can never be satisfied with an education in which God, and the Bible, do not have a central place. To go one step farther, faith in Jesus and a good, responsible, godly life are related to each other as roots and fruits, or, in the words of Jesus, as vine and the fruit-bearing branches. "I am the vine, ye are the branches, He that abideth in me and I in him, the same bringeth forth much fruit: for without me ye can do nothing."[20]

If today there is a cry from social workers, teachers, parents,

147

governmental agencies that make, interpret and execute laws, for something to help teen-agers to grow up, to stabilize them, to make them responsible and mature young people, why not remember that God, operating through Christ, through Christ's Word, through faith, through the power of the indwelling Holy Spirit, through the influence of the local congregation of believers, and not through the social matrix of unbelieving individuals, through the influence of the Christian home, has in the past, is today, and can and will in the future prevent further moral and spiritual corrosion and restore reasonable community safety and decency in this land of the free and home of the brave. Walking on the streets at night will no longer be the hazard which it is today.

To relate this concept of values and the manner in which education can cultivate a practical appreciation of these values, let us recommend these things to all that are seriously interested in the finest education for all young people in our land.

As a means to the ultimate end and universal good for all men, we could enumerate, besides cars, airplanes, telephones, all mass media of communication; money and things that money can buy as very valuable and very good: as means to the end. But God's people insist that when the means become ends in themselves, and are worshipped and glorified and trusted and valued as ends, we have arrived where the nomad Israelites were when they worshipped the golden calf. Intelligence, a high intelligence quotient, all the competencies, such as economic, civic, social, artistic, linguistic and generally academic skills, all are valuable to be appreciated and cultivated zealously, also in Christian schools and colleges, but always not as ends but as means to the end of more fully becoming united with God and more effectively sharing that life of supreme meaning and joy in God with others, with all members of the exploding world population.

The reader has not missed the point, we are sure, that what has been presented in the foregoing about the summum bonum of human existence, was recommended highly when Jesus said: "Suffer the little children to come unto me, and forbid them not, for of such is the kingdom of heaven."[21] The reader will also understand why the picture of Mary and Martha, just as that of Jesus Blessing

148

Little Children, is usually found in a Christian classroom. Martha's service was valuable, but Mary's sitting at Jesus' feet, listening to a sermonette on eternal values was even more valuable in the scale of values that Jesus had been setting up. Service projects are good, but worship and learning His Word is even better. Jesus tagged it with the memorable sentence: "One thing is needful. Mary hath chosen the good part. That shall not be taken from her."[22]

Jesus' scale of values is tersely expressed also in some of his parables, such as the one recorded in Matthew 13:45-46: "The kingdom of heaven is like unto a merchant man seeking goodly pearls, who when he had found one pearl of great price, went and sold all that he had and bought it." And again in the same chapter: "The kingdom of heaven is like unto a treasure hid in a field; which when a man had found he hideth, and for joy thereof goeth and selleth all he hath and buyeth the field."[23] All the man's possessions and the field are secondary in value. God in Christ, and with it, eternal life, a life to come with God and a high quality of life here and now, that is the ultimate value.

To philosophers whose thinking is centered in matter, to the exclusion of an eternal and unchanging, holy and merciful God, to the exclusion even of the values of idealistically oriented philosophers, God-centered values are a fiction. Men who go on the basic assumption that all the universe is exhausted with physical entities and phenomena, also in the lives of human beings, will scarcely be impressed with the belief that God is central and necessary in the good education of the person. However, idealists, such as Herman Horne, or Theodore M. Greene, or even men who are realists such as John Wild, or of men like John S. Brubacher, who are aware that our culture has lost something vital feel that something radical should be done about it.[24] We ask them, why not acknowledge that the heritage of historic Christianity is worth preserving and that something must be done before our whole culture is thoroughly impoverished and bereft of God and all that is associated with God.

We have indicated that philosophies of education, also with reference to values, overlap and that in this point the Christian

149

heritage and the heritage of idealism has much in common. Both agree, I am sure, that some values are not man-made. They are pre-existent. They are eternal. They inhere in the very nature of the universe.

> Lay not up for yourselves treasures upon earth, where moth and rust doth corrupt and where thieves break through and steal. But lay up for yourselves treasures in heaven where neither moth nor rust doth corrupt and where thieves do not break through nor steal. For where your treasure is there will your heart be also.[25]

The values and truths revealed in the Word are regarded as absolutes. They do not change from one year to the next. They do not vary from one culture to the next. As the Word is the Word of God and as God is the Creator of all men, it has the same message to proclaim to all men, the same standards to set for all. The Christian's insistence upon divinely revealed absolute values and absolute truths must not be understood in the sense that the Christian religion permits and encourages riding in horse-drawn carriages as good and God-pleasing while considering the inventions, such as the automobile (and airplane and space ships) to be inventions of the devil. God permits a great amount of liberty with regard to the material elements of our culture.[26]

In *Values That Last,* Clovis Cappell quotes I Corinthians 13: 13.[27] "Now abideth faith, hope and charity. These three. But the greatest of these is charity." Love. Other values and joys, even the joy of the newly weds, passes away. Beauty, strength, youth, a thick purse full of one hundred dollar bills, the latest model sports car, none of them abide. Loving and being loved, being wanted, being recognized and honored, they all pass. Tongues of angels, effective communication skills, scientific knowledge, intelligence, scientific knowhow, space control, all are values for which we can afford to pay 50 billion dollars a year. Yet, even these values can lead to suicide and self destruction. God is love. The greatest good is love. Love of God and love of fellowman. Nothing is great without love, either in the classroom, in the home, in the interracial strife and in the world. Christ for man and God in man through faith in Him. Union and fellowship with God. Here are values that last. Here is God and here are God's people, sharing in God's freedom,[28] and sharing in God's immortality.[29]

Perhaps we should stop here, having set forth the source and nature of the greatest of values. We could, but the disturbing fact is that these values are no longer known or not valued. Idealism does not accept the real source of these values, a personal God as we know him in Christ the Son of God. And, materialistically oriented thinking has relegated these values to the limbo. Tax supported education is all but devoid of these values and idea-centered philosophy of education is making a relatively futile attempt to salvage absolute and eternal values in a world which is increasingly secular, changing, and in a state of uncertainty and flux. We shall take a closer look at both, but first at idea-centered scales of values in education.

C. IDEA-ORIENTED VALUES: IDEALISM

Plato is generally regarded as the father of idealism. He believed reality to be dual in nature: matter and idea. The former could be sensed, the latter could be apprehended by reason. Kant appears to have continued Plato's distinction between the "phenomenal" and the "noumenal" realities. The former realities are temporal, changing, passing; the latter are pre-existent, eternal, unchanging, absolute. One arrives at the abiding concept of Beauty, e.g., by observing many samples of beautiful things or persons. The eternal reality of Justice is arrived at by observing the nature of justice in particular cases. The highest of all is the idea of the Good, which is also the Beautiful, which is God. God is the sum of all that is GOOD.

Herman Horne is probably the most consistent philosopher of education in recent years to take up the Platonic concept of the duality of reality and to spell out the implication of the same for education. "Are values cosmic, or only human?" Horne asks in an article contributed to the 41st Yearbook of the National Society for the Study of Education, entitled "An Idealistic Philosophy of Education."[30]

> Are values newly created as man experiences them in the temporal order or are they already realized completely in some superhuman eternal experience? Here philosophies differ. Naturalistic philosophies (including realism and pragmatism) say the former. Idealistic philosophies say the latter, i.e., that all human values are but temporal expressions of an eternal order which has value in itself. This eternal order is spiritual, non-material, in character and changeless in nature. It is the world of essential ideas and ideals. It is the world of Platonic ideas, the deity of Aristotle, the Jehovah of Moses and the Hebrew prophets, and the Heavenly Father of Jesus.[31]

Virtue, and justice, and the good life are closely associated, if not identical in the idealistic philosophy. Crito in the dialogue by that name asks: "May I say then that not life but the good life is to be chiefly valued?" And the answer given was: "Yes, and the good life is equivalent to a just and honorable one. — I will not escape death if it is against my better judgment," said condemned Socrates when tempted to make his escape from prison.[32] "Virtue is the supreme good, and for it I will die," stated Socrates in the same connection.

Spinoza was among those who perpetuated the idealistic philosophy of values.

> I finally resolved to enquire whether there might be some real good, having power to communicate itself — which would enable me to enjoy continuous supreme and unending happiness. Riches, fame, pleasures of the sense? No, they are but obstacles in the way of a search for something different and new. All are perishable. — Happiness and unhappiness is made wholly to depend on the quality of the object we love. — Knowledge of the union existing between the mind and the whole of nature, and to help others to arrive to the same knowledge.

Spinoza was (of course) a Pantheist and this philosophy comes to the surface here. It is a further development of idealism. He arrives at the point where he identifies nature and God, and thus arrives at the statement that "the love of God is the highest Good and the ultimate aim to which all our actions should be directed."

This no doubt included in his thinking, actions as represented in the teaching-learning process.[33]

Greene is a contemporary philosopher of education who represents idealism as modified by the liberal Christian viewpoint.[34] "All objective value is rooted in God."[35]

> I believe in Truth, Goodness and Beauty, as objective values. Also I believe in that dynamic Being who is worshipped as God in the Christian faith.[36]

"I believe in objective reality, in coercive order. — Values are imbedded in reality itself."[37]

> Man seeks to apprehend these values. — Man is good in proportion as his search for values is successful. — Therefore I am against authoritarianism in education. I am for the open door policy, for maximum freedom of choice and a maximum incentive to responsible maturity.[38]

Tillich appears to persue a similar direction when he defines religion as the "ultimate concern for the Ultimate."[39]

George D. Santayana voices similar beliefs in "Ultimate Religion."[40] He extols Health and Knowledge and states, "We love health and knowledge. Ours is a religion of boundless sympathy with the universe. The Good is whatever increases our perfection."[41]

The humanistic tendency in idealism becomes increasingly articulate. In humanism the focal point of attention is no longer on God, nor even on absolutes, but rather on man and the human personality. "Personality has ultimate worth. We know and can think of nothing higher or more valuable than selfhood, or personality," states Horne.[42]

The culture of the whole man and not a partial efficiency in a particular occupation comes to be the goal of education as suggested by Arthur Moehlman from L. P. Jacks, *The Education of the Whole Man*.[43]

Maximum opportunities for children and youth to realize their full potential for a creative life. Such and similar expressions are used in the latest White House Conference and in the follow-up magazine called *Children,* and in many other educational articles and books.

A relatively new movement in religion is known as *Existentialism.* In the Kierkegaard version of existentialism God together with Self are still both central. Man comes into existence with a leap of faith by which he discovers that he exists as an independent existant. Later non-theistic existentialists eliminated God and "described man as filled with zeal, having freedom unguided by norms, and reaching a crisis of negation without positive solution."[44]

> The autonomous function of the pupil's mind and the habitual exercise by him of a character that is free, charitable, self-moving — and thus becoming adjusted to his finiteness, his homelessness, his lostness. . . .

That is the goal of man's education, as seen by existentialism.

Man, the maximum development of the whole man in all of life situations, this is perhaps the closest we can come to a common ground among the heirs of historic Christianity — Catholic, Lutheran and Protestant, idealism and secularism — when it comes to values in education. Closely associated with the concept of man as an individual is the concept of man as a group. Idealism is probably the most important source and force in making the ideal society a reality.[45] It is the origin of Johnson's utopian plan of a Great Society. This brings us to the consideration of democracy with freedom and justice as a near ultimate if not the ultimate value in American secular education.

The relative position of the individual and society presents an issue on which the free world and the communist world are at loggerheads. The free world places the emphasis on the value of the individual. The latter thinks of man as a means toward the end of a powerful, classless and eventually peaceful society. At this point we come very close to saying that both the free nations and the communist nations meet on common ground: Peace, a permanently peaceful world. Of course, a permanently peaceful world could mean a dead world, a cemetery-like peace. Dead also because of a world without individual freedom. For the present, let us try to describe the importance of democracy and freedom as ultimate values.

Idealism seems to lie at the roots of our very Constitution.

> We hold these truths to be self evident, that all men are created equal, that they are endowed by their Creator with certain unalienable rights, that among these are Life, Liberty and the Pursuit of Happiness. That *to secure these rights, Governments are instituted* among men, deriving their just powers from the consent of the governed.

It appears to be very obvious that society, or the State, is not the ultimate good or goal. It is a means to an end, namely the end of the individual's welfare, freedom, rights, and individual development. The Introduction to the Report of the President's Commission on National Goals emphasizes the same relationship between individuals and the group as organized into a government, in America. "The paramount goal of the United States was set long ago. It is to guard the rights of the individual, to ensure his development, and to enlarge his opportunity."[46] Such key words as "self-fulfillment," "rights," "liberty," "opportunity," seem to make it clear that government is still *a means to an end*, or value, by itself.

It is significant that even Maritain, a spokesman for Thomism and Catholicism, rejects the idea that the Church is the supreme and the ultimate good and pleads for an education designed to "develop in people the capacity to think correctly and to enjoy truth and beauty, i.e., an education for freedom, or, a liberal education."[47]

Individual, personal, maximum development, together with a socially coherent unity, dedicated to the democratic charter is a must. If both goals are to be attained "a sound pluralism (of religious and cultural values) must obtain in the means," that is in the government and in government schools and universities.[48]

Whether worship of any kind is permissible and desirable in the interest of personal development in a country that has been

155

committed to separation of church and state seems debatable. Horne thinks it is a very desirable value in education.

"At the top of a scale (of values) would come worship as bringing man into conscious relationship to the Infinite Spirit of the Universe."[49] In a somewhat similar vein the Goals for America states toward the end of the Introduction,

> The very deepest goals for Americans relate to the spiritual health of our people. The right of every individual to seek God and the well springs of truth, each in his own way, is infinitely precious. We must continue to guarantee it, and we must exercise it for ours is a spiritually based society.[50]

In view of the chaotic condition of ethics and morality in our society the urge to retain moral standards and to transmit them to the next generation is a matter of great concern to all, also to the secularists. However, they expect to accomplish this without religion and without God, either the God of the Idealists or the God of the Christian believers. Bower states the issue clearly in *Moral and Spiritual Values in Education.*[51]

> The Kentucky Movement of Moral and Spiritual Values in Education is unalterably committed to the strict separation of Church and State and unequivocally is opposed to teaching religion in the public schools in any functional cooperation with the churches or their clergy.[52]

Believers of the Christian faith are equally certain that morality and good conduct must have the sanction of God and God imbedded in conscience. They are quite sure that attempts to teach morals and good conduct have always been part and parcel of public education, ever since religion as such was eliminated from tax supported schools beginning some 100 years ago. But that attempt to teach morality without God and a sensitized conscience has brought us to where we are with our teen-age problems of delinquency and general lawlessness. We are not suggesting that this void in the curriculum and purposes of the tax-supported schools is the only contributing factor in today's moral chaos among Americans, but we suggest it is one and we think the principal basic deficiency in the education of America's youth. And now to have "spirituality" without God and God's Word borders on the inane. It's a pious wish, of course. But the attitude of youth today expressed in a cynicism of "So what?!" and "Who said so?" is in part the product of an a-moral secularism, a non-moral education that cannot get beyond the selfishness of "What do I get out of it?"

Of course, Bower, even as John Dewey and Durkheim, has an answer to the question, How do you propose to develop a serious appreciation of moral and spiritual values?

> Moral and spiritual values come into being in and are conditioned by the experience of the whole self in inter-action with its total environment. A school that seeks to discover and develop moral and spiritual values in public education and young people must seek to establish under-standings and effective cooperation with all the constructive agencies of the community that in one way or another influence their attitude and behavior. Destructive agencies, as taverns, road houses, organized gambling, sexual de-bauchery, must be eliminated or rendered ineffective.[53]

Here we are back to puritanism and control from without, instead of concentrating on control from within, self control! Mr. Bower means well. But we don't think that he has the answer; perhaps that goes in a totalitarian state, but not in a country that is dedicated to free, permissive, democratic, creative America. And that brings us to a brief consideration of values, intermediary and ultimate, in a matter-centered culture.

D. VALUES — AXIOLOGY — IN A MATTER-ORIENTED PHILOSOPHY: MATERIALISM

Bower, in *Moral and Spiritual Values*, provides the transition from a quasi-idealist to a materialistic evaluation of morals and values.

We are now confronted by the necessity of finding moral and spiritual values within man's continuum of earthy experience as he lives his life in the constant context of social, scientific and human relations.[54]

Morality and spirituality are qualities that are potentially inherent in any and every experience of growing persons in their interaction with their natural, social, cultural and cosmic world. — These values are therefore inherent. They are indigenous to the school community and the learning process and are not to be injected into the school by some outside agency. As they are being generated in the school experience, the school must identify them, develop them with the resources available to the school, and carry them into action in actual school situations.

Unfortunately for Bower his fine proposals conflict with history, with age-old experiences, and with God's revelation about human nature.

St. Paul evidently had a firsthand knowledge of morals and values in a decadent Rome. In his letter to the Romans he said: Moreover, since they considered themselves too high and mighty to acknowledge God, he allowed them to become the slaves of their degenerate minds, and to perform unmentionable deeds. They became filled with wickedness, rottenness, greed and malice: their minds became steeped in envy, murder, quarrel-someness, deceitfulness and spite. They became whisperers-behind-door, stabbers-in-the-back, God-haters; they overflowed with insolent pride and boastfulness, and their minds teemed with diabolical invention. They scoffed at duty to parents; they mocked at learning, recognized no obligations of honor, lost all natural affection, and had no use for mercy. More than this — being well aware of God's pronouncement that all who do these things deserve to die, they not only continued their own practices, but did not hesitate to give their thorough approval to others who did the same.[55]

What are the values in a naturalistic, materialistic, secular culture? In summary: The good is what satisfies biological and social cravings. Brubacher states it thus: "Whatever promotes life, or in other words, biological survival, becomes the measure of value."[56]

"Beliefs about values are pretty much in the same position in which beliefs about nature were before the scientific revolution," said John Dewey in *The Quest for Certainty*.[57]

The fact that value judgments are subjective has kept some from becoming too articulate about values and a defensible scale, or hierarchy of values. Feigl,[58] among others, raises this question:

> The central issue for any theory of values is clear: Can value judgments be justified as valid and if so, what is the basis and what is the method of such justification? Are value judgments propositions in the same sense in which empirical statesments are empirical? Do value judgments have intersubjective validity? Or is it true that 'degustibus non est disputandum?' (About tastes it is useless to argue.)

> "Experimentalism," says Geiger, "prides itself on continuity. Therefore it must address itself above all to a naturalistic explanation of value." This is what John Dewey was doing for more than two decades.[59]

> From Aristotle on intelligence has been classically delineated as the summum bonum. It has come to be regarded as the core of the experimentalist theory of value. Intelligence is the quality of relating ongoing activities to ends in view. Intelligence is never outside of a context. It does not operate in a vacuum. There is nothing stable in that context. There are no fixed points of orientation. Education is a moral affair. It is pre-eminently a value enterprise.[60]

Man is the measure of all things. This Greek principle of evaluation finds a ready acceptance among naturalists, and materialists.

> Like naturalism, modern materialism is opposed to any other criterion of value than human needs and aspirations. It combats all forms of authoritarianism in morals and arts. It rejects the appeal to any supposed extra-natural

experiences. With the removal of a supernatural perspective, man must stand consciously on his own feet. Let him rise to his full stature and dignity.[61]

The time-honored criteria of values as found in Scriptures, both Old and New Testament, as well as the similarly time-honored source of values as expressed in idealism have come under severe criticism ever since the days of Darwin, Spencer and Huxley. The evolutionary theory, though unproven, has tended to dissolve the absolute, eternal, preexistent unchanging, standards of value. Evolutionary materialism and secularism has lost no time in offering devastating criticism against values as conceived in Pre-Darwin days.

"To take evolution seriously is to be a naturalist," writes Geiger in an article titled, "An Experimentalist Approach to Education."[62] Geiger responds to the accusation that evolutionary criteria of value "lead to moral anarchy and to vicious relativity" by saying,

> When any value is put above all else, outside the reach of criticism and emendations as the only true and right value then it is consistent to sacrifice to it (no criticism about that) and to the diabolism of the end justifies the means. This is a logical follow through. The absolute value may be the salvation of an immortal soul or it may be the classless society.[63]

The escape from both types of fanaticism, he thinks, is in a persistent use of intelligence in all problem situations in life. The naturalistic approach to the concept of values must "choose between a better and a lesser good as means to an end. This calls for intelligence. This is a key word, and, in fact, the summum bonum of modern man."

"Scientific thinking, resulting in reliable, precise, coherent concepts, as against theological, animistic, or metaphysical thinking, this," states Herbert Feigl, "is the way to arrive at valid concepts of values. And the supreme value then is intelligent thinking and intelligent action."[64]

"A more mature and a more fully integrated life, that is our ultimate value," he goes on to say. "This calls for clearer thinking, elimination of tender-minded, wishful, pre-scientific thinking, to do justice to the scientific outlook."[65]

> The dogmatic other-worldly, supernaturalistic, tender-minded, rationalistic, parochial preconceptions must be abondoned and replaced by critical, worldly, naturalistic, fact-minded, empirical, experimental and universally applicable ways of thinking.[66]

Feigl calls this, and probably it is just that, "scientific humanism," and adds, "the distinction between itself and previous 'value concepts' is itself one of the main results of logical empiricist reflections and is the way and a means to maturity."

Bertrand Russell expresses a similar belief (for beliefs they are, as much as the Christian believer's faith) in speaking on the development of the good life: "Vitality, courage, sensitivity and intelligence, men and women so educated might produce a new world," says Russell as quoted with approval by Arthur Moehlman.[67]

In saying that, both have taken sides in behalf of a good society as contrasted with a good individual, as the ultimate value. It appears not unfair to conclude that they take sides with a typical communist belief that a good society, a classless society, is the ultimate good, and, at the same time the means toward changing and improving individuals to make them contented, care-free individuals. "The gradual evolution of organized society through the effect of society on education and education on society." This describes both the ultimate value and the means of attaining this value through education. The supreme value is democracy in action.

This naturalistic, pragmatic, instrumentalist philosophy of values in education has been in operation in formal and informal movies, books, etc., in American education during the past one hundred and more years. With what results in terms of law-abiding happy individuals? Not only the avowed heirs of historic Christianity, but men who stand out in the field of educational philosophy, are disturbed. John S. Brubacher, among others, lists a series of six

161

reasons for *"anxiety"* among church people and among educators, legislators and others operating within the machinery of government. "There is a current anxiety that modern education is adrift without rudder, chart, or compass."[68] Roy Sellars holds out hope that, in effect, "we have only begun to fight." He states, "A democratic way of life is not a gift of the gods. It demands favorable conditions and willingness to plan the extension and development of these conditions as a means to the end."[69]

But there is a continued strong and supported belief that it is not the slums in the community but the slums in the hearts of unregenerate teen-agers that are the source of these "anxieties" in American education. And the solution is still believed by many to be indicated in the words of the Great Teacher who said: "Except a man be born again, he cannot see the Kingdom of God."[70] "Can the Ethiopian change his skin, or the leopard his spots?"[71] The answer is No. But what man, even when he stands resolutely on his own feet, as suggested, cannot do, that God the Holy Spirit has done, is doing in Christian schools and can and will do whenever educators and parents are humble enough to try the means whereby God operates on the hearts and minds of learners: Word and Sacrament. There are men and women, youth and aged, who are truly educated since they are "born again, not of corruptible seed, but of incorruptible, by the Word of God which liveth and abideth forever."[72]

So far we have said little or nothing about Marxism and communism, operating in the land where materialist values have been made the basis of a new education and presumably a new and a better world. Perhaps this is because the article on Marxism in Education says nothing about ultimate values.[73] All of the ten authors of articles in this 54th Yearbook of the National Society for the Study of Education were asked to write a section on Aims and Values. All did except the author of the article on Marxism. Is this omission significant?

In 1959 Washington sent a Commission to the USSR to study education in the Soviet World.[74] A report from the mission gives a very good description of what the Commission evidently regarded as a good educational program. It states among other things, "The one fact that most impressed us in the USSR was the extent to which the nation is committed to education as a *means of national advancement.*"[75] They reported one leading Soviet educator saying, "We believe in a planned society, you in individual initiative. Let time tell."[76] The State appears to be the focal point and the supreme value in education, rather than the development of the individual, as in American education.

> From infancy, children are taught that *the highest* good is to serve the State; school children through their clubs or circles, in classes, and in games are taught *to identify all good things with the State.*[77]

Among the curricular offerings from kindergarten to graduate studies, science rates easily as the most important. Students evidently are trained to regard the sharing of their blessings under communism as of great importance and value to them. In its visits to schools the Commission was usually greeted with bouquets of flowers and a speech in English by a student, concluding usually with the wish: "In the name of the pupils of our school I ask you to give our Pioneer (Lenin) and our ardent regards to all the children of the United States of America."[78] The task of "evangelizing" the world for communism appeared to be uppermost in the minds of Russian children.

Continuing on a more philosophical note we quote Robert S. Cohen, "On the Marxist Philosophy of Education," to the effect that "The source of value lies only in the human labor expended."[79] Dialectical materialism seems to concentrate on man, human welfare, and is therefore similar to the "scientific humanism" spoken of on previous pages. While not idolizing intelligence in so many words, the Soviet emphasis on "identifying, counselling and aiding" the mentally gifted future citizens indicates that a high and ever higher degree of intelligence is of primary value to them. This intelligence should operate in the natural sciences, but primarily also in the economic structure. Expressions such as "attaining the truth about man," "the oneness of man," "the oneness of society," "the communal life," "the science of society," "the economic structure of society," "a classless society," "an end

163

of exploitation of men by men," in fact another Utopia appears to be the summum bonum of Soviet philosophy of education. The value of capitalism, as an economic structure for "maximizing of financial profit on investments" is conceded, but only as an intermediary step toward the goal of eliminating capitalism. "The Marxist vision of man sees him as united with himself, his comrades and his world."[80] They claim and they frankly admit that every system of pedagogy is *"an instrument of national policy"* and the final state of a permanently peaceful society, and classless, is one in which is operative the principle: "From each according to his ability and to each according to his need."[81]

Except for the *method* of attaining the final value and goal the ultimate value and end result in education in communism and in American democracy is very similar, if not identical. This no doubt explains why the intellectual elite on college campuses is often the center of fermentation for greater understanding of communism and its objectives. John Dewey put it this way: "The school is a form of community life designed to aid the child to inherit the resources of the race and to use his own powers to *social ends."*[82] Charles Beard, eminent social philosopher, expressed it in a similar way: "The maintenance and improvement of American society — so as to contribute to the good life for each person."[83]

The great value, the ultimate value, is social progress, a wholesome attitude toward both order and change, orderly change, improvement of society, calling for good citizenship.[84]

E. EDUCATIONAL IMPLICATIONS AND SUMMARY EVALUATION

The implications of the three major theories of values have been persistently referred to in the previous presentation. We ask again in conclusion, What shall the heirs of historic Christianity, and, more specifically, what shall the heirs of the Reformation say? How should they feel about peace, a permanently peaceful society? Are Christian believers indifferent to, or even opposed to, progress and peace? Far be it from that. "Seek ye the peace of the city."[85] that is the guiding principle in their citizenship responsibilities. With Lincoln they act on the principle: Can a house divided against itself survive? The current racial riots and racial discrimination are a disgrace to our fair land. There is much that can and should be done to make "civil rights" legislation operative in every community. But, a more permanent basis of peace must be sought not in legislation but inwardly, in a change of heart on the part of all concerned. Unfortunately, humans are stuck with the heritage of sin. Hence we are skeptical about human nature. We are more than skeptical. As realists we have our fingers crossed about Lenin's, Dewey's, and Johnson's Utopian dream about improving the nature of man by changing his environment, economic, social and in high rising new apartments to take the place of shambled cottages. We feel compelled to remember still on the basis of man's past experiences and on the basis of the revealed Word, which came from Him who is the Way, the Truth and the Life; "Out of the heart proceed evil thoughts, murders, adulteries, fornications, thefts, false witness, blasphemies."[86] Every page of the morning paper, even the statistics of J. Edgar Hoover, throws this truth glaringly on our mental screen. Confronted with Utopian dreams which hold out the prospect that improvement of the environment, social, economic, political, does not change sinners into saints, the rhetorical question still stands: "Can a leopard change his spots? Can the Ethiopian change his skin"[87] The answer still is: "Ye must be born again. Except a man be born again he cannot enter into the kingdom of heaven."[88] Christian educators still quote unabashedly: "The fear of the Lord is the beginning of wisdom."[89] And therefore they remind all social planners, dreamers of a Utopian society: "Trust in the Lord with all thine heart and lean not on thine own understanding."[90] "Righteousness exalteth a nation but sin is a reproach to any people."[91]

Civic righteousness can be and should be the concern of all and each educator whether his thinking is oriented around the Atom, the Idea, or God. Real righteousness is found through faith in him of whom it is written: "The Just for the unjust, to bring them to God."[92]

Peace, within man's own heart, escape from the guilt complex, peace among members of one family and with neighbors, peace within a nation, yea, peace, within the human family dwelling with us on the same satellite, peace of man with God, is found in forgiveness. And forgiveness is found through faith in Jesus the Savior from sin. And we still say with David: "Blessed is he whose transgression is forgiven, whose sin is covered."[93] Since God the Holy Spirit operates through the means of grace, Word and Sacrament, and indirectly also through the "koinonia," the body of Christ, the Church, and the Christian family, we have here a summary of Christian values, the ultimate good, as seen by those whose educational thinking is God-centered, and not either matter-centered with Paul: "Now abideth faith, hope and charity; and the greatest of these is charity,"[94] or love. Through faith we are united with the God of love. There we learn to love God and love also our neighbor. LOVE is therefore the ultimate value.

Undaunted by obstacles such as the Supreme Court ruling which follows the Soviet trend of excluding God and prayer from tax-supported education, undismayed by the deeply entrenched secularism and naturalism in our culture and therefore in our public education, tenaciously on guard against the invasion of naturalism in the theology of today, by theologians such as Bultman[95] and Tillich,[96] the heirs of Historic Christianity will not be outdone by the "missionary" zeal of communist school children to share their values with all of humanity.[97] If anything, Christian families and Christian churches will be more than ever determined to keep God and the Supreme Good in the education of their youth. Currently their emphasis in education is concentrating on eliminating the disparity that has too often been found between the beliefs which Christians profess and the lives they live. There is a growing firm determination that, with the help of God the Holy Spirit, the love and good will of God toward even the undeserving, will manifest itself and become observable in the living products of God-centered education.

The "artificial separation" of the "knowing subject" from the "known object" will be increasingly eliminated, not primarily to please Marx and Hegel, who have pointed to this as the greatest fault of Western culture, but to please the God who has created, redeemed, and sanctified us to grace, through faith, as a gift of God. And all to the greater glory of God.

CHAPTER V

ETHICS AND MORALITY

What is right? And what is wrong? What is good and what is evil? What is virtue and what is vice? What is an adiaphoron? Does the Golden Mean represent more than an escape from making a decision between right and wrong? What is the difference between ethics and morality? How are mores and customs related to both of these? What is the nature of the penalty for following the wrong way? What are the rewards, if any, of following the right way? Why are the prisons filled to overflowing in all parts of our fair land? Is there any identifiable reason why American youth should be more lawless than, say the Canadians? How do we distinguish between original and actual sin? What is the difference between moral law, natural law and human law? Why did they burn persons for heresy in the past centuries? Why is a traitor to his country considered most menial? These and other questions are to be considered in this chapter.

It is a crucial subject because the bars of restraint have been let down in practically all facets of our culture.

The problem of maintaining standards of ethics and of morality is acute and nationwide. Many factors contributed to the demoralization in the present Western world.

"Many Christian leaders were dead to the cries of the persecuted (under Castro and Mao) because they were muffled by social reform. They were blind to the atheistic ideology and the bloody records of the leaders. Then when power was secure, naked dictatorship and slavery quickly became evident."[1]

Power itself is neither good nor bad. The manner and purpose for which it is used is the thing that matters.

> Science and technology can be used in two ways, in the service of mankind and to the detriment of mankind; to improve health and standard of living or for the development of weapons of great destructive power. . . . The evil and the good that thus becomes possible are not property of science and technology, but they are two choices facing man. . . . The decisions required are not scientific decisions, but moral decisions. . . . What is needed is an acknowledgment that we are not making this moral grade ourselves. Not only others, *we* are sinners. It is here that the Christian message enters in. It aims at convincing us that we are sinners. . . . That means it does not drive us into despair but revives in us the hope and makes it possible to work quietly toward a solution of the problems that face us.[2]

The corrosive element of secularity and atheism has permeated all facets of our culture, particularly also the area of the fine arts. Virginia Held[3] is among those who speak of the current dismay and alarm; of the moral malaise; of derangements in politics and morals. Ruth Nanda Anshen speaks in a similar tone.[4] She states: "Modern art is on the verge of spiritual and moral insanity and having lost the sense of who and what he is, man fails to grasp the meaning of his followmen, of his vocation, and of the nature and purpose of life itself."

Virginia Held quotes various prominent leaders to support her cry of alarm. John F. Kennedy is quoted as saying: We have gotten soft; General Eisenhower as saying to the Committee on National Goals: We are in an era of moral fatigue. We have no stamina to fight. We cannot expect to compete with a strong-willed purposeful Soviet Union. Cicero said: Law is the bond of civil society. Lippman is quoted: We must have it (morality) or else! Krutch says: We are not merely the product of circumstances. There must be a way out! God is dead? But we must believe in something. There must be a re-affirmation of religious faith. Back to God. Back to God's Word. To objective principles. Roman Catholic Bishops in Conference are quoted as saying: Accept the

169

reign of God. Quit arguing. Agree on values.[5] Paul Tillich says: Be ultimately concerned about the Ultimate. Ethics must be rejuvenated. Youth wants a new content of ethics and morality.

Denis Hawkins expresses concern about trends in sex life, promiscuity, homo-sexuality, birth control. etc.[6]

Edith Kermit Roosevelt is concerned because "Hitler is dead. But the totalitarian mentality lives on among the social engineers in our midst," especially also in matters of regulating sex behavior.[7]

Station WMAY released an editorial on September 10, 1964, that reveals public concern about the trends in sex permissiveness:

> Cook County Welfare Director Raymond Hilliard has predicted expansion of the current birth control to include birth control dissemination to unmarried teen-age girls. Such information currently is given only to married female relief recipients. 'The wind is blowing' says Hilliard. We think this is an asinine trend. If we are going to concern ourselves with the morality of an oncoming generation, how can we condone pre-marital relations by the very act of teaching unmarried teen-age girls how to avoid pregnancy?

Large questions are raised here. How is behavior according to good standards developed? What erodes good behavior patterns? Is it bad company? Bad movies? Bad reading? Bad example? Or is it basically a bad philosophy of ethics and morality? We think the latter is it, a faulty understanding of human nature. If we didn't, we would not be writing this chapter on Ethics and Morality in a Philosophy of Education.

Differences in philosophies stem from different basic assumptions, or beliefs. Materialists begin with a basic belief that all reality is made up of physical entities only; that nature is autogenetic. Idealistic philosophers begin with the basic assumption that all existence is fundamentally made up of ideas; of something akin to mind. And heirs of historic Christianity, though they differ in many ways in spelling out the implications of their belief nevertheless begin philosophizing with God. The Scriptures from beginning to end present God as angry because of sin, and yet ready to forgive, and pleading with man to follow God's rules of good behavior. Redemption, justification and sanctification are key words in the ethics of both Old Testament and New Testament. One philosophy is matter-centered; the other is idea-centered, and the third is God-centered. Which is right? We'll say with Lenin: Time will tell.

These three families of philosophies have their implications also for ethics and morality. Let's see what the God-centered believers say, and why they say about ethics and morality what they do say.

B. ETHICS AND MORALITY AS SEEN BY HEIRS OF HISTORIC CHRISTIANITY

Christian believers have several basic things in common about ethics and morality. The basic ethical principles came from God, they believe. The principles of morality are revealed. They apply to all men at all times and in all places. They are a part of God's self-revelation. They stem from the holiness, the justice and the righteousness of God. They stem also from the love, the mercy, and the kindness of God. They present Law and Gospel. They are God-originated. In Exodus, Chapter 20, we read: And God spake all these words saying: I am the Lord thy God. Thou shalt have no other gods before me. And thus we received the Ten Commandments, known as the Decalogue, from God.[8] In Matthew, Chapter 5-7, we have a record of Jesus' interpretation of the Decalogue. It is a study in depth of the Decalogue. In the Life of Him who is "the express image of the Father,"[9] The Christians have "Him who is the Way, the Truth and the Life."[10] That means Jesus is the Christian's example in ethical conduct.

The Christian's pattern of behavior was evidently the most distinguishing observable mark of the believers because they were known in their community as persons of "that way."[11] The Proverbs are a collection of practical ethics and morality and wisdom; they were designed to give instruction in wisdom, justice, judgment and equity.[12] "The fear of the Lord is the beginning of wisdom" is the keynote.[13]

171

In the centuries of 800 to 400 B.C. the prophets applied the principles of the Decalogue to economic, political and social issues. Isaiah, Amos, Hosea, Micah and Jeremiah, they all preach Law and Gospel, repentance and faith, and exhort to godly conduct. Social justice, righteousness, mercy, love, these are key words in these Old Testament books. Ecclesiastes, the Preacher, seems to propose the views of Epicurean materialists, suggesting that there is nothing better than carnal enjoyments and the pleasure of this life, but he ends up with the more God-centered appeal: "Fear God and keep his commandments for this is the whole duty of Man."[14]

Much of the New Testament, especially the letters of Paul and Peter and James, concern themselves with the problem of man's restoration in a proper, close and filial relationship to God, by the road of repentance, faith, commitment, and re-dedication to sanctified living. These letters are a powerful answer to those who are today asking: What can be done to restore maturity, a sense of responsibility, law-abiding citizenship? Nowhere do these inspired writers resort to mere legalism, formalism, codes of conduct. Persistently they call for repentance, faith and holiness of living, not as a means of being saved and justified and united with God, but as a fruit and outgrowth of the fact that they have been saved and justified and born again into a new existence and a new life, by grace, without the deeds of the law, through faith, a faith that is the gift of God, developed by the Holy Spirit, through Word and Sacrament. "Walk worthy of your vocation."[15] "Walk circumspectly."[16] "Walk in love."[17] "Walk worthy of the Lord."[18] "As ye received Christ, so walk in Him."[19] "Walk after His commandments."[20] James does not overlook repentance, faith and justification, but his major emphasis is on practical religion, on ethics and morality, on faith that worketh by love.

During various periods in the history of God's people there have been times in which morality and sanctified living were neglected, while the emphasis on true doctrine was greatly stressed. Then theologians wrote about the problem of "dead orthodoxy." There have also been periods of extreme emphasis on piety, to the extent of growing into a sickly pietism. Today there is observable an awareness among God's people that the unbeliever reads the lives of His people rather than the books on Christian ethics and morality. So that the Way may be less badly spoken of, and in order to prepare the way, as it were, for witnessing and recommending the Gospel, we have had occasion to observe a refreshing new emphasis on The Life in Christ, on conduct worthy of the Gospel. In fact, the emphasis on stewardship of time, talent, treasure, stresses the hope and the prayer of leaders in the church today that Christ may increasingly have the pre-eminence in all things, and in the whole character and personality of the Christian. In this new emphasis on Christ-like conduct laymen and laywomen are considered equal with the clergy. In this connection the reader may want to read Chapter 4 from Paul's Letter to the Galatians. Also the famous charity chapter in I Corinthians 13. The 23rd chapter of Matthew makes timely and helpful reading at a time when church going, tithing, and sundry types of good conduct in contemporary Christianity, are being urged in the churches.

"The essential and paramount interest of Christianity is the Christian life itself," writes Chr. Ernst Luthhardt. "The scientific comprehension and elucidation of this is the chief function of modern theology. To avoid a sterile emphasis on dogmatics and systematics, theologians must find here the central emphasis."[21]

Martin Luther, even as Thomas Aquinas before him, devoted much of his preaching and writing to *good works,* their nature, their origin and their place in God's plan of salvation.[22] The teaching of Luther that any and every honorable kind of "vocation" is pleasing to God and has the nature of good works was revolutionary and did much to destroy the common belief that life in a monastery or in a convent had special merit because such lives were considered especially good and holy. The Catholic Catechism, Luther's Small Catechism, and the Heidelberg Catechism are still powerful textbooks, commonly used in all types of Christian education on Christian ethics and morality. There is much, very much of ethics and morality in these treatises.

Among the multitude of books and treatises which have been written about Christian ethics and morality in more recent years, is

173

The Quest for Holiness, by Koeberle.[23] This study was designed especially to defend the Gospel against attempts to equate
it with a new morality, as this was attempted by Kant's categorical
imperative, and later by Ritschl. Barth made his influence felt
among theologians by quickening the conscience of theologians,
warning them not to confuse the Gospel with pragmatic moralism,
with psychology and with conception of idealistic philosophy.

Martin Marty, in *The Hidden Discipline,*[24] calls attention to
the Christian's motive for moral conduct. He insists self-discipline
begins with the joy of forgiveness. He stresses the fact that true
morality and good conduct are the result of justification, not a
means toward justification. Legalism, moralism, formalism, leads
to Pharisaism and hypocrisy, not to a God-pleasing life worthy
of the Gospel.

James D. Smart, in *The Teaching Ministry of the Church,*[25]
deplores the trend in Sunday School materials and the teaching in
church agencies, to identify the Gospel with a new code of conduct and calls for a redefinition of the goals of Christian education
in terms of a reunion with God, rather than giving information
about God. Walther's study on Law and Gospel still provides
reliable guidelines for the presentation and the application of
both Law and Gospel in the interest of making true disciples;
of fostering a life of daily repentance, re-acceptance of Christ as
Savior from sin, and re-commitment to a life that is truly sanctified, moral and ethical.[26]

Having said this about morality and ethics among the heirs of
historic Christianity, we turn to a consideration of two philosophies
which tend to inject pagan ideas into the Christian heritage. One
is idealism. The other is materialism, pragmatism, instrumentalism,
secularism and communism. They are a threat to bury the heritage
of Moses and the prophets, of Jesus and the Church.

C. ETHICS AND MORALITY IN IDEALISM

Sometimes the differences between right and wrong are not
clearly identifiable. This was made the subject of a study by
Graebner, in *Borderline of Right and Wrong.*[27] This area of ethics

and morality is a kind of no man's land, or the area of "adiaphora." This is the field of ethics in which Scriptures, or the laws of the land, do not say either that it is right or wrong.

Similarly the line of demarcation between the ethics of historic Christianity and idealism is not always clearly marked. The two philosophies do have elements in common, though they have arrived at similar results from two distinctly different presuppositions, and by two distinctly different approaches. Idealism, also in ethics and morality, is based on the assumption that certain ethical truths are inherent, you might say, natural, in the universe. Certain "ideas," as Plato believed, are pre-existent, eternal, absolute, unchanging, the same everywhere, at all times and under all circumstances. The mind of man, in the process of reflection, has over a period of centuries, uncovered these pre-existent, non-material entities. Thus, for instance, concepts and ideals, such as honesty, chastity, obedience, loyalty, charity, contentment, are regarded by idealists as eternal, pre-existent, and never-changing. They existed long before man's thinking discovered them or before they were experimentally discovered. This characteristic of idealism makes it a strong bulwark against the materialistic concept of continuing change. Historic Christianity and idealism are here seen as close allies in the struggle to retain moral stability and to hold back the floodwaters of moral chaos.

Since idealism does not build on the assumption of a personal God, but only on the absoluteness of eternal principles, it follows that idealism is not really a religion, but a system of ethics and morality, evolved in the last analysis by the mind of man, without benefit of either revelation or the experimental method. This major emphasis of idealism on ethics rather than on a God-centered viewpoint, is widely recognized. Idealists, however, frequently use the term "god," even with a capital "G" but they do not really mean what the heirs of historic Christianity designate with the term "God." And so they also use and claim for themselves the term "religious" even though they do not admit or claim to be a religion. Theirs is not a theology so much as a sociology.

The fountainhead of this emphasis on reason and ethics is found among the Greeks, especially the Stoics. Epictetus, in answering the question, Wherein consists the essence of the Good? stated:

> God is beneficial. Good also is beneficial. It should seem then that where God is, there too is the essence of good. What then is the essence of God? Flesh? By no means. An estate? Fame? By no means. Intelligence? Knowledge? Right reason? Certainly. Here then, without more ado, seek the essence of the good.[28]

Without tracing the history of the relationship between ethics and religion through the ages, we quote Soe.[29] "Die Religion findet ihren Abschluss in der reinen Lehre der Sittlichkeit" (Religion finds its termination in the pure doctrine of ethics and morality). Critically he observes "the absolutely binding on the man is holy. If man finds this in his own personality this means that man makes himself into a deity."[30] Affirming a more conservative belief he states: "Conscience is the voice of God in man."[31] "Religion and ethics are two independent manifestations which are, however, so closely related as to bring them into vital mutual interaction."[32] Soe appears to summarize his belief in saying: When I am integrated, made one, with the "Urgrund des Daseins" (foundation of reality) I have been made one with ultimate reality, the final ultimate goal of idealistically oriented education.

The concept of "conscience" holds a central place in the morality of both the Christian religion and in idealism. Paul speaks of the Gentiles as not having the law and yet doing by nature the things contained in the law, "which show the work of the law written in their hearts, their conscience also bearing witness and their thoughts the mean while accusing or else excusing one another."[33] Soe suggests that the concept of "suneidesis," knowing together, grew on the soil of humanism.[34] The "guilty conscience," or guilt complex, has come to be, in the age of psychology and psychiatry, a very basic problem in the therapy of the mind and soul where it is still accepted as a real existent. It is at this point the Good News of complete "forgiveness" as found in the Gospel joins in the quest for mental health.

176

Currently, and particularly since the moral monstrosities that have been committed in materialistically-oriented ethics of fascism, naziism, and communism have aroused the concern of free nations, the Western and free nations have become intent on preserving the idealistic basis of our culture. This concern, heightened no doubt by a rapid rise in lawlessness here in our own country, has prompted the President to appoint a Commission on National Goals. In their report they say, among other things. "Above all, Americans must demonstrate in every respect of their lives the fallacy of a purely selfish attitude — the materialistic ethic. Indifference to poverty and disease is inexcusable, in a society dedicated to the dignity of the individual. So also is indifference to values other than material comfort and national power. Our faith is that man lives not by bread alone but by self respect, by regard for other men, by convictions of right and wrong, by strong religious faith. . . . A basic goal for each American is to achieve a sense of responsibility as broad as his world-wide concerns and as compelling as the dangers and opportunities he confronts."[35]

This sounds very good. But it really gets us nowhere beyond Kant's categorical imperative. It is a morality based on sound reason. It is idealistic. It lacks motivation. It lacks sanctions beyond human reason. It is pure moralizing. It is a far cry from the compelling urge of God and of God's people to be enthused about a program of action characterized by active love, the love that sacrifices itself for the benefit of fellowmen. Kant's fundamental idea in his Prolegomena to his main work, *A Critique of Pure Reason,* was the reduction of religion to morality.

Heirs of Historic Christianity have not let go of their belief that *human nature* is perverse; that it is helpless to initiate any good works of its own. Here a paragraph should be inserted about the will of man, and the problem of a free will. We can best say what needs to be said about man's natural perverseness and his ability to decide and carry out what is good and right by quoting on the relationship between "civil rightousness" and "free will" the Apology of the Lutheran Confessions:

177

We do not deny liberty to the human will. The human will has liberty in the choice of works and the things which reason comprehends by itself. It can to a certain extent render civil righteousness or the righteousness of works; it can speak of God; offer to God a certain service by an outward work, obey magistrates, parents. In the choice of an outward work, it can restrain the hand from murder, from adultery, from theft. Since there is left in human nature reason and judgement on objects subjected to the choice between these things, the liberty and power to render civil righteousness are also left.[36]

"Neither the evening star nor the morning star is more beautiful than righteousness. And God also honors it with bodily rewards. Yet it ought not to be practiced with reproach to Christ." The writers of the Apology of the Confessions were concerned about keeping distinct and clear the doctrine of salvation by grace. Any concession to "merit" was deemed by them, and rightly so, as a "reproach" to Christ, as if he had not fully and freely made available the righteousness by faith by which sinners are justified before God. And while the Apology insists on the total depravity of the human nature and its total lack of freedom to choose the right, they nevertheless concede that in matters of civic righteousness man has a free will and can prefer the right rather than the wrong. So, there appears to be reason and hope for a better society, at least outwardly and eventually if not now. In this sense morality can be taught, also in the public school, without religion. But, the effectiveness of such teaching of morality is still very much in doubt. Current upswing in crime statistics do not support the thesis. "Religion and ethics are two independent manifestations which are, however, so closely related as to bring them into mutual vital interaction."[37] Soe contends that idealism, bereft of religion, "threatens us with ethical relativism, indifference and moral chaos."[38]

"All ethical thinkers," writes Theodor Culmann in *Christian Ethics,* "are agreed that their discipline (ethics) is of a practical nature. It has to do with the realization of Christian principles in life and activities. Gradually they come to the conclusion in practical things the purely theoretical truths are as useless as mere

178

theoretical errors are harmful. In either case they are unfruitful and may therefore be ignored."[39] "The ultimate Why for doing the right and avoiding the wrong is God. . . . God is not concrete but he is the ground of the concrete. It is God's very good nature to divide the Good from the Evil."[40] It is well and good for Horne to say: "Idealism holds that the goodness of man's individual and social life is the conformity of the human will with the moral administration of the universe."[41]

If Soe is right when he declares that "Die Ethik ist ihrem Wesen nach Theologie."[42] (Ethics are in their very nature theology), then we must conclude that only theologians, only the Church, can teach morality and ethics. The state and the state schools, being without God and without theology cannot.

D. ETHICS AND MORALITY AS SEEN BY MATERIALISM

Since idealism has not proven itself to be an effective way of educating morally responsible and morally mature teenagers, what about the materialist's approach to good and predictable behavior? Really, the materialistic approach to the definition and propagation of ethical behavior includes a wide variety of "philosophies," all of which however have in common that they recognize no supernatural ties; their viewpoint is entirely this-wordly, naturalistic, entirely secular. God and eternity have no place in these "Weltanschauugen." They include naziism, fascism, communism; also pragmatism, instrumentalism, positivism, scientism, secularism.

"Nature does not know political frontiers. She first puts the living on the globe and watches the free game of energies. He who is strongest in courage and industry receives as her favorite child the right to be the master of existence."[43] Here we have the spokesman of a bloody, brutal, extremely brutal, chapter in the history of man who spells out for us the ethics of Darwin. It is the survival of the fittest. And the fittest are the ones who are strongest. Of course, Hitler's revolution in ethics and morality was not the first time man rebelled against and sought to dethrone God and God-centered morality. "The world is the house of the strong," said Diderot, during the French Revolution.[44] Might is

179

right. That is the logical terminus of evolutionary morality. That is the logical terminus of materialism. In *The Moral Code of Communism,* Sullivan presents a long list of instances which illustrate the morals of communism.[45] "The liquidation of Kulaks (landowners) as a class in 1929 resulted in ten million deaths. In 1936 armed forces were sent to Spain, to support a 15 deputy minority, out of 473. When the Republic collapsed, $550 million dollars in gold was shipped to Russia. . . . The Hitler-Stalin pact for the partition of Poland in 1939 stands as the most depraved act of dictatorship aggression in modern history. In 1956 came the sack of Budapest. At Hitler's convenience, the Hitler-Stalin pact was suddenly disrupted, followed by a ruthless attack." These are but some examples to illustrate that Lenin uttered more than a theory when he stated in 1918: "Promises are like pie crusts. Made to be broken."

How can totalitarian morality ever justify the horrors of Dachau[46] and Bellshausen?[47] The idea that this was necessary to solve the "Jewish problem" is very, very weak indeed. Of course, it was in the interest of survival for the pureblooded Nordic race! Perhaps Bentham would have said: "Prudent calculation."[48] "The only sanction which the ethics of the future can recognize is the pleasure of venturing," says Hoeffding.[49]

"Ethics is the doctrine of means with the help of which the end proposed by nature itself, the increase and preservation of life, can be reached."[50] Francis Hackett reported on the Eichmann trial in Jerusalem. "It is an amazing spectacle that he has given us since he proposed it in Mein Kampf, right before our eyes, like something on a screen, the vast social fabric of familiar Germany has crumbled, and with it the moral Germany that stood the test since Martin Luther."[51]

We dare to account for these monstrosities in behavior by saying that it is an application of the idea that only matter exists. And matter is constantly in a state of flux and change.

> The most obvious attribute of the cosmos is its impermanence. It assumes the aspect not so much of a permanent entity as a changeless process in which naught endures save

the flow of energy and the rational order (sic) which pervades it.[52]

Basically all materialistically oriented ethics and morality are similar. They express it differently. Marx and his disciples had a special axe to grind, to promote an economic revolution. He put it this way: "Morality is that which serves to destroy the old exploiting society and to unite all the toilers around the proletariat which is creating a new communist society."[53]

Over Radio Moscow, Lenin is reliably reported to have stated: "From the point of view of communist morality only those acts are moral which contribute to the building up of a new communist society."[54] "We do not believe in eternal morality and we expose all the fables about morality."[55] Again, "Law, religion and morality are so many bourgeois prejudices behind which lurk in ambush just as many bourgeois interests."[56] "The Bible is a collection of fantastic legends without any scientific support. It is full of dark hints, historical mistakes and contradictions. It serves as a factor for gaining power and subjugating the unknowing nations."[57]

It is most astonishing that the communist ethics which denounces the perfidy of Biblical ethics, is itself the very personification of perfidy, treachery, of broken treaties, and of persistent conquest by force of its innocent neighbors.

"The Communist record in systematic, diplomatic treachery is tabulated in a list of more than 1000 treaties of peace, amity and commerce which have been violated ruthlessly and repudiated by Communist Russia since 1917."[58] Following are some of the instances of broken treaties:

Agreement with Central Powers, Brest-Litovsk. Made 3/3/18. Broken 11/3/18.
With Finland. Made 12/31/17. Broken 12/3/39.
Estonia Armistice, 12/31/19. Incorporated with Russian 6/16/40.
Lithuania was wiped off the map on August 3, 1940.
Latvia was dealt with similarly on August 5, 1940.

181

Since 1917, 1,086 treaties were broken. Seventeen countries were absorbed. 732 million people lost their freedom. And all despite of "peace treaties." Action was based on the negation of every principle of honor and good faith. In 1919 Zinoviev stated: "We put no trust whatever in the piece of paper we sign. For us it is a breathing space in order to gather our strength." Stalin's shocking purges in 1936, Khrushchev's brutal crushing of Polish, Hungarian and East German revolts in 1953-56 confirms a pattern of *irresponsible ethics.*[59]

How does communism account for its irresponsible behavior before the tribunal of world public opinion? "Wait until we have abolished temptations," they say. "We have not yet passed beyond class morality. . . . This becomes possible only after class contradictions have been overcome and forgotten in practical life," wrote Engels in his Anti-Duehring papers.[60]

Lest we point fingers pharisaically at communism only, and lest we think that secularism is not guilty of irresponsible behavior, let us quote an example from secular American community life. In an article on "This Is Gracious Living," appearing in the Chicago Tribune, there appeared pictures of nine mansion-like homes in the most respectable suburban areas of Chicagoland, owned and lived in by Chicagoland hoodlums, gangsters, racketeers, Chicago Crime Syndicate men, Loop gambling supervisors. These men can testify — although testimony is not their strong point — that there is a deep and abiding satisfaction in knowing that in this great democracy of ours even a hoodlum can live in a style to which 92% of our population is unaccustomed.[61] The same issue of the Chicago Tribune carried another article by Norma Lee Browning titled, "Do Suspended Sentences and Easy Paroles Produce Chronic Offenders?" in which she answers her question by saying: "90% of all criminals sentenced to federal prisons are repeaters; 50% started as juvenile offenders." In the same line of concern the Illinois State Journal[62] carried an editorial titled "Appalling Increase in Crime," saying: "J. Edgar Hoover, Director of the FBI reported an appalling upswing in crime, consistent in all areas. Crime in the U.S. is increasing five times faster than our population growth."

The most recent authentic summary of the crime rise in our own country is found in "Crime in Our Streets" by J. Robert Moskin an article in Look Magazine, June 1, 1965, in which Nicholas de B. Katzenbach, Attorney General for the U.S. is quoted as saying: One of my three major tasks is to discover some remedy for the flood tide of crime which has been rising five times as fast as our population.

Today your city streets and parks are fearfully unsafe. — Organized crime, as the Mafia, is not a fiction. It wrecks businesses and destroys people's faith in their local law enforcement agencies. It tends to corrupt government. — Crime among young people is often blamed on poverty; on poor housing and on unemployment. But, it's up in the suburbs; it's a matter of parents who are interested more in themselves than in their children.

From this evaluator's viewpoint the parents themselves are at this time products of an education in which God, as a source of motivation and guidance, had no place. A feeling of irresponsibility and immaturity is a mark of parents as well as of their children and teen-agers. "Society is going to have to create substitute parents. Institutions will have to do the jobs which parents are unwilling to do," says Attorney General Katzenbach.

One would think that those who believe in materialistically oriented ethics, as naziism, communism and secularism do, would be aroused from their slumber and think seriously about finding a more stable basis of morality. And, it seems that Huxley, once an ardent exponent of evolutionary ethics, did adjust his theory in the years of the World War II and thereafter. In 1947, T. H. and J. Huxley expressed opposition "to that which leads to success in the cosmic struggle for existence, e.g., ruthless self-assertion, lack of self-restraint, treading down competition; and recommended respect and helping others in the struggle for the survival of the fittest, fitting and helping as many as others to survive."[63] He protested against unbelievable brutality in Europe and also in the U.S. Tolerance? Yes. But violence, wanton destruction, sexual license? No. But by no means have all experienced that change in heart. In 1947 Erich Fromm wrote:

> Psychology must debunk false ethical judgments and build objective and valid norms of conduct. . . . I have written this book with the intention of reaffirming the validity of human ethics. Man's aim is to be himself. The condition for attaining this goal is that man must be *for* himself.[64]

Everywhere we still hear the echo of pragmatism and instrumentalism as propounded by James and Dewey.

> A moral law, like a law in physics, is not something to swear by and stick to at all hazards; it is a formula of the way to respond when specified conditions present themselves. . . . Beliefs, creeds, moral laws are tools, and only tools, instrumentalities of directions. Therefore the same scrupulous attention should go to the formation of ethical principles as now goes into making of precision instruments in technical fields.

There are those who feel that something vital has been lost in our culture through the loss of God and God-centered ethics. Walter Lippman quotes Aristophanes: "Whirl is King, having driven out Zeus."[65] And continues, "Among those who no longer believe in the religion of their fathers, some are proudly defiant, many are indifferent. Some feel a vacancy in their lives."[66] They no longer have a foundation for their behavior. They are bent on satisfying their appetites. But appetites become jaded. Then they find themselves in a meaningless whirl. He quotes Dostoievsky as saying: If God is dead, everything is allowed.

Both materialism and idealism have now been weighed in the scales that evaluate morality and have been found wanting. Idealism lacks the powerful motivation that is generated in a personal attachment to a personal God.

"The doctrine of adjustment or adaptation explicitly excludes any consideration of Standards. The adjustment must take place whether the environment is good or bad. An educational system that is based on this theory must therefore ultimately become a system without values and without morals," says Robert Hutchins, in *The Conflict in Education.*[67]

"Conscience becomes an echo of social custom rather than divine command," says Brubacher.[68]

There is not much consolation, or hope, even in Kant's sense of duty. "To have moral worth an action must be done from duty."[69] "I am never to act otherwise than so that I could will that my maxim should become universal law. . . . Man will find rest nowhere but in a thorough critical examination of our reason. An a priori synthetic practical proposition is a pre-requisite to freedom."[70]

Whitehead is among those who are far from satisfied that a valid answer to the problem of morality will be discovered by science and scientism. He speaks of "the fallacy of dogmatic finality."

> The universe is vast. Nothing is more curious than the self-satisfied dogmatism with which mankind at each period of its history cherishes the delusion of finality of its existing modes of knowledge. Skeptics and believers are all alike. At this moment scientists and skeptics are the leading dogmatists.[71]

It would appear then that both the State in its attempts to "maintain outward decency and good behavior" and the Church, which in too many instances has succumbed to the wiles of a this-worldly idealism, are fighting a relatively hopeless battle as long as their influential philosophers and novelists say, as did Markun, in *The New Revolution,* in 1963: "And now, young people, citizens of the future . . . as a last bit of advice, let me say this: Pursue life as you see fit and have faith in the future. Leave behind the deep darkness of the mediaeval past — the church with all its unfounded unreasonable oppression — and walk forward uninhibited into the golden sunlight of your scientific future."[72] "Individual self-reliance, pacifism, liberalism, free thought, and following the golden rule are the wisest course for man."[73] Undoubtedly the universal mind will not be misled."[74]

Is there hope for a reversal of ethical thinking in Soviet Russia?

185

Sometimes the leaders lead one to believe there is a change of heart. But the long term purposes and intentions of education in communist morality are not likely to change for the better as long as wishful and prayer-like ambition of a sixth grade pupil is approvingly quoted in a text book for teachers in Soviet Russia: *I Want to be Like Stalin.*[75]

Lest some reader has still not grasped, or not accepted, the claim that the evolutionary theory has done more than any other single factor to upset the apple cart in our God-centered house of ethics and morality, we dare to bring one more quote. This from an earlier than 1947 presentation by Thomas Huxley: "Man, the animal, has worked his way to the headship of the sentient world, and has become the superb animal which he is, in virtue of his success in the struggle for existence. . . . The self-assertion, the unscrupulous pouncing upon all that can be grasped, the tenacious holding of all that can be kept, which constitute the essence of the struggle for existence have answered. For his successful progress throughout the savage state, man has been largely indebted to those qualities which he shares with the ape and the tiger; his exceptional physical organization; his cunning, his sociability, his curiosity and his initiative; his ruthless and ferocious destructiveness when his anger is aroused by opposition."[76]

The wide-spread attempt to make the ethics of evolutionary humanism to take the place of God-centered ethics and morality, an effort that must be associated with the history of public schools in America for a period of 100 years and more, has left many thoughtful parents and educational people very depressed about the future.

"The number of illegitimate babies born in America is reaching alarming heights," writes Rinehart, in a *Look* article titled "Mothers Without Joy."[77] "The cost to support mothers and their illegitimate children in one state (Illinois) was $180 million dollars in one year. One of eight babies born in the U.S. in 1963 was born out of wedlock. Seven million Americans are now born to unwed mothers." Reason given? Too early dating. Going steady. Our society condones it; it contrives and consumes enticements. The attitude seems to be: Sex is fun. This idea permeates our novels, our films and our plays. Dr. Clark Vincent is chief of the National Social Sciences Section of the National Institute for Mental Health. He says: "The beauty queen is the centerpiece from football to trade fairs. Girls begin dating at 10 and 11 years. Ten million teen-age girls spend 25 million dollars on deodorants, twenty million on lipstick, nine million on permanent waves. The assumption is: If you buy the right bra, happiness is yours. And these figures hold for both sides of the track, for white and black. The IQ of unwed mothers is no lower than the median. Birth control contraceptives, especially if made available as now in convenient pill form, is not the answer," says Vincent. What is the answer? The next move?

E. CONCLUSION AND SUMMARY

What is the answer? Education, BETTER education, of course! Federal Aid to Education, all education, public, private and parochial, we hear. "There is a seething discontent with public education," writes the Editorial Board, including Reinhold Niebuhr and John C. Bennet.[78]

Leaders in education are quoted as saying: "Break the religious knot!"[79] "Church-sponsored schools should not be excluded from aid."[80] "No preferential aid but they need not be excluded from aid."[81] We have made exceptions (military chaplaincy, GI Bill, etc.). We urge Protestants, Catholics, Jews and secularists to begin moving on education. What shall we say? More of the same thing? Shall we try the shared plan? Liberal financial support, even if this were forthcoming, is not the answer. A frank reexamination in answer to the question: How did we get to where we are now? as recommended by at least two of the authors of articles in the 54th Yearbook of the NSSE: *Modern Philosophies and Education.*[82] As a minimum that could result in a much more systematic attempt to foster "civic righteousness." Conceivably it might open the door to allow the heirs of historic Christianity to take the floor in behalf of God and Godliness in Education. For the present and immediately foreseeable time it should result in Christian parents who make their homes centers of God's workshop in moral behavior. And Christian churches, if indeed they are not yet among the lost heirs of historic Christianity, to gird their loins anew to spell out in the education of their children, their teen-agers, and their adults, their belief that God is the beginning, middle, and end of human existence, and in fact, of all reality, and certainly in ethics and morality.

In the world-wide concern for an end to war and a reign of peace, we quote a piece of poetic-like prose, which might have its application also to our problem of cultivating godliness as against individual licentiousness and libertinism. Lin Yutang writes: "Our rulers are cavorting with the harlot and while peace sees them through the windows and hears the mad laughter, the bawdy noisiness, the clanking of champagne glasses inside, she will turn her steps away and never come. . . . For peace is a lady and she comes to our house only when she knows she is loved. But those who are guiding the nations' destinies are hypocrites; they love not her but the wench, Power. Therefore her face will be hidden from us until she knows that we love her truly, and not the wench, Power."[83]

If we truly love godliness and refinement in good behavior, let us show that we love the ways by which God leads little ones, teen-agers and adults, toward the goal: Using in education, in the homes and in the churches, if not in tax-supported schools, the Word and Sacraments; leading to personal faith in the Savior from sin; thus leading to a daily and grateful awareness of forgiveness; and thus to a life of imitation of Him; to Christ dwelling in us and we dwelling in Christ; to an awareness of being personally one with God and with His body, the Church.

Let those who love the Lord and are interested in promoting the best possible kind of education, insistently spell out the implication of their love in their goals and objectives in the curriculum and in extracurricular activities for their schools; in their methods and their motivations for learning, in their instructional materials; in their administrative procedures, and also in their measuring and evaluation of progress. Let it become everywhere evident you are striving for a truly God-centered education.

Chapter VI

THE GOOD LIFE

A. THE PROBLEM

The subject matter of this chapter is closely interwoven with the statement on educational objectives. At the ultimate level of objectives all education is designed to stimulate and to aid each educand to share as fully as possible in the good life. The statement of ultimate objectives in education is based on basic assumptions. These we have learned to see as being based on three distinctly and basically different basic assumptions regarding reality. The basic beliefs are oriented either around matter, or around ideas, or around God. That is to say that this universe of which our planet and man himself is a part can be accounted for materialistically, idealistically, or as a reality in which God is the beginning, the core, and the end. Our conception of the Good Life will vary with these fundamentally different world views, or "Weltanschauungen."

B. GOD-CENTERED CONCEPTION OF THE GOOD LIFE

The heirs of historic Christianity do not agree with Epicurus. "According to Epicurus philosophy must be a cure for the mind and soul; it must be a guide to happiness. He taught that pleasure was the beginning and the end of the blessed life."[1]

Nor can the God-centered believers be satisfied with the Dewey version of the intellect as an instrument leading to the good life, i.e., intelligent action, and to more of the same kind of education.

Nor can the heirs of the Protestant segment of historic Christianity agree that reason supplemented by the grace of God re-

189

presents the royal road to the good life, as Thomists appear to hold. It is not reason supplemented by the grace of God, but rather the grace of God in Christ Jesus, informed by reason, that holds the key to the good life in sound Protestant theological and educational thinking.

In speaking of the virtuous life as essentially the good life, it should be noted that while Thomism does stress, with idealism, the intellectual virtues, it does consider the moral virtues as most indispensable to the good life. States Father W. Farrell: "While the intellectual virtues (understanding, knowledge, wisdom) and the practical virtues (prudence and art) need to be stressed in an education which is designed to lead into the good life, the moral virtues are pre-eminently designed to lead into the good life. While the intellectual virtues perfect a man in this or that way, it is the moral virtues alone which perfect the whole man. . . . There is nothing, humanly speaking, in this present life of ours outranking the moral virtues in importance."[2]

Pope Pius XI stressed the moral virtues similarly in any education sponsored and controlled by Catholic educators. He emphasized that the moral virtues exceed in importance the intellectual virtues. Hence the former ought to be stressed as much as, if not more than, the latter in the work of the school. "Man whole and entire . . . soul united to body in unity of nature, with all its faculties, natural and supernatural, such as right reason and revelation show him to be."[3] Thus this encyclical on Education of the Youth stresses the education of the whole person, with emphasis on the moral virtues.

Unfortunately the conception of the good life in Catholic theology is only partly Scriptural. Partly it is Thomistic. Aquinas used Aristotle and Revelation. The result is also in its answer to the question of the nature of the good life, a Catholic conception is partly Christian and partly Greek philosophy.

In stating the Scriptural, Protestant point of view about the good life, and stating it tersely, in the fewest possible words we would say this:

God is all in all. Christ is the Alpha and the Omega of existence. When God becomes operative "im Sitz des Lebens" (where life is lived) and when it can be truthfully said: "Es ist nur noch Gott auf dem Platz" (only God remains where life is lived) there the good life has been initiated. The Good Life centers in God. Where man's thinking, feeling, valuing and overt behavior has its origin, focus and end-point in God, there we find the good life. Inseparable union with God, through faith in Christ, is therefore the very core of the good life, and that is therefore the ultimate goal of a good education. Since God is love, the good life expresses itself in active neighborly love.

The one factor which alienates man from God is sin. A separation from God, through a sense of shame and guilt before God, is the one basic hindrance to a good and happy life. God has thrust Himself into the life of humanity, by becoming a brother to man, a servant to man, so as to save man from sin. Those who believe in Jesus Christ, accept Him as their Savior from sin and from all that is evil in this present life, are free from the guilt of sin. They are inwardly united with God. They share in the holiness, the love, the mercy, the purity, the power, yea, in the very nature of God. That is blessedness. That is the good life. It is marked by peace of mind, fearlessness, optimism, "faith, hope and charity." God is the perfection in all manifestations of life. And so this concept of the good life embraces indeed the moral virtues such as holiness, obedience, cleanliness, honesty and uprightness; peace within, peace with God, and peace and goodwill toward all men.

It is in this theological context that the Beatitudes must be understood. The Greek word for "blessed" is *makarios*. The dictionary defines it as "blessed, fortunate, happy." The Sermon on the Mount begins with the Beatitudes, addressed not to anyone, but to those who have insight into the ideal relationship between God and Man; i.e., to His disciples.

> Blessed are the poor in heart: for theirs is the kingdom of
>   heaven.
> Blessed are they that mourn: for they shall be comforted.
> Blessed are the meek: for they shall inherit the earth.
> Blessed are they which do hunger and thirst after right-
>   eousness: for they shall be filled.

191

Blessed are the merciful: for they shall obtain mercy.
Blessed are the pure in heart: for they shall see God.
Blessed are the peace makers: for they shall be called the children of God.
Blessed are they which are persecuted for righteousness' sake: for theirs is the kingdom of heaven.
Blessed are ye when men shall revile you, and persecute you, and say all manner of evil against you falsely, for my sake.[4]

If this seems like a negativistic, introverted, conception of the good life, we must set alongside of the Beatitudes the magnificent exhortations and guidelines toward a truly virtuous life as we find them in the Epistles, usually the latter half of the Epistles. In the first part of the Letters of Paul and Peter and James we find the basic assumptions, or beliefs, or doctrines which provide a basis for repentance, faith, baptism, newness of life which has come into existence through the power in the Holy Spirit. This is followed by guidance and exhortation on how to express that new life, "im Sitz des Lebens," where life is lived. The interested reader is here referred to such readings as found in Romans 1:16-32; Romans 12:15; I Corinthians 15:16: II Corinthians 7:11; Galatians Chapter 5; Ephesians 4.5. and 6; and others.

It should be noted that the appeal to live and practice the morally good and virtuous life is invariably based on God's great mercy and generosity to man. Nowhere in the literature, religious and non-religious, of all the world is there anything like this unique motivation for the good and virtuous life.

The believers' response to God's unbounded goodness to undeserving man is first of all God-ward. It expresses itself in praise and thanksgiving and in the desire to understand still more fully the mercy, the power and the will of God, as we find these in worship, in private, family and in corporate worship, in the assembly of the saints in church services. When we analyze the constituent elements of the good life of the Christian in terms of a response to the goodness of God, we find in them such concepts as freedom, hope, a cheerful optimism, worship, peace, security, self-control, action in the area of services to society, active neighborly love.

192

We have no hesitancy to speak here of the manifold natural and divine gifts and their maximum use for the glory of God and for the benefit of society. The heirs of historic Christianity strive prayerfully not to be self-centered, pious, praying people who blithely can pass by on the other side when from many parts in our own country and still more loudly from underdeveloped countries come the cries for help. Let us identify these widely acclaimed results of a good education in America, particularly to see in what respect they fit into the good life as conceived by Christians.

Among various conceptions of the Good Life we find those whose living, thinking, hoping, aspirations, are centered in God. Those whose principal joy in life comes from the awareness of God and of being united in intimate fellowship with God do appreciate many of the things that money can buy. They value a good standard of living as measured by the yardstick of possessing those things which satisfy biological needs. But again it is a matter of first things first. They do appreciate and enjoy the establishment in practice of broad and universal ideas and ideals of honesty, charity, justice, peace among men, civic righteousness. But even if and when such values surround them, they still regard God, the understanding of God, faith in God, sharing fully in the life of God, as the primary source of joy. And here they find the fountainhead of the Good Life.

We call attention to several other ingredients of a believer's good life. First among these is *freedom*. No one other philosophy of life is so basically concerned about freedom as are the Christian theologians. That is because one of the basic qualities of God is freedom. God is free. That is a far cry from arbitrariness. Order is heaven's first law. God is predictable. Those persons who through faith in the Son of God are united with God are also free. And they cherish this freedom very highly. "If ye continue in my word, then are ye my disciples indeed, and ye shall know the truth and the truth shall make you free. . . . If the Son therefore shall make you free ye shall be free indeed."[5] Sin, a sense of guilt, the fear of punishment, anticipation of reward, eternal death, these are the slave drivers in Christian

193

theology. In the Gospel of free grace believers find a new life and a new freedom. Christians cherish and applaud the great Emancipation Proclamation issued by the great humanitarian, Abraham Lincoln on January 1, 1863. But they cherish with even greater enthusiasm and joy the proclamation made by Paul when he stated: "By grace are ye saved through faith; and that not of yourselves: It is the gift of God; not of works lest any man should boast."[6] Hence Paul, writing to the Galatians, pleads with them: "Stand fast therefore in the liberty wherewith Christ has made you free, and be not entangled again with the yoke of bondage."[7]

But are not Christians expected to do the will of God? Yes. But they do the will of God and conform to God's morality and ethics, not because they must; not because they fear punishment if they don't; not in anticipation of reward; but the new nature in them motivates them to do God's will freely. They share Christ's attitude: "This is my meat to do the will of my Father."[8] Doing the will of God, that is one of the sources of satisfaction and joy for the Christian believer. It is an important ingredient in his good life. The worst sort of slavery into which everyone is born by nature is the slavery to one's own desires and passions. The heirs of historic Christianity have found the way to self-control.

The Reformers, and especially Luther, are referred to sometimes as the great liberators. Luther's contribution to widely cherished political and civil freedom, and the establishment of civil rights, lies in the fact that he re-discovered the Gospel. Therein he found the courage to stand for liberty and freedom, even in the face of over-powering forces of the Church and the State. And so the appreciation of freedom rates high among the objectives of a good Christian education. The fear that we may lose an appreciation of freedom in our current secular culture, and that totalitarianism is a constant threat, is warranted. Eternal vigilance is the price of liberty. Even now an occasional voice is heard among the heirs of democracy and freedom: Better Red than dead.

Hope and *charity* are two inseparable elements in the Christian's good life. "Faith, hope and charity" are the three cardinal elements in the believer's life. Charity, or love, said the inspired writer, is the greatest of these.[9] But hope, hopefulness and cheerful optimism, even in all the vicissitudes of life, including even death, is the prized possession of the heirs of historic Christianity. Paul stresses this ingredient of the good life of the believers in his letter to the Romans, "For whatsoever things were written aforetime, were written for our learning, that we through patience and comfort of the Scriptures might have hope. . . . Now the God of hope fill you with all joy and peace in believing, that ye may abound in hope, through the power of the Holy Ghost."[10]

Cheerful hope is closely related to an ingredient of the good life which appears to have all but disappeared in our atomic and space age, that is a feeling of *security*. Both a feeling of security and of heroic *courage* is found in a large measure among those who put their confidence not in the resourcefulness of man, not in mighty arms that all but wiped out Hiroshima and Nagasaki, not in the abundance of things, but rather in the Lord. Christians comfort each other with such words as: "Commit thy way unto the Lord, trust also in Him. He shall bring it to pass."[11] Also, "It is better to trust in the Lord than to put confidence in princes."[12]

In our Western culture, and particularly also in Colonial America, this latter basis and source of enjoyment was very prominent. The Pilgrim Fathers are generally believed to have migrated to America so they could worship God freely without interference. With the advent of a new and different conception of the universe, the concern about God has tapered off. Today our culture is essentially secular, naturalistic, non-theistic. The supernatural element in our total environment is either completely denied or at best is bypassed, ignored, as not a significant factor in the Good Life. With the rather general acceptance of Marx's concept that the universe is "autogenetic," the discovery, possession and worship of a source of valuable things is found in this world alone. Other-worldliness, a God outside of this material world, is an anachronism. God and His friendship is therefore no longer considered to be a part of the Good Life. We believe that this represents a great loss, and a great impoverishment in the so-called Good Life in the Western world, including America. It represents a calamitous impoverishment of the curriculum in State-sponsored education, at all age levels.

C. THE IDEALISTICALLY ORIENTED CONCEPTION OF THE GOOD LIFE

Corroborative evidence that the merely natural, secular, this-worldly, non-theistic and non-idealistic approach to the goal of the good life is inadequate has been accumulating over a period of several centuries. Hutchins, former President of Chicago University, has given voice to the disappointments into which secularism, science and naturalism has led our culture.

"We do not know where we are going, or why. And we have almost given up the attempt to find out. . . . We have more information, more means of getting more information, than at any time in history. And yet we are bewildered."[13] And he might have added that we suffer from anxiety, from fears and frustrations. Current literature expresses the pessimism bordering on nihilism which characterizes our culture today.

Aristotle found the full functioning of that quality of life which is uniquely human, in contradistinction to qualities which man has in common with the animal kingdom. *Reason being that* unique characteristic of homo sapiens, or man, it followed for Aristotle that the life and activity of reason is the essential and the "sine qua non" element in the good life of man, and education ought therefore above all else cultivate that life of reason. Virtue is indeed very important in Aristotle's philosophy of this Good Life. But the roadway to virtue was for Aristotle the life of reason.

As a further development of the life of reason, Aristotle found the pathway to the good life in the *avoidance of extremes.* Adherence to the Golden Mean in all things was characteristic of the Good Life. Every virtue overdone tends to become a vice. Thus thrift overdone becomes avarice. Goodness always fluctuates between two extremes. Half-way between moroseness and buffoo- nery we find good humor. Hence, "alles mit Mass," "eis ton meson," moderation between extremes, that is the road which leads to happiness and to the good life.

However, particular life situations call for or permit excessive degrees of whatever is called for in a given critical situation. This modification of the Greek concept of "soophrosune" (reasona- bleness, good judgment, German exegetics translated it with "Nuchternheit"), as it is also called, came into the political ar- guments in connection with the Goldwater-Johnson, Democratic- Republican, campaign in the fall of 1964. The opponents of Goldwater called him an extremist. His rejoinder was that ex- tremism may be a very good thing in certain life situations. He cited war and bloodshed on the battlefield in defense of freedom and democracy as an instance when extremism and excess in courage and patriotism are indeed very excusable and desirable.

Happiness is never a means to an end. It is the ultimate end of all human effort. The summum bonum of both individual and social idealism is still the greatest happiness of the greatest num- ber.

With Aristotle the attainment of happiness is within reach of man with his natural powers. Man is a continuum with nature. Natural phenomena have their destiny and self-realization in themselves. Self-fulfillment, maturation, is therefore very central in the Greek concept of the good life.[14]

"The good of man is a working of the soul (reason) in the way of excellence in a complete life. . . . As one swallow does not make Spring, so it is not the action of one day which makes man blessed and happy, but rather the *'habitus,'* the way of life, that brings man into the realm of the good life."[15]

The pursuit and attainment of the good life, and happiness, is very largely an individual matter. To say this does not mean that the society, and the government under which an individual's life is lived is a matter of very secondary significance. The practice of high ideals in government (USA) is traceable to idealistic concepts in government.

Democracy has its roots basically in the Gospel. As seen in

the light of the Gospel, all men are equal. The individual is of paramount importance as an end in himself, never a means. God went to very great lengths, even to self-sacrifice, to make possible the inner freedom of man, freedom from the law, and from fear of punishment, freedom from his own passions, self-control. As one studies the documents which still lie at the very foundation of American and English democracy, one cannot escape the conclusion that idealistic concepts were widely invoked for the defense of democratic structures and functions of government. Hence, in this section of this chapter we place such eternal, pre-existent, unchanging, self-evident concepts as freedom, justice for all, equal opportunity for all to share in the good life, peace, the pursuit of happines, goodwill, tolerance. When the Preamble and the Constitution of the USA were written in 1789 high ideas and ideals of government were emphasized as indispensable factors for more people to share in the good life as conceived by idealism. The purposes of government in the new regime were stated to be: To form a more perfect union; to establish justice; to insure domestic tranquility; to provide for the common defense; to promote the general welfare; to secure the blessings of liberty to ourselves and our posterity. Since that time the Bill of Rights, and more recently the Civil Rights Bill, were passed to secure equal educational, social and economic opportunities for all Americans.

In the light of these truths and emphases in our society we readily understand why democracy, good citizenship, should constitute the very core of a good public education in America. No educational efforts, whether privately sponsored or church sponsored, can afford to omit from their goals and curricula these same objectives if they wish to be rated as good American institutions.

Beginning with Aristotle and continuing through to the present in secular and in humanistic thinking, the concept of maturity holds a central place in the good life. Aristotle gave much thought to the nature of man. He concluded that the ability to think, to remember, to image, to classify, to draw logical conclusions, to meditate, these were among the traits that distinguish man from lower forms of animals. It is easy to follow him when he concludes that the life of *intellectual* activity is the heart of the good life for man. Feigl, as a proponent of logical positivism, brings this conception of the good life up to the present when he suggests that the good life is a life that is more mature, more fully integrated.[16]

D. THE MATERIALISTICALLY ORIENTED CONCEPTION OF THE GOOD LIFE

Let us say Mr. X's thinking, feeling and behavior is oriented materialistically. Mr. B's life is oriented idealistically. And Mr. C's "Weltanschauung" is God-centered. This does not necessarily mean that each one's concept of the good life is unique, distinctive, to the exclusion of everything that may be found to be characteristic of another philosopher's understanding of the good life. They do overlap. To a very large extent it is a matter of emphasis. The question is, what are the priorities in a man's life, and in his educational philosophy. Biological gratifications, for example, are an ingredient of presumably every person's conception of a good life. They all get a certain amount of pleasure and enjoyment out of food, perhaps even stimulating drinks, shelter and a well appointed home; decent and confortable clothing. Biological perpetuity of the race and physical survival have deeply rooted drives to support these goals. It is difficult to picture anyone having no satisfaction from sex life. The good life has in it also a large element of the feeling of security.

The thought that individual happiness is possible only in a social *environment* that provides the fullest and freest opportunity is frequently interwoven with ideas about the good life. Thus, Bertrand Russell in *Education and the Good Life,* enumerates, as most men who have given this problem sustained thought do, that "certain things are indispensable to the happiness of most men. These are simple things: food, shelter, health, love, successful work and respect of one's own herd. To some people parenthood is also essential."[17] Unhappiness he attributes to self-encasement; self-centeredness; self-pity. At this point Russell is putting in his oars for participation in the emerging environment, particularly in group life. When the ideal society, or as now referred to, The Great Society, comes into the picture of the good life, we rightly suspect the presence of utopian dreams in which everyone will have his wishes granted without effort on his part. Hence, the newly declared war on poverty. Russell combines the two elements of the good life as these are found in the individual and in society when he states, "vitality, courage, sensitivity and intelligence — men and women so educated might produce a *new world.*"[18]

The Science of Society, particularly the economic structure of society, the classless society, an end of exploitation of men by men, a permanently peaceful society, these and similar concepts have their origin in Marx's philosophy of the good life.[19] Man united with himself, with comrades and with his world, will be a happy man. "From each according to his ability, to each according to his need," is a widely quoted Marxist description of the good life.[20]

The importance of *society* as a factor in the attainment of the good life was persistently advocated by John Dewey. Maximum development of the individual to the extent of his native capacity and aptitudes in a self-repairing evolutionary society, that summarizes his goal and his conception of the good life and a good education. Beard summed up Dewey's picture of the good life in the following words: "The maintenance and improvement of American Society so as to contribute to the good life for each person."[21] As a thoroughgoing instrumentalist Dewey does not, however, regard the intellectual life as an end in itself. He is not an idealist. Intelligence for him should be spoken of not as a noun, but rather as an adjective or adverb. Intelligence represents a function in the organism. Its purpose is to make action intelligent. Intelligence brings ends and means into harmonious relationship. Hence, of course, the purpose of a good education is to develop the skill and habit of thinking, solving the problem or relating means to ends. This conception of intelligence and intellectual activity is quite far removed from the idealistist's conception of intelligence, as an end in itself.

The materialist's conception of the good life was recently expressed quite incidentally, in a report which was designed to explain Khrushchev's sudden disappearance from public life in Soviet Russia. It stated, "the Khrushchevian promises of the good life for all have fallen far short of performance." Obviously, the good life in the Marxian ideology means an abundance of food, clothing, shelter, and other elements among the list of creature comforts.

We find the scientific emphasis throughout the history of modern man. Clear thinking, elimination of tender-mindedness and wishful thinking, elimination of escapes from reality, these are marks of amateurs. One who aspires to share in the good life must do full justice to the scientific outlook. Scientific humanism offers the best possibility of the good life. The habit of scientific thinking is to the logical empiricist the surest, and in fact the only way toward a truly good life.

An interesting deviation from this road toward the good life is found among the early Greeks, the Stoics that is, and among many other peoples of the Orient, and also among Westerners. This approach to the reasonably good life appears in periods of national defeat, and general frustration. "The apathetic acceptance of defeat and the effort to forget defeat in the arms of pleasure (or in the philosophy of self-denial) were theories as to how one might be happy (and enjoy the good life) though subjugated or enslaved (or impoverished), precisely as the pessimistic Oriental stoicism of Schopenhauer and the despondent epicureanism of Renan were, in the 19th Century, the symbols of a shattered Revolution and a broken France."[22]

"The secret of peace (of mind) is not to make our achievements equal to our desires, but to lower our desires to the level of our achievements."[23]

The Roman Stoic Seneca likewise emphasized the other side of the coin when he said: "If what you have seems insufficient to you, then, though you possess the world, you will yet be miserable."[24]

An echo of this approach to happiness and the good life is found also in the source book for Christian viewpoints in life. Paul counseled a young pastor by writing: "But Godliness with contentment is great gain. For we brought nothing into this world and certain it is we can carry nothing out. And having food and raiment, let us be therewith content. But they that will be rich fall into temptation and a snare and into many foolish and hurtful lusts which drown men in destruction and perdition. For the love of money is the root of all evil."[25]

The coexistence of this approach to the good life in both Stoicism and in the Christian heritage must not be looked upon as something to belittle inspiration of the Scriptures. Inspiration may at times utilize existing cultural elements in the contemporary world without exposing itself to the charge of having copied from another source.

The man who gave the name to epicureanism, namely Epicurus, needs a word of defense. He is unique among those who counsel crass hedonism as the essence of the good life. Epicurus, following Democritus, was a thoroughgoing atomist, materialist. He might have been expected to grant free course to libertinism as an approach to the good life. But, said he, "permanent absence of pain, rather than joy and debauchery; self-control; prudence, these are necessary for the pursuit of happiness." So Epicurus was really not an epicurean! "It is not in the continuous drinking and revellings nor the satisfaction of lusts. . . . which produce a pleasant life, but sober reasonings, searching out motives for all choice and avoidance of mere opinions, to which are due the greatest disturbances of the spirit."[26]

E.   SUMMARY

No man, or few if any, are ever so wholly concerned with either material things or ideational things as to find enjoyment in their possession alone, to the exclusion of enjoyment of other things. This applies even to the God-oriented persons. They all share to some extent in the gratifications that are derived from sources other than those in which they have a special interest. It is always a matter of priority. Idealists too enjoy the gratification of biological needs. So do the God-oriented persons. But only the materialists give prior consideration to the gratification of such biological urges while the idealist puts the ideas and ideals first on his scale of values and satisfactions. In the idealist's conception of the Good Life neither material things nor the personal God nor good relationship with Him rate as of prior importance. In his conception of education not the natural sciences but the humanities, the ideas and ideals, the law, that have engaged the attention of mankind in its long history, are given priority rating.

Chapter VII

A GOOD EDUCATION

A. PROBLEM AND INTRODUCTION

All persons strive for the best kind of life. Is there a nation that does not strive for the best kind of life for all its citizens? Of course, their conception of what constitutes a really good life varies widely. Whatever the conception of the good life, education is the means toward attaining it. Broadly speaking an education is good to the extent that it does what it is supposed to do. This definition of goodness holds good whether it is applied to matter-centered, to idea-centered, or to God-centered education. The differentiating factor among the educational philosophies is expressed tersely in a short descriptive phrase. Those philosophers who begin with the basic assumption that all existence is material, atomic, and nothing but material will add to the maximum growth concept the limiting phrase "in the physical organism." Those who begin with the assumption that all existence is ultimately idea, or mind, will add the phrase "in intellect." And those philosophers and theologians who believe that God is all in all, from the distant past into the equally distant future, will add the phrase "in God." Because the heirs of historic Christianity believe in Christ as the Messiah they add the significant phrase "in Christ." These are permanent and universally applicable principles.

B. THE GOD-CENTERED VIEW OF A GOOD EDUCATION

In the God-centered view of the universe God-in-Christ is the same yesterday, today, and forever. He is the Alpha and the Omega. He is the ultimate reality. He is the doorway through which a person enters into the Kingdom of God. Through faith in the unique Son of God and the only Savior from sin a person finds forgiveness. He is justified before God. He is born again. He is a new creature, born in the image of God. He shares in the life of God. He participates in the very nature of God. That gives to his life here and now a unique, distinctive quality, i.e., godliness. He is united again with God in a Paradise-like fellowship of God. True he is *"simul sanctus et peccator"* (saint and sinner at the same time). But through daily repentance, renewed faith, and renewed commitment to God, a man of God is continuously in a state of becoming. The person is a new creature. He is united with God, but he remains an individual existent, even as God is neither absorbed, nor enriched, nor impoverished, nor merely immanent, nor adjusted, nor made more and more in the image of man through this intimate union with man. This process resembles a branch being grafted into the main stem of a fruit tree. Thereafter, the grafted branch bears the kind of fruit that the tree bears, i.e., he thinks, feels, and acts as God does into whom the individual has been grafted.

The God-believers are not unmindful of the two main sources through which a person becomes what he is and what he may come to be: *heredity* and *environment.* There is not much that even God-fearing parents can do about heredity, except to make the most of it. Brain washing to make saints of sinners will hardly do it. Parents can, of course, counsel their teen-agers in the dating and mating days, to make reasonably sure that their grandchildren will be physically fit, mentally alert, and that they will grow up in a God-centered home environment. God Himself takes a long-range view of heredity. He promised to those parents who love Him and who keep His commandments that He will show mercy unto thousands of their subsequent generations.[1] Individuals continue to be responsible for their actions. "The son shall not bear the iniquity of the father, Neither shall the father bear the sin of the son."[2] Each person is morally responsible for what he says and does. None of the six or more "defense mechanisms" through which persons seek to shelter their ego will work before God. The significance in this sequence of events is expressed in the words, "if the wicked shall turn from all his sins that

205

he has committed . . . he shall surely live. . . ."³ This means that repentance and recommitment to God is a highly significant "habitus" in the education of the young, and in the continued life-long growth of adults toward greater Godliness, toward the Good Life.

A causal relationship between God-centered education of youngsters and their eventual contribution to the total welfare of mankind is drastically expressed in the case of Abraham, called the father of believers. Abraham's faith in God and his concern for transmitting this knowledge and faith to his descendants is definitely related causally to the blessings which God through him bestowed upon all the nations of the world.

"Shall I hide from Abraham that thing which I do? Seeing that Abraham shall surely become a great and mighty nation and all the nations of the earth shall be blessed in him. For I know that he will command his children and his household after him, and they shall keep the way of the Lord, to do justice and judgment."⁴ Abraham's biological descendants constitute to this day a family that enjoys a high degree of physical fitness, of family coherence, of mental alertness, and of financial and legal acumen. The principal source of that promised blessing came upon all men in the person of Jesus Christ, a distant descendant of Abraham. Unfortunately when the promised Messiah did come He was not accepted by His people. Thus they alienated themselves from the Living God and from His spiritual descendants. Here is the point of difference between Christian and Jewish education.

God-centered parents and pastors are not unconcerned about the dating and mating habits of their young people. At a time when moral permissiveness and promiscuity is tolerated among married and unmarried persons; when the number of unwed mothers is on the increase; when syphilis has proliferated among large segments of teenagers, despite medical progress in combating this dreaded social disease; at a time when rape and murder occupy wide headlines in our newspapers and magazines; when pornographic pictures and literature, as well as TV programs, offend the decent-minded; at such a time the concern of godly parents, pastors, and counselors shows good judgment.

The proper prenatal care of prospective mothers is a concern of medical men. At the time of birth every care is taken that all goes well; that e.g., the supply of oxygen has free passage to the infant's lungs. It is alleged by men who know that many cases of mental retardation are the result of failure at this point. Mother love in the early stages of the infant's life, even to the extent of physical contact between mother and child, is rated to be an important factor in the normal or non-normal development of the child. Proper nutrition is considered similarly a factor in the total of optimum conditions for maximum growth.

All parents follow a similar pattern of attitude and conduct in the interest of maximum development. A parting of the ways in the conception of a good education begins at this point. It is based on different conceptions of reality, of the nature of man, of truth, of ethics, of values, and of the good life, as shown in previous chapters.

Before the child gets to be many weeks old, the heirs of the Judean heritage bring their male child to the temple for circumcision. The Christian parent heeds the invitation, "Suffer the children to come unto me and forbid them not."[5] They want their child to get a start in the right direction, toward a God-centered education. They want their child to be adopted, blessed, regenerated by the Savior. They choose sponsors for the Sacrament of baptism, who will aid the parents in spelling out the implications for this "washing of regeneration."[6] Among these implications is the matter of regarding their child as having been born again, that it is a new creature, that a new life has begun in it, and that it is now their task to "bring up the child in the nurture and admonition of the Lord."[7] Prayer, inner communion with God with whom the child has been united in the Holy Sacrament of Baptism, is common practice in the home of believing parents at bedtime and in times of crisis. God's Word is used around the family altar, as was the practice of Godfearing people in all Christian lands prior to the blight of secularism and atheism. Although the frame has been broken, the picture of that ideal Christian family circle, painted by Robert Burns in "The Cotter's Saturday Night," is still with us in the Christian family of today:

And "Let us worship God!" he says, with solemn air.
The priest-like father reads the sacred page,
How Abram was the friend of God on high;
Or Job's pathetic plaints, and wailing cry;
Or rapt Isaiah's wild, seraphic fire;
Then kneeling down, to Heaven's Eternal King,
The saint, the father, and the husband prays:
Hope "springs exulting on triumphant wing,"
That thus they all shall meet in future days.
From scenes like these old Scotia's grandeur springs,
That makes her loved at home, revered abroad.[8]

To bring the combined resources and services of the Church and the God-centered home to bear on the development of their offspring the child is commonly enrolled in the Cradle Roll of the Day or Sunday School; parents are provided with relevant instructional material. Increasingly the parents' Sunday morning Bible class takes up for study in depth the same lesson material that the child learns in the Sunday School lesson, in order thus to encourage dialoging in the home circle on topics of mutual concern in a given week.

Wherever possible the child is then enrolled in a God-centered *Day School* where all the factors which affect the teaching-learning process in all required subject matter fields are given attention and correlated in one unit of work in religion. In such a School the child's thinking, feeling, and behavior is oriented to God. This means a school in which the *objectives* as anticipated outcomes are centered in God and His Word; where the *curriculum* is God-centered; where *extra-curricular activities* are similarly oriented to God; where the instructional materials, including the *library,* and various other audio-visual *aids* to learning are similarly selected in keeping with the school's philosophy of education; where teacher *training and qualification* includes the criterion of understanding and accepting what God has revealed about Himself and His manner of working in the hearts of individuals, families, and social groups; where *methods* of instruction are derived from the Great Teacher even though these have become informed by research in educational psychology.

Leisure time activities are similarly oriented to the goal of growth in God. *Administration* and *discipline* among staff members and students is enriched by the concepts of a God-centered faith, hope, and charity. *School plant and site,* including supervised playgrounds, are likewise kept in accordance with the principle of optimum conditions for growth in God. Finally, also the evaluation of progress and reports to parents reflect the school's concern about progress and growth in the God-ward direction.

Through frequent *parent-teacher* conferences the student is permitted to grow up in a climate and under conditions in which there is no conflict between the philosophy of education that guides the school and the home life of the student. This is in the interest of integrity in educational programs, from kindergarten to graduate work at the university. The broad goals are the same throughout the formal education period of the student, and they need adjustment only in keeping with different stages of maturity and of age levels. Eventually, and fairly early, the student, with the help of a God-centered counselor, in cooperation with Godly parents and pastors, makes his choice for a vocation that is socially significant and suited to his native abilities.

The tie-up with all branches of the natural sciences, beginning with the thoughtful observation and control of a budding and blossoming plant to the most intricate phenomena of chemistry and physics, in biology, and in the behavior in all phases of nature helps the student to discover unity in the great diversity in his enviroment. This in turn contributes toward the development of an integrated personality. From the beginning to the end of his studies through college and graduate education, his attention is directed to the important role of *love,* redeeming love, as this has shown itself in the incarnation and the redemptive work of God among men. He is continuously provided with a stimulating environment and school curriculum to help him to grow in understanding the power and the sanctifying *work of the Spirit of God,* working mostly through Word and Sacrament. The student will thus mature, but he will never exhaust nor reach the endpoint of the great religious concepts of creation, redemption, and sanctification.

Included in this ongoing "optimum condition for maximum

growth in God" is the student's expanding understanding and acceptance of "a way of life" of the will of God as revealed in the *Decalogue,*[9] in the Sermon on the Mount,[10] and in the life of Jesus. Instead of growing up in an atmosphere of unlimited permissiveness the learner discovers that some ways of behaving are right, others are definitely wrong. Parents and teachers will remember that a garden has to be weeded.

Having learned to know, understand, and accept as important the very God who has revealed Himself in nature, in Revelation, and in the history of nations; having been conditioned to trust in and love God, to stand in reverence and awe before Him; not to despise the sacred Scriptures but to continue to love, learn, and live the Word, to observe His day and to attend regularly His house, the student is surrounded by an environment in which God is a stimulating and guiding factor in the maximum development of the student.

In such an educational environment the student is gradually conditioned to honor and *respect his superiors,* in the home, the classroom, and in government. He is obedient and cooperative not only because he is expected to do so, but for conscience sake.

He is filled gradually with the desire to contribute as much as possible to his own *physical development* and that of everyone else's physical fitness, preservation in danger and suffering; in short, to lengthen and to sweeten the life of every human being, whether he lives next door or in the jungles of Africa.

He learns that human life is sacred. He is trained not to kill through carelessness. Four hundred fifty traffic deaths on the highways over a single week-end prompt him to drive with double care. He is not taught to be a pacifist. He will not tear up his draft card. But he will work for peace and for settling of disputes on the playground and among nations at the conference table. He strives 'not to kill.' He appreciates no end the contribution of the medical science toward the preservation of life and the elimination of pain. He is thankful for Medicare as a means of re-assuring the aged and sick.

He learns to regard *sex* and *sexual experiences* as a gift of God, to be used within the limits imposed by the will of God. Promiscuous sexual intercourses have temptations also for God's people, as we learn from the example of David. But, when tempted to deviate from time-honored standards of acceptable sexual behavior they learn to say No! with firmness. They know where to draw the line in petting and to say with Joseph who, when similarly tempted by Potiphar's wife, simply picked up and left the room saying "How can I do this great wickedness and sin against God?"[11]

While in attendance at a God-centered school where the Decalogue is constantly in operation, alongside of the Gospel, the student will learn at an early age to distinguish between *mine and thine,* as the class studies the commandment: "Thou shalt not steal." He will learn to keep his fingers off the candy counter and to keep his fingers off the public purse when in later life the opportunity presents itself to do so.

Even an incurably optimistic humanist like Norman Vincent Peale recently wrote in *Sin, Sex, and Self-control* and was quoted in an article titled "Today's Disease: Dishonesty" carried in the *Chicago Daily News:* "Every year in this country employees steal at least 1 billion dollars in cash or merchandise from their employers. Every single day white collar workers get away with about $4,000,000. One insurance company estimates that over one thousand businesses failed last year because of losses caused by dishonest employees."[12]

Does this mean that the secular schools where 90% of these thieves received their education taught them to steal? Positively not. But, the schools failed to have in their curriculum the adequate corrective for these natural tendencies. Human nature being what it is, a good education should have in its curriculum an adequate antidote to such human weaknesses.

But there have been dishonest people in all cultures and nations at all times. Granted. But, the percentage of dishonest people in the U. S. A. is much higher than it was 10, or 20, or 30 years ago, says author Peale.

Over and over again America's chief crime recorder reports that crime, among the poor and among the rich, in government and

211

industry, embezzle not dimes and single dollars but thousands, if not millions of dollars.

With the authority of God's justice and with the motivation of God's love more, if not all, persons must have an education in which they learn to think and feel and say and do, "It is my delight to keep Thy commandments."[13] Again the question arises why should parents be penalized by having to pay their entire tax dollar for an education other than where God and the doing of His will is a daily ingredient in their curricular activities?

To pursue the *Decalogue* further: a student in a God-centered school learns early not to bear false witness against anyone; *to discipline his thought and his speech about others,* for conscience sake. Rules of fairness are rather well observed in sports. The accused shall be considered innocent until he is proven guilty, is a rule deeply ingrained among the people in the covered wagon days, as every TV viewer knows. But, the widespread custom of calling on the Fifth Amendment, to protect the guilty, reflects on the reliability of witnesses in court. Perjury, though the witness gives a solemn oath that he will tell the truth and nothing but the truth, is committed lightly. When those things that were considered in an earlier stage of our culture to be sacred become altogether secular, there is reason for Brubacher's "anxieties."

The student learns early, with a motivation that stems from faith in God, *to be content* with such things as he has, not to covet and fret about those things that are beyond his reach without however neglecting to strive ambitiously for excellence in whatever he undertakes to do. Throughout this process of growing in understanding and acceptance of the *Decalogue,* he echoes frequently his response to God's Law: O God, be merciful to me a sinner, for Thy mercy's sake. And with equal frequency he again and again pledges himself to strive for greater moral excellence, this time with the added notation "with the help of Thy Holy Spirit."

God's people are "the salt of the earth" (Matthew 5:13) to preserve from corruption the moral life of the groups of which they are a part. Thus they add flavor and good taste to group life. But salt must be spread into the areas of living which it is to preserve. This means that God's people must mix with and share their unique character with others on the job, in the professions and vocations. This calls for penetration into the various competencies that education in America is designed to develop.

COMPETENCIES as Educational Outcomes determine the goodness of an education. Webster defines competency as knowing, understanding, accepting as important, and as the habit of using skills to apply such knowledge in every life situation. The competencies which American education strives to cultivate can be used for various purposes, some high and noble, others less so, and even for vicious purposes. The three philosophies under consideration here all aim to develop competencies: Personal, social, economic, civic, cultural, academic, moral and spiritual. But the motivations for learning these skills are different and unique and the use the students will eventually make of his competencies will reveal deep seated differences in their philosophy of life.

For the heirs of historic Christianity *personal competence* means physical fitness, mental alertness, emotional maturity, and above all a personal affectionate attachment to God-in-Christ. It means God-centered personalities, godly characters — dedicated, ready to serve God and neighbor.

Social competence refers to the ability to get along with people. God-centered students are concerned about others. They make friends easily, they gain the respect, confidence, and loyalty of others. This pattern of growth in social competence is modeled after the example recorded in Luke 2:52 where it is said: "Jesus increased in wisdom and stature, and in favor with God and man." The student's willingness to adjust to the social life of his peers will be cordial, but limited by the fact that he is adjusted to, and loyal to, God and His standards of conduct. Adjustment to the moral standards of unregenerate teen-agers, or adults, may be fatal to character.

Development of *economic competence* begins early in the family circle. The young of the household learn to abhor waste; to share in kitchen and garden duties; to lay by a part of his earnings for a rainy day. He tends to become indignant and angry when he hears or reads about the problems of overproduction and surplus foods while in less fortunate countries people go to bed hungry.

213

Humaneness is his middle name. When someone has fallen among thieves, robbed, and half killed, he has compassion on him, and does something about it, as the Good Samaritan did.

In a godly home and in a God-centered school each member learns to develop *civic competence*. He learns to obey rules and laws for conscience sake. If he shows an aptitude for it, his parents and teachers will encourage him to practice an acceptable kind of leadership in *citizenship*. The significant and unique contribution that God-oriented education makes consists in giving to God and godliness a central position in the development of these competencies. God and God's people are always on the side of equal civil rights for all citizens of a community and country. With that deep-rooted persuasion goes their vote in favor of equal educational and occupational opportunities. It cannot be otherwise, for their "God so loved *the world* that he gave His only begotten Son" (John 3:16). God's people have national loyalties but also global concerns. Love and humaneness is central also in their goals of good citizenship.

This also applies to the development of *academic skills*. If Johnny can't read, there may be several factors that hinder his progress in reading. But the will to learn to read is markedly strengthened by the student's awareness that God wants him to develop that and other academic skills. He develops skills of communication, such as speaking and writing, in order to share his faith in God in tactful and effective ways. The student is motivated and he seeks to excel in his preparations for a profession such as being a lawyer, a doctor of medicine, a physicist, a teacher, a sociologist, or other profession. Success in the preparation for such professions requires not only native ability above average but a high degree of motivation and will power that can best be attained by a high sense of duty and service to God and neighbor.

Cultural competence is an important ingredient of a good education. A brief look around among the paintings, music compositions, literature, novels, drama, TV programs in the contemporary secular world and a comparison with the products of the fine arts in a day when God was still an important factor and inspiration among artists and art admirers is enough to remind us that the trend toward secularization has impoverished and debased the fine arts of today. The origin of such cheapening of the fine arts reflects on the emphases in secular education. In the God-centered home the music, the pictures, etc. will reflect godliness.

Church-sponsored schools and colleges still place a strong emphasis on *parish competence*. In late years particularly participation of the laity in the worship and work of the parish has emerged, even in denominations which until recently were strongly clergy-dominated. Adult education has come to be a major concern in the civic community among the people of God. A text from Paul's letter to the Ephesians has helped to shift the emphasis on education of children to education of adults. "And he gave some apostles; and some prophets; and some evangelists; and some pastors and teachers; for the perfecting of the saints for the work of the ministry for the edifying of the body of Christ."[14] It is significant that the comma after ministry has been dropped in later and more scholarly editions. This means that the laity needs to be educated to exhort, to comfort, to cheer, and to edify the fellow members of the body of God, the church. Furthermore, the laity is increasingly trained to bear witness to the Risen One in personal contacts with their neighbors and with those with whom they come in contact in their professional and vocational life. This kind of parish competence is receiving much more emphasis also in the objectives of schools, elementary and high, and in colleges maintained by the people of God.

FACTORS affecting the Teaching-Learning Processes can make or break the reputation of a school. It is less from philosophers and more from psychologists that education has been alerted to the fact that education is a very complex development, influenced by many previously neglected factors.

OBJECTIVES. First and foremost among these factors are the objectives and the *anticipated outcomes*. For God's people these objectives are summarized in the manifesto given the disciples on the day of His ascension. "All power is given unto me in heaven and in earth. Go ye therefore and disciple all nations, baptizing them in the name of the Father and of the Son and of the Holy

Ghost, TEACHING them to observe all things whatsoever I have commanded you; and lo, I am with you alway even to the end of the world."[15]

This is not a manifesto for the building of an empire, even though the note of evangelism is strong. The Kingdom of God is within. The objectives of Christian education focus attention on saving, enriching, ennobling, sanctifying the lives of individual persons. It aims at developing life to the utmost here and now, for greatest blessing and the greatest happiness of the greatest number here and now.

"Faith, hope, and charity. These three. And the greatest of these is charity," wrote St. Paul to the Corinthians.[16] Love. Active love for God and equally active love for fellow man. This is the core of the ultimate objective in a good education as seen by God's people because "God is love."[17]

The CURRICULUM is the principal means of reaching educational objectives. All schools and colleges, to be accredited, will of necessity teach all of the required subjects appropriate for the age level of their school.

However, there are differences in the curricula of schools based on a different philosophy of existence and of life. Thus the people of God, intent on having a good school, will give a place in the daily schedule for learning to know God and for understanding His will. Relevant projects in which students learn to do His will are attached to every unit of work.

INSTRUCTIONAL MATERIALS, text books, work books, A-V aids help to spell out the philosophy of the school, provided these aids to learning are chosen intelligently. To the extent that they are in harmony with the school's basic objectives, and are effectively used, the school is a good school. This means that the God-centered viewpoint, with the standards of right and wrong, good and bad that are approved of God, when used purposefully, go a long way toward making it a good school and providing a good education.

The TEACHER is, next to objectives and curriculum, a most important factor affecting the teaching-learning process. To be rated a good, or superior, school it must be staffed with well

216

trained, dedicated teachers. This training includes not only familiarity of subject matters stressed in keeping with a school's basic philosophy, but it calls for teachers who are sold thoroughly on the assumptions, or beliefs, which underlie its philosophy of education. This means that teachers and administrators in a school or college sponsored and supported by God's people and not by taxes, will employ, or call, teachers who are men or women of God; who believe in and who are affectionately attached to the Lord of their life, and of their church; whose lives will be, not perfect, but exemplary for the students, and whose record of professional growth shows perseverance.

ADMINISTRATION AND LEADERSHIP will reflect the basic philosophy of a given school. Administration will be good to the extent that it applies the philosophy of that school. The administration of a school or school system will be similar in some respects in all schools, since in America all schools are dedicated to the application of democratic principles. Differences will show up in the area of human relations, and in the procedure followed in case of discipline. The climate and atmosphere in administration and leadership, the staff and line procedures, will reflect in a God-centered school the manner of God's dealing with men. No good school in any philosophy, will today in the U. S. A. follow through with the rigidity of military administration, or the authoritarianism of a dictator.

EVALUATING AND TESTING is an area where goodness depends on the objectives of a school or a school system. Reliability is a test characteristic that is the same for all schools. If reliable, a test measures consistently whatever it measures. Validity is different. A school, or a school system will develop and use valid tests and criteria of measuring goodness. That is to say, a God-centered school, an idea-centered school, and a science-centered school will use measuring devices that reflect the objectives and goals of their particular kind of school, with distinctive elements in its objectives, and curriculum that are different and unique. A school's system of measuring progress that does not reflect the objetives of that school is not a good school, at least it is not in the area of measuring progress toward its goals.

217

This brings us to the focal factor in any school, the LEARNER. All other factors, including the building itself, are there not for the teacher, the administrator, the evaluator, but for the sake of the learner. Schools are maintained for the sake of students. The learner in adult life represents or is the product of the educational efforts. In American education we have nearly gone overboard for pupil-centered education while making light of curriculum content. It seems right though that a school should accept the student as he is, with his past experiences, native abilities, be they 90 IQ, or 130 IQ, and with his interests.

Where *God's people* maintain a school, God and His Word, the needs of community and parish, are important. But the teacher nevertheless keeps his eye on the learner as he is. Whether baptized or not yet baptized, he looks upon the learner as an organism with three facets of body, mind, and soul, and as one organism with unlimited potentialities. God and God-centered teachers do not superimpose on the learner. Rather the teacher stimulates, shepherds, and guides. Like a gardener he cultivates the soil, waters it, and waits for beautiful blossoms and perhaps for marvelous fruits. He provides opportunity for the New Life to find expression in his students. God-likeness is the anticipated end result of a God-centered education: maturity, Christian character, with all the competencies which have been described. While God is the initiating and motivating factor in learning, the learner and learner activities remain in the foreground.

By this time two things bearing on three philosophies of education are emerging. Our three philosophies begin with different basic assumptions regarding the nature of reality, and therefore regarding the nature of a good education. Yet, while different, they have much in common. What has been said about competencies and about "factors affecting the teaching-learning process, needs to be repeated briefly as seen from the viewpoint of idealism and by materialism. Philosophy's function is to focus attention on competencies and factors. These are different largely in the motivation for developing them and more particularly in the use that graduates are expected to make of skills and abilities.

Idealism continues to make its contribution to education in America largely through an emphasis in education on ideas, principles, and ideals that are regarded as permanent, pre-existent, unchanging. Private schools and colleges which stress the humanities in their curriculum are among the more tangible remains of a fading idealism. Idealism has made its major contribution to education in the area of civic competence, and citizenship, community, national and international citizenship. The four faces of American statesmen hewn out of the rock in the hills of South Dakota's Badlands are a permanent and eloquent testimony to the contribution of idealism in American citizenship. The immortal words of one of these men, great if not the greatest, found expression in the well known Gettysburg Address. On that occasion President Lincoln on Nov. 19, 1863, stated: "Fourscore and seven years ago our fathers brought forth on this continent a new nation, conceived in liberty, and dedicated to the proposition that all men are created equal. . . . We here highly resolve that these dead shall not have died in vain, that this nation, under God, shall have a new birth of freedom and that government of the people, by the people, for the people, shall not perish from the earth." Here is a cornerstone of democracy, of freedom, and of equality of opportunity.

One may concede that in the wars fought by America in its history, from the War of Independence, through the War of 1812, the Spanish War, the Mexican War, and the First and Second World Wars, the Korean War, and the current Viet Nam War, the motive was not ever purely idealistic but was always permeated with elements of a selfishness often economic in nature, yet these wars were defended on ideological grounds with a large measure of validity. Current parades of protests, largely by student groups, protesting against the participation in the Viet Nam War, reveals that many Americans do not believe that this or any war was ever fought on purely ideological grounds. But that does not alter the fact that ideals have been a basic reason for a display of patriotism and a high regard for the permanency of high ideals of citizenship: freedom, equality, justice for all.

The liberal arts colleges today uphold the emphasis on idealism in education. Wherever one finds that the humanities get priority over the natural sciences, idealism still holds the fort for permanency and for eternal values. The reaction to Sputnik in 1957 has resulted in a major thrust in behalf of the natural sciences through the 1958 National Defense Education Act. However, the humanity studies survive.

"The future of Western civilization is intimately connected with the future of education. The citizens need the skill to distinguish between the true and the false, the good and the ill. The education of the Western man, however, much as it must be scientific, must also be humanistic," states Arthur C. Cohen in his introduction to *Humanistic Education and Western Civilization* essays.[18]

Since idealistic philosophers begin with the belief that Mind is the ultimate in Reality, their educational efforts will give priority in any statement of the school's objectives to the development of the *mind*. Intellectual activities are at the core of their objectives. Conformity to eternal, uncreated, universal, absolute ideas, and ideals, stand at the head of the list of objectives. Through intelligent correlation of all subjects intellectual achievement will be fostered throughout the courses.

Idea-centered educational institutions give prominence to the humanities, a continuation of the social studies in elementary grades.

A similar relationship between goals and instructional materials, including the aids offered by the library is called for in idea-centered education.

In an idealistically-oriented school or college, the teachers will be expected to be familiar with the best in literature and other fine arts and in their classroom technique they will proceed according to the Socratic method, stimulating their students to think, to reason logically, and to appreciate creative intellectual activity.

Where the philosophy of *idealism* prevails, the learner's mind gradually becomes adjusted to the Great Mind. He learns to understand and appreciate universal, unchanging, absolute, ideas and ideals.

The major emphasis in the development of idealistically oriented competencies will throughout be on the development of the mind and will concentrate on intellectual activities.

D. A GOOD EDUCATION FROM THE VIEWPOINT
OF A MATERIALISTICALLY ORIENTED PHILOSOPHY OF EDUCATION

The educational process is complex. The ultimate outcome is the result of many factors. These factors vary in content with the basic assumption of *reality* and with the resultant image of man. In general the competencies in naturalistic education are similar to the competencies which have been identified in a previous section of this chapter. However, it places prior emphasis on man, on man's ability to think and his ingenuity to act intelligently in any situation. For this reason the student's ability to think scientifically and to solve his problem by his resourcefulness ranks very high among the anticipated outcomes of his education. It is not difficult to wax enthusiastic about the effectiveness of this emphasis in education. We see the evidences for superiority of this approach to education all about us: in transportation, in communication, in the art of healing, in the exploration of space, in exploring the behavior of the atom, and in harnessing its unheard of powers either to build or to destroy. We could add to the praises we have sung to the power that has become useable by man through his knowledge of science, the natural sciences in particular. This would seem to indicate that a good education as conceived by the materialistically oriented philosophy will usher in Utopia, but sure and soon! We need not at this time again belabor the statistics about rising crime rates, broken homes, signs of deterioration, personal and social.

> No one will deny that the signs of the times are portentous. The symbol of its perpetuity is the nuclear stockpile, here and also over there, undestroyed and perhaps indestructible, destined to permanent presence a hidden threat to the future of civilization.[19]

Because matter and energy centered thinkers go on the assumption that existence is made up of matter, and nothing but matter,

221

it stands to reason that a good education in their book will give first place to the development of the scientific man, and to a science-centered culture.

The matter and energy centered schools and colleges will concentrate on courses which grow out of the belief that all that matters is matter.

In a science-centered school the relationship between goals and instructional material forms one of the criteria for evaluating the school and reporting it to be good or not so good.

The secular and science centered educational institutions will seek to engage teachers who are thoroughly conditioned to the scientific method in discovering the truth and rejecting non-scientific opinions and beliefs. The laboratory, and the experimental method, engaged in by the learners, will be a particular trait of teachers who are rated superior. The assembling of data, the classification of observed and counted facts, resulting in warranted conclusions and generalizations will characterize the teacher and his methods.

In a science-centered school the learner's development to maximum potential, with growing curiosity and understanding of the powers in the physical universe will be fostered.

The competencies and factors which affect education whether its philosophy is atom-centered, mind-centered, or God-centered, is very similar except for basic conceptions regarding the nature of reality of man and of truth. Certain it is that secular education is not concerned about spiritual and parish competence. It is questionable whether a strictly secular and scientific education is at all concerned with the use that man makes of the powers and competencies given to him by the natural sciences. Even if it had concerns, it is doubtful whether it would have the power to direct the uses of such competencies to good purposes.

"We know what goodness is," says Milton Mayer.[20] Moses knew. And Machiavelli knew. "But we do not know how to make men good." Secular education lacks something. It cannot and it does not supply all of the crucial needs of youth today. Secular education is based on a fragmentary conception of reality.

God's people have the answer. They still sing about it in the words of Cecil Alexander: "He died that we might be forgiven. He died to make us good."

E. SUMMARY

Shall God have a place in education? In America some say No! Others say Yes! Which shall it be? Whither goest thou, America? What can those who answer with an emphatic Yes! do? They have the longstanding principle of separation between church and state. They are faced with a predominant trend toward secularism among educational philosophers. Now even the U. S. Supreme Court in 1962 and 1963 ruling has joined the chorus of those who say No!

There is much in idealist education and very much in science-centered education for God's people to admire and appreciate. But they are uneasy of an education which touches only a segment of reality and leaves their children and teen-agers in moral and spiritual matters "without rudder, chart, or compass." An education without God and Godliness is not enough, and it may be very misleading. Secularism will not do, because

> the works of the flesh are plain: immortality, impurity, licentiousness, idolatry, sorcery, enmity, strife, jealousy, anger, selfishness, dissension, party strife.
> The activities of the lower nature are obvious. Here is a list: sexual immorality, impurity of mind, sensuality, worship of false gods, witchcraft, hatred, quarreling, jealousy, bad temper, rivalry, factions, party spirit, envy, drunkenness, orgies, and things like that.[21]

No. Parents who have God dwelling in their home want an education in which the Spirit of God is educationally active, through the Word, and where He produces

> the fruit of the Spirit which is love, joy, peace, patience, kindness, goodness, faithfulness, gentleness, self-control; against such there is no law.[22]

We conclude our radical re-examination of basic assumptions

and beliefs undergirding *Three Philosophies of Education in America* with a recommendation to God-believing parents and educators to do what can be done at this time in order to keep God in the formal education of their youngsters.

A MANIFESTO AND A STRATEGY
FOR GOD-BELIEVING EDUCATORS

1. Theologically stated, the strategy of God's people in educational matters must grow out of the Manifesto as this is recorded in Matthew 28:18-20. The central and ultimate goal of discipleship, of intimate personal fellowship and union with God, is contained in this statement.

2. Philosophically stated, in terms of means to ends, provide optimum conditions for maximum growth in Christ, for the maximum number of persons, in any and all parts of the globe.

3. Continue frankly and with firm determination, but in patience with those who cannot yet believe and agree, to sponsor and maintain full-time God-centered elementary, secondary schools, and colleges.

4. Aid parents in their attempts to obtain the legal right to retain a part of their tax dollar for education, so that they may be able without great sacrifice to use and support a school that keeps God central in its program of education.

5. All parents and tax payers shall, however, pay taxes toward the support of America's one, public, free, secular school system, so that all of its citizens will receive an education in good citizenship.

6. Help to keep public schools secular, nonreligious, in keeping with the Supreme Court's direction. Do not try to use, nor allow others to use, the public school to attain the goals of their religious group, be it Catholic, Protestant, Lutheran, or Jewish. Also, help to keep public schools free from anti-God teaching.

7. Increase your efforts in adult education, particularly parent and family life education. But do not rely on the home to do the job of the parish or the community school.

8. Encourage liberal financial and moral support for all accre-

dited forms of education, both public, parochial and private. Education is no luxury. Education is a condition of survival, and of growth, particularly in a free country where ballots, not bullets, decide crucial issues and among God's people where the ballot in the local congregation by the laity decides vital issues.

9. Encourage leadership in both public and parochial education to cooperate and coordinate their efforts, as far as feasible, in the training of informed, participating, responsible citizens, particularly in projects that aim at the solution of specific contemporary community problems, such as delinquency, burglary, vandalism, sexual promiscuity among teen-agers, unwed mothers, integration, elimination of slum housing conditions.

10. Solicit, in collaboration with representatives of other interested religious groups, Catholic, Jewish, Protestant, public school administrators' willingness to carry out church-sponsored week day, released time, shared time, Saturday school and confirmation instruction.

11. Aid public school leadership to recognize that secular public education, even if it integrates so-called "moral and spiritual values," cannot and does not meet all of the crucial needs of America's youth.

12. Be concerned about and be ready to participate in purposeful self-study of your educational efforts, with a view of improving the processes and the products. Let quality education be closely related to quantity. Give attention to individual differences; make special provisions for the mentally retarded and for the gifted.

13. Support, use, and participate as voluntary teachers in the various part time agencies of God-centered education as: Released time, Sunday School, share time, confirmation instruction, vacation Bible school, Bible classes for students and adults, and summer camp.

14. Be ready to discuss and explore the possibilities of cooperating in inter-parish educational efforts, such as inter-parish or central day schools, so as to make it possible for small groups of God's people, as mission parishes and blighted inner-city parishes to share in the blessings in God-centered education.

15. Be prepared to encourage and to guide current church-wide movements, such as ecumenism, as far as the Lord of the Church in His Word makes this possible, particularly as this has a bearing on the widest possible participation in the blessings of a full-time God-centered school, high school, or college.

16. Keep in touch with current attempts of Citizens for Educational Freedom to help create a favorable atmosphere for the establishment of Parent's Civil Rights.

17. Acquaint yourself with the strategy of education:
   a. In Canada, where parents choose between separate and public schools and pay their taxes for the school of their choice.
   b. In Free European Countries where the Bible is studied at all age levels in all public schools, and where in addition the state supports parochial schools, up to 65% and 80%.

18. Methods make a difference. Two grain fields may lie across the road from each other, of the same or very similar soil exposed to the same amount of rain and sunshine, and yet produce differently, one 30, the other 90 bushels per acre. Why? It's the difference in methods of farming including the use of hybrid seeds, fertilizer, etc.

The real difference in education, secular and God-centered, lies in the curriculum. But there are different ways of fostering curriculum assimilation. Educational phychology says: Begin where the learner is. Consider his past experiences. Proceed from the known to the unknown, from the concrete to the abstract, from the material to the spiritual, from the interesting to that in which you want to interest the learner. Begin with the recent and the nearby. Pose a problem situation. Give them time to think. "Open your book on page 67. Here we are told that . . . etc." Book teaching, assignments for rote learning, regurgitation — this method refuses to die. Even the instructional method of "new math" was recently reported to have slipped back into the traditional method of memorizing tables and forms. Visualize your objectives in terms of the living product. Remain ever "zielbewuszt," goal conscious. To do this, plan your own units of instruction.[23] Consider the needs of your learners, their life in home, community, and parish. Aim ever at improvement. Keep knowing and doing closely associated.[24] Knowledge is a means of making achievement intelligent and God-related. Correlate subject matter. Select relevant instructional material from many sources. Start the unit with a thought-provoking overview. End it with a self-evaluation.

Have a minimum of an annual self-study.[25] Ask: what are we trying to do? Why? How do we hope to attain those objectives? Did we? If not, why not? Plan to improve.

Faith, hope, and charity are gifts of the Great Teacher, the Holy Spirit. Pray over your unsolved problems. Praise God for observable evidence of success.

19. Pray without ceasing that God may be retained to the fullest extent possible in the education of youth and in the culture of the Western, yea, the whole world.

"Then were the disciples glad when they saw the Lord" (John 20:20). In the glow of Easter morning, we can move forward with joy and with optimism!

NOTES TO CHAPTER ONE

1. Genesis 1:1.
2. 2 Tim 3:15.
3. Luke 24:27 and 31.
4. John 1:14.
5. 2 Peter 1:4.
6. Galatians 2:20.
7. Hebrews 13:8.
8. John 3:36.
9. John 4:12.
10. Ryan, Francis A., *A Catholic Philosophy of Education*. Milwaukee: Bruce Publishing Co., 1956.
11. Henry, Nelson B., *Philosophies of Education*. Chicago 37, Ill: National Society for the Study of Education, 5635 Kimbark Avenue, 1942.
12. *Ibid.,* p. 269.
13. *Ibid.,* p. 269.
14. Plato, *The Republic*, Cambridge University Press, James Adams, 1963.
15. Santayana, George, *Platonism and the Spiritual Life*, N. Y.: Scribner's, 1927.
16. Descartes, René, "Two Meditations" reprinted in *Readings in Philosophy*, J. H. Randall, Jr., et al., N. Y.: Barnes and Noble, Inc., 1946.
17. *Ibid*, p. 29.
18. Quoted from N. Sri Ram, with approval, in *An Approach to Reality*. The Theosophical Publishing House, 1956, p. 2.
19. N. Sri Ram, *An Approach to Reality*. Madras, India: The Theosophical Publishing House, p. 175.
20. *Ibid*.
21. Leibniz, Gotfried Wilhem, *Discourse de la Metaphysique*. Translated by George Montgomery, Reprinted in D. D. Runes, *Treasury of Philosophy*, New York: Philosophical Library, 1955.
22. Brubacher, John S., "The Challenge to Philosophize about Education." *Modern Philosophies and Education*. National Society for the Study of Education. Chicago: University of Chicago Press, 1955.
23. Weber, Alfred., *History of Philosophy*. New York: Charles Scribner's Sons, 1925.
24. Horne, H. H., "An Idealistic Philosophy of Education." *NSSE 41st Yearbook — Philosophy of Education*. 1942, p. 144ff.

25. Greene, Theodore M., "A Liberal Christian Idealist Philosophy of Education." *Modern Philosophies and Education — NSSE 54th Yearbook*. Chicago: University of Chicago Press. 1954, p. 93.

26. Roywood Sellars, et al., *The Future of Philosophy*. New York: The Macmillan Co., 1949. (Foreword, pp. 6-9).

27. Marx, Karl, *Das Kapital*. Introduction to the First Volume, Encyclopedia of the Philosophical Sciences. I, 25. Sec. 25-28. Chicago: Encyclopaedia Britannica, 1955.

28. Hook Sydney, "Studies in the Intellectual Development of Marx." *Hegel to Marx*. N. Y.: The Humanities Press, New York University, 1958.

29. Darwin, Charles; *The Origin of Species*. New York: Collier, 1909. (1859).

30. Sellars, Roywood, et. al., *Philosophy of the Future*. New York: The Macmillan Company, 1949. (Foreword, p. 7.)

31. Lunacharsky, Commissioner of Education, USSR, Recorded in the Congressional Record, Vol. 77, pp. 1539-1540.

32. Webster, *Unabridged Dictionary*.

33. Lin Yutang, *From Pagan to Christian*. New York: World Publishing Co., 1959.

34. Feigl, Herbert, "Aims of Education of Our Age of Science: Reflections of a Logical Empiricist." *Modern Philosophies and Education — NSSE 54th Yearbook*. Chicago: University of Chicago Press 1954.

35. Lehman, William, Jr., "Educational Philosophy and Religious Implications." *Lutheran Education*. River Forest, Illinois, January, 1960, p. 237.

36. Lin Yutang, *Op. cit.*, pp. 175-176.

37. Dehovre, F. and Jordan, D., *Catholicism in Education*. Benziger Bros. New York, 1934. p. 34. Quoted in Redden and Ryan, *A Catholic Philosophy of Education*. Milwaukee: Bruce Publishing Co., 1956, p. 16.

38. Dewey, John, *A Common Faith*. New Haven: Yale University Press, 1934, p. 2.

39. *Ibid.*, pp. 8-9.

40. James, William, *Pragmatism*. New York: Longmans Green & Co., 1907.

41. Peirce, Chas. S., *Collected Papers*. Hartshorne & Weiss. Cambridge: Belknop Press of Harvard University.

42. Dewey, John, *Studies in Logical Theory*. New York: Philosophical Library, 1903.

43. Darwin, Charles, *The Origin of Species*, 1859, and *Descent of Man*, 1871. Chicago: Encyclopaedia Britannica, 1955.

44. *Ibid.*

45. Childs, John L., *Education and the Philosophy of Experimentalism*. New York: The Century Company, 1931.

46. Brameld, Theodore, *Patterns of Educational Philosophy.* New York: World Book Co., 1950, pp. 109-110.
47. Superintendent of Documents, Government Printing Office, Washington 25, D.C.
48. Pike, The Right Reverend James A., "Has the Supreme Court Outlawed Religious Observance in the Schools?" Debate by William J. Butler and Rev. James A. Pike. *The Reader's Digest,* October, 1962, pp. 78-85.
49. Brubacher, John S., "The Challenge to Philosophize about Education". *Modern Philosophies in Education — NSSE 54th Yearbook.* Chicago University of Chicago Press, 1955, p. 16.
50. Wild, John, "Education and Human Society: A Realistic View." *Modern Philosophies and Education — NSSE 54th Yearbook.* Chicago University of Chicago Press, 1955, p. 54.
51. *The Christian Century.* New York: Association Press.
52. Reissner, Edward H. "Philosophy and Science in the Western World" *Philosophies of Education — NSSE 41st Yearbook.* Part I. Chicago: University of Chicago Press, 1942.
53. *Ibid.*
54. Galatians 5:22-23.
55. Galatians 5:19-21.

NOTES TO CHAPTER TWO

1. I Corinthians 15:42-57.
2. Genesis 1:26-27.
3. Disraeli, quoted in Buckle, *Life of Disraeli,* Volume 4, p. 374.
4. Henry R. Luce, "To Ike the Wall Rises Between Opposing Ideas of Man." *Life* Magazine, September 8, 1961, p. 46.
5. Pascal, as quoted by Reinhold Niebuhr, *Pious and Secular America.* New York: Charles Scribner's Sons, 1958.
6. J. D. Smart, *The Teaching Ministry of the Church.* Philadelphia, Pa.: Westminster Press, 1954.
7. *Question 7.* Film produced by Lutheran Films, Inc., New York.
8. Genesis 1:26-27.
9. Acts 17:26.
10. Genesis 3:23.
11. John 1:1.
12: John 1:14.
13. John 1:12.
14. John 17:3.
15. I Corinthians 15:55 and 57.
16. I Corinthians 15:44.

17. Luke 23:43.
18. John 8:36.
19. Hebrews 13:5.
20. W. McGucken, *The Catholic Way in Education*. Milwaukee: Bruce, 1934.
21. Pope Pius XI, *Encyclical on Christian Education,* quoted in McGucken, pp. 260 and 261.
    Also in Seven Great Encyclicals, New York: Glen Rock, 1963.
22. Smart, *Op. cit.,* p. 159.
23. John Dewey, *A Common Faith.* Yale, 1934, p. 5.
24. H. Heine, *From Luther to Kant to Hegel.* Stuttgart: Sämtliche Werke. J. G. Cotta (1797-1856).
25. Rev. Mrs. Maud Kellog, Pastor of Unity Church in Evanston, Ill., as reported by Dave Meade, *Chicago Daily News.*
26. Herman Horne, *Philosophies of Education.* 41st Yearbook, NSSE, 1941, p. 155.
27. H. E. Wornom, General Secretary, Religious Education Association, 545 West 111th Street, New York 25, N. Y.
28. Hugh Elliot, *Modern Science and Materialism.* New York: Longmans, 1919.
29. Charles Darwin, *Origin of Species.* Harvard: Harvard Classics, 1909.
30. Lewis H. Morgan, *Ancient Society.* Harvard: Harvard University Press, 1907.
31. Revelation 7:16-17.
32. Caitlin Thomas, *Leftover Life to Kill.* Little, Brown, 1957, Autobiography.
33. John Osborne, *Look Back in Anger.* New York: Dodd, Mead, Drama, 1947.
34. Tennessee Williams, *Camino Real, Baby Doll,* and *Cat On a Hot Tin Roof.* New York: James Laughlin, Theatre Arts Magazine, June, 1957.
35. Romans 1:23-32, J. B. Phillips translation.
36. Romans 1:14-17.
37. John S. Brubacher, *The Challenge to Philosophize About Education* 54th Yearbook, NSSE., Chicago, 1954, p. 14.
38. Matthew 22:21.
39. Breed, Fredericks, *Philosophies of Education*: "Education and the Realistic Outlook." 41st Yearbook, NSSE., 1942, Chicago: 1951.
40. Roger L. Shinn, "The Story of Man and the Image of Man." An address to the National Convention of the Religious Education Association, Chicago, Nov. 25, 1957.
41. *Ibid.*
42. Gustav Weigel, S. J., "The Christian as Humanist." An address to the National Convention of the Religious Education Association, Palmer House, Chicago, Nov. 25, 1957.

43. Pope Pius XI, *Op. cit.*
44. Theodor Brameld, *Toward a Democratic Faith* as quoted in Education for an Emerging Age, *Patterns of Educational Philosophy.* New York: World Book Co., 1950, p. 13.
45. E. L. Thorndike, *The Original Nature of Man.* New York: Columbia University, Teachers College, 1913.
46. Robert E. Clark, *Darwin: Before and After.* Grand Rapids, Mich.: Grand Rapids International Publications, 1958.
47. Karl W. Keller, "The Basic Aims of Education," in *Lutheran Education.* St. Louis, Mo.: Concordia Publishing House, Sept. 1957, pp. 6-19.
48. *Ibid.*
49. Smart, *Op. cit.*
50. Paul E. Klopsteg, in *Living Philosophy,* "This I Believe." Address given to the Sunday Evening Club, Orchestra Hall, Chicago, April 17, 1963.
51. "Die heute am weitest verbreiteten Auffassungen beziehen dass biologisch Fassbare des Humanen stets auf das hoehere Saeugtier als Norm und schnuren zu diesem Zweck von vornherein das Nichtvergleichbare, das Besondere, als Geistiges, von diesem Menschen ab." A. Portmann,
     Biologische Fragmente zu einer Lehre vom Menschen B. Schwabe & Co., Basel, 1951. (Quoted in *Natural Sciences* and *The Christian Message* by Van Der Ziel, Minneapolis: T. S. Denison & Co., 1960.)
52. Rudolph Bultmann, "Der Moderne Mensch." *Die Theologie des Neuen Testaments,* Tubingen, 1948.
53. Martin H. Scharlemann, Director of Graduate Studies, Concordia Seminary, Editor in Chief of *What Then Is Man?* A Symposium of Theology, Psychology and Psychiatry. St. Louis, Mo.: Concordia Publishing House, 1958.
54. *Ibid.,* p. v.
55. Martin Luther, Weimar Edition. II 263ff.
56. John 15:15.
57. Martin Luther, Weimar Edition, 13, 550.
58. Emil Brunner, *The Great Invitation.* Lutterworth Press, 1955. Quoted in E. H. Robertson, "Man's Estimate of Man," Richmond, Virginia: John Knox Press, 1958.
59. Martin Luther, *Op. cit.*
60. Joseph W. Krutch, *The Great Chain of Life.* Houghton, 1957. Lloyd L. Ecremont, *Man, The Bible and Destiny.* Grand Rapids, Mich.: Eerdmanns Publ. Co., 1961.
61. Jacques Maritain, *Thomist Views on Education* In Modern Philosophies and Education, 54th Yearbook, NSSE. University of Chicago Press, 1955, p. 64.

62. I Peter 3:18.
63. Lin Yutang, *From Pagan to Christian*. New York: World Publishing Co., 1959.
64. William Ernest Hocking, *What Man Can Make of Man*. New York: Harper, 1942, p. 31.

NOTES TO CHAPTER THREE

1. Dostoievsky, Fedor, *The Brothers Karamazov*. Translated by Constance Garnett. New York: Modern Library, 1950.
2. Jack Allen and Clarence Stegmeier, *Civics*. Chicago: American Book Company, 1959.
3. Plato (427-347 B.C.), *Euthyphro*. Chicago: In Encyclopaedia Britannica, 1952.
4. Felix Adler, *Creed and Deed* (1878); Robert Maynard Hutchins, *Conflict in Education in a Democratic Society*. New York: Harper, 1953.
5. Ralph Harper, *Significance of Existence and Recognition for Education*. 54th Yearbook, National Society for the Study of Education, 1954, p. 238.
6. Karl Marx, *Das Kapital*. New York: International Publishers Co., 1939.
7. John Dewey, *The Quest for Certainty*, A Study of the Relation of Knowledge and Action. Minton-Balch, 1929.
8. Franz Pieper, *Christian Dogmatics*, Vol. I. St. Louis: Concordia Publishing House, 1917.
9. Constitution of the United States. Washington: Government Printing Office, Norman J. Small, Ed., 1964.
10. Report of Committee on Un-American Activities, Hearings on *The Communist Mind*. Washington D.C., May 29, 1957.
11. G. W. F. Hegel (1770-1831), *Phaenomologie des Geistes and Wissenschaft der Logik*. Translated by Benjamin Rand, *Phenomenology of the Spirit*. Boston: Houghton, 1924.
12. Karl Marx, *Op. cit.*
13. Francis Bacon (1561-1626), *The Advancement of Learning*. Chicago: Encyclopaedia Britannica, 1952.
14. David Hume (1711-1776), *Treatise on Human Nature* (1739). Eliot, C. W., ed. The Harvard Classics. Collier, 1909.
15. Immanuel Kant, *Critique of Pure Reason*. Chicago: Great Books of the Western World, Robert M. Hutchins, ed. 1871.
16. John 14:6, also 8:32.
17. Hebrews 13:8.

18. John Henry Newman, *An Essay in Aid of a Grammar of Assent.* New York: Longmans, 1870.
19. John Dewey, *Op. cit.,* p. 300.
20. John Dewey, *Logic, The Theory of Inquiry.* New York: Holt, 1938, p. 513.
21. Theodore M. Greene, "A Liberal Christian Idealist Philosophy of Education". 54th Yearbook, NSSE, 1954, p. 99.
22. Corinthians 5:15.
23. James 2:20.
24. Frederick S. Breed, "Education and the Realistic Outlook," 41st Yearbook, NSSE, 1942, p. 119.
25. *Ibid.*
26. *Ibid.*
27. Jacques Maritain, "Thomist Views on Education," 54th Yearbook, NSSE, p. 118.
28. Frederick Breed, *Op. cit.,* p. 133.
29. *Ibid.,* p. 124.
30. *Ibid.,* p. 125.
31. Frederick S. Breed, *Op. cit.,* p. 88.
32. *Ibid.,* pp. 87-91.
33. Erwin L. Lueker, Editor in Chief, *Lutheran Encyclopedia.* St. Louis: Concordia Publishing House, 1954, p. 511.
34. *Ibid.*
35. 2 Timothy 3:14-117.
36. John 20:31.
37. 2 Timothy 3:15-17.
38. Revelations 22:18-19.
39. The literal sense is one.
40. Scripture interprets Scripture.
41. Analogy of faith.
42. One Holy Church.
43. Fellowship.
44. John 8:32.
45. John 10:10.
46. John 3:16.
47. Genesis 1:1.
48. Deuteronomy 6:1.
49. Isaiah 56:1.
50. Joshua 1:5-9.
51. Genesis 18:18-19.
52. Deuteronomy 6:6-9.
53. Deuteronomy 6:12.
54. Deuteronomy 6:4-5.
55. Deuteronomy 12:10-13.

56. Deuteronomy 32:4.
57. Psalm 146:5-6.
58. Hebrews 6:17-20.
59. Acts 17:22.
60. I Corinthians 1:22-25.
61. Hebrews 1:1-3.
62. John 1:1-5.
63. Romans 1:4.
64. Hebrews 13:8.
65. John 17:3.
66. John 8:36.
67. Acts 2:42-45.
68. Martin Luther, *Diet at Worms,* in Roth & Kramer, *The Church Through the Ages.* St. Louis: Concordia Publishing House.
69. Franz Pieper, *Op. cit.,* p. 190.
70. *Ibid.*
71. John Toland, *Christianity Not Mysterious.* Stuttgart: Fromm Verlag, 1964.
72. W. E. H. Lecky, *History of the Rise and Influence of the Spirit of of Rationalism in Europe.* New York: Longmans, Green and Company, 1904.
73. Herbert Feigl, "Logical Empiricism," *Modern Philosophies and Education.* 54th Yearbook, NSSE; Chicago: University of Chicago Press, 1954.
74. Jaroslav Pelikan, *The Riddle of Roman Catholicism.* New York: Abingdon Press, 1959, p. 193.
74. *Ibid.*
75. *Ibid.,* p. 199.
76. Jaroslav Pelikan, *From Luther to Kierkegaard.* St. Louis: Concordia Publishing House, 1950.
77. Karl Barth, *Kirchliche Dogmatic.* Translated by G. T. Thomson, *Dogmatics in Outline.* New York: Philosophical Library, 1949.
78. Erwin L. Lueker, *Op. cit.,* p. 1026.
79. J. Bronowski, et. al., *Science.* Garden City, New York: Doubleday and Company, Inc., 1960.
80. Johann Andreas Quenstedt, *Theologia-polemica, sive systema theologicana.* Wittenberg, 1696
81. A. M. Ramsey, *An Era in Anglican Theology.* New York: Charles Scribner's Sons, 1959.
82. 1 Timothy 3:16.
83. Albert Van Der Ziel, *The Natural Sciences and the Christian Message.* Minneapolis: T. S. Denison and Co., 1960, p. 217.
84. *Ibid.,* p. 243.
85. *Ibid.*

86. *Ibid.*, p. 237.
87. Genesis 1:28.
88. Genesis 1:26.
89. Alfred O. Fuerbringer, "Our Newest Frontier: Theology," *A Symposium of Essays and Addresses Given at the Counsellors' Conference.* Valparaiso, Indiana: Valparaiso University, Sept. 7-14, 1960, pp. 137-138.
90. *Ibid.*
91. Book of Documentation: "State of the Church Conference." Milwaukee.
92. George G. Beto, Editorial, "The Springfielder," Summer, 1961.
93. L. B. Meyer, *An Evaluation of the State of the Church Conference and the Documentation.* St. Louis 2, Mo., 210 N. Broadway: Luheran Church, Missouri Synod.
94. Dr. Martin Scharleman in L. B. Meyer, *Op. cit.*
95. O. P. Kretzmann, "Campus Commentary," Valparaiso, Indiana: Valparaiso University, April-May, 1959.
95a. Hans Küng, *That the World May Believe.* Translated by Cecil Hastings, New York: Sheed and Ward, 1963.
95b. Milton S. Terry, *Biblical Hermeneutics.* New York: 1884.
96. Herman H. Horne, "An Idealistic Philosophy of Education," *Modern Philosophies in Education.* 41st Yearbook, Part I, NSSE; Chicago: University of Chicago Press, 1942, p. 139.
97. Alfred Weber, *History of Philosophy.* New York: Charles Scribner's Sons, 1925.
98. Plato, *Theaetetus. Dialogue of Plato.* Great Books of the Western World, R. M. Hutchins, ed., Chicago.
99. *Ibid.*, (Quoted somewhat non-literally).
100. Plato, *Dialogue with Parmenides on The Doctrine of Ideas.* Robert M. Hutchins, ed., Great Books of the Western World, 1952.
101. Plato, *The Republic.* Translated by B. Jowett; Chicago: Modern Library.
102. René Descartes, *Meditations.* Great Books of the Western World, R. M. Hutchins, ed., 1952.
103. Immanuel Kant, *Critique of Pure Reason* (1781); *Critique of Practical Reason* (1788); *Critique of Judgment* (1790). Chicago: Great Books of the Western World, R. M. Hutchins, ed.
104. David Hume, *Treatise on Human Nature.* Chicago: Great Books of the Western World, R. M. Hutchins, ed.; also in Encyclopaedia Britannica, 1952.
105. Immanuel Kant, *Op. cit.*
106. Immanuel Kant, *Prolegomena,* p. 14., *Op. cit.*
107. Oliver J. Thatcher, New York: The Library of Original Sources, University Research Extension, 1907.

108. George Berkeley, *A Treatise Concerning the Principle of Human Knowledge*. Dublin, 1710.
109. *Ibid.*
110. John Locke, *Essay on Human Understanding*. (1960). Benjamin Rand, ed., Boston: Houghton, 1924.
111. Herman H. Horne, *Op. cit.*
112. Theodore M. Greene, *Op. cit.*
113. Herman H. Horne, *Op. cit.*
114. *Ibid.*, p. 152.
115. *Ibid.*, p. 154.
116. *Ibid.*, p. 259.
117. *Ibid.*
118. *Ibid.*, p. 269.
119. Karl Marx, *Das Kapital* (Introduction to the First Volume), *Op. cit.*
120. Herman H. Horne, *Op. cit.*, p. 259.
121. Theodore M. Greene, *Op. cit.*, p. 91.
122. Scott Buchanan, *Essay in Politics*, New York: Philosophical Library, 1953, pp. 182-185.
123. Theodore M. Greene, *Op. cit.* (In consultation with Professor Donald Butler, Princeton University.)
124. Andrew Krzecinski, *Is Modern Culture Doomed?* New York: Devin Adair Company, 1944.
125. Herman H. Horne, *Op. cit.*, p. 289.
126. Paul Henri Baron D'Holback, *An Examination of Supernaturalism*, (Quoted from *Common Sense,* as trans. by H. D. Robinson, in *Readings in Philosophy*. New York: Randall, Buchler, Shirk, Barnes, and Noble, Inc.).
127. Hugh Elliott, *Modern Science and Materialism*. New York: Longmans, Green, and Company, 1919, Chs. 5-6.
128. *Ibid.*
129. Roy Wood Sellars, et. al., *The Future of Philosophy,* Foreword, p. vi, New York: The Macmillan Company, 1930.
130. Psalm 139:14.
131. Psalm 19:1-,2.
132. Francis Bacon, *Novum Organum*. Quoted in *From Descartes to Kant*. Smith and Greene, p. 38. Also in Benjamin Rand, *Modern Classical Philosophers*. Boston: Houghton, 1924.
133. John Wild, "Education and Human Society: A Realistic View," *Modern Philosophies and Education*. 54th Yearbook, NSSE; Chicago; The University of Chicago Press, 1954.
134. Geoffrey O'Connell, *Naturalism in American Education*. New York: Benziger Brother, 1938. p. xxiv, Introduction.
135. *Ibid.*

136. *Ibid.*
137. Martin Scharleman, *What Then Is Man?* St. Louis: Concordia Publishing House, 1958.
138. Charles Saunders Peirce, *Grand Logic,* in Philosophical Writings. New York: Ed. Justus Buchter, Dover Publications, 1955.
139. William James, *Pragmatism.* New York: Longmans, Green, and Company, 1907.
140. John Dewey, *The Quest for Certainty, Op cit.*
141. George R. Geiger, "An Experimentalist Approach to Education," *Modern Philosophies and Education.* 54th Yearbook, NSSE; Chicago: University of Chicago Press, 1954.
142. John L. Childs, *Education and the Philosophy of Experimentalism.* New York: The Century Company, 1931.
143. *Ibid.,* p. 141.
144. Lawrence G. Thomas, "The Meaning of Progress in Progressive Education," Educational Administration and Supervision, October, 1946, pp. 385-400.
145. Charles Saunders Peirce, "The Ways of Justifying Beliefs," *Popular Science Monthly* (1877). Also, *The Faith of a Liberal.* New York: Holt, 1946.
146. David Hume, *An Inquiry Concerning Human Understanding* (1748), Ch. 10. Harvard (Colliers), The Harvard Classics, 1909.
147. William H. Kilpatrick, "Philosophy of Education from the Experimentalist Outlook," *Philosophies of Education.* 41st Yearbook, NSSE; Chicago: University of Chicago Press, 1942.
148. Philip P. Wiener, *Evolution and the Founders of Pragmatism.* Cambridge: Harvard University Press, 1949.
149. *Ibid.,* p. 35. Herbert Spencer (1820-1903), *What Knowledge Is of Most Worth.* New York: *Education,* Intellectual, Physical. Hurst. Also: *First Principles.* New York: A. L. Burt. 1880.
150. C. O'Connor, *Naturalism in American Education.* New York: Benziger Brothers, 1938.
151. William James, *Op. cit.,* p. 54.
152. Martin Luther, The Preface in *Enchiridion: The Small Catechism.* St. Louis: Concordia Publishing House, 1912, p. 6.
153. *Ibid.,* p. 48B.
154. Philip P. Wiener, *Op. cit.,* pp. 125, 127, 99.
155. *Ibid.*
156. William James, *Pragmatism: A New Name for Some Old Ways of Thinking.* New York: Longmans, Green and Company, 1907.
157. *Ibid.,* p. 53.
158. *Ibid.,* p. 89.
159. John Dewey, *A Common Faith.* New Haven: Yale University Press, 1934, p. 32.

160. *Ibid.,* p. 33.
161. John Dewey, *The Quest for Certainty, Op. cit.,* pp. 288-289.
162. Henry J. Boettcher, *An Experimental Study of Activities in Religious Education,* To Determine the Relative Effectiveness of Two Methods of Teaching Religion, In partial fulfillment of the requirements for the doctoral degree (copy in University Library). Minneapolis: University of Minnesota, 1949.
163. John Dewey, *Op. cit.*
164. Herbert Feigl, "Aims of Our Age of Science: Reflections of a Logical Empiricist," *Modern Philosophies and Education,* 54th Yearbook, NSSE; Chicago: University of Chicago, 1954, pp. 305-306.
165. *Ibid.*
166. *Ibid.,* p. 325.
167. *Ibid.*
168. *Ibid.,* p. 311.
169. *Ibid.,* p. 326.
170. S. Alexander, *Space, Time, and Deity.* 2 vols. London: Macmillan and Company, 1927.
171. Karl Marx, *Das Kapital* (1876). Garden City, N. Y.· Doubleday and Company, 1946.
172. Dagobert Runes, *Treasury of Philosophy.* New York: Philosophical Library. (Notes on *Das Kapital,* p. 790).
173. Robert S. Cohen, "On the Marxist Philosophy of Education," *Modern Philosophies in Education.* 54th Yearbook, NSSE; Chicago: University of Chicago Press, 1954, p. 175.
174. Karl Marx, *Op. cit.,* p. 175.
175. N. S. Timascheff (1917-1942) *Religion in Soviet Russia.* New York: Sheed and Ward, 1942, p. 10
176. *Ibid.,* p. 13. (Quoted from *Minister of Education in Soviet Russia* by Yaroslawski.)
177. *Ibid.,* p. 110.
178. Robert S. Cohen, *Op. cit.,* p. 185.
179. Karl Marx, Introduction to a *Critique of Hegel's Philosophy of Law. Op. cit.*
180. N. S. Timascheff, *Op. cit.*
181. John S. Brubacher, *"The Challenge to Philosophize about Education,"* *Modern Philosophies and Education.* 54th Yearbook, NSSE; Chicago: The University of Chicago Press, 1954, pp. 4-16.
182. Francis Bacon, *Advancement of Learning. Novum Organum.* Chicago: Encyclopaedia Britannica, 1955.
183. Plato, *Dialogues.* Chicago: Encyclopaedia Britannica, 1952.
184. John W. Klotz, *Genes, Genesis, and Evolution.* St. Louis: Concordia Publishing House, 1951, p. 547.
185. J. Edgar Hoover, FBI Director, *Springfield State Journal,* July 24, 1961.

239

186. Scudder & Bean, *The Twenty Billion Dollar Challenge.* New York: G. P. Putnam, 1961.
187. Everett C. Olsen, Geologist and Editor, *The Journal of Evaluation.* Washington, D.C., 2633 16th St. NW.
188. John Brubacher, *Op. cit.,* p. 16.
189. Alfred Van Der Ziel, *Op. cit.,* p. 176.
190. Mark 2:27.
191. John Brubacher, *Op. cit.*
192. Theodore M. Greene, *Op. cit.*

NOTES TO CHAPTER FOUR

1. *Large Catechism,* Translation by R. Malmin. Minneapolis: Augsburg Publishing House, 1935.
2. Matthew 6:24.
3. *Ibid.*
4. Francis Bacon, "The Four Idols," *Novum Organum,* reprinted in *Readings in Philosophy.* New York: Barnes and Noble, Inc., 1946, original in 1861.
5. *Third International Dictionary,* Unabridged. Springfield, Mass.: G. and C. Merriam, Publisher, 1961.
6. Lin Yutang, *Between Tears and Laughter.* New York: John Day Company, 1943, p. 187.
7. Frederick Nohl and Frederick A. Meyer, *A Curriculum Guide,* Vol. I, for Lutheran Elementary Schools. St. Louis: Concordia Publishing House, 1964, p. 12.
8. Aristotle, "Pleasure and Happiness," *Nichomachean Ethics,* p. 356. Translated by H. Rackham. Cambridge: Harvard University Press, 1955.
9. William Clayton Bower, *Moral and Spiritual Values in Education.* Lexington: University of Kentucky Press, 1952. The Kentucky Program of Moral and Spiritual Values in Education.
10. Dr. Wm. Graham, "Power Over the Air," *Decision,* Vol. 5, Nov. 9, Sept. 1964. Minneapolis: 1300 Harmon Place.
11. I John 4:8.
12. R. R. Kaemmerer, "The Nature and Attributes of God," *The Abiding Word.* St. Louis: Concordia Publishing House, 1947, II, 59-77; and quoted in *The Lutheran Cyclopedia,* Erwin L. Lueker, Editor.
13. Psalm 19.
14. II Corinthians 5:17-21.

15. Psalm 90.
16. Romans 8.
17. Kaemmerer, *Loc. cit.*
18. Romans 3:23-25; Titus 2:11-14.
19. Romans 10:17.
20. John 15:5.
21. Matthew 19:14.
22. Luke 10:42.
23. Matthew 13:44.
24. Cf. *Modern Philosophies and Education, NSSE Yearbook,* 54th. Chicago: University of Chicago Press, 1955.
25. Matthew 6:19-21.
26. Karl W. Keller, "The Basic Aims of Education," *Lutheran Education,* Sept. 1957, pp. 6-19.
27. Clovis Cappell, *Values That Last.* Nashville: Cokesbury Press, 1939.
28. John 8:36.
29. John 17:3.
30. Herman Horne, "An Idealistic Philosophy of Education," *Philosophies of Education, NSSE Yearbook,* 41st. Chicago: University Press, 1942.
31. *Ibid.,* p. 183.
32. Plato, Crito, 1871. Trans. by Benjamin Jowett, *The Dialogues.* Oxford: Clarendon Press, 1953.
33. Benedict Spinoza, "Reflections on the Good of Man," as reproduced in *Readings in Philosophy,* J. H. Randall, J. Buchler, Evelyn Shirk. New York: Barnes and Noble, 1946, pp. 255-258.
34. Theodore M. Greene, "A Liberal Christian Idealist Philosophy of Education," *NSSE Yearbook,* 54th. Chicago: University of Chicago Press, 1955, pp. 97ff.
35. *Ibid.,* p. 135.
36. *Ibid.,* p. 97.
37. *Ibid.,* p. 105.
38. *Ibid.,* p. 110.
39. Paul Tillich, *Dynamics of Faith.* New York: Harper and Brothers, 1957, pp. 1ff.
40. J. H. Randall, J. Buchler, Evelyn Shirk, *Readings in Philosophy.* New York: Barnes and Noble, 1946.
41. *Ibid.,* p. 74.
42. Horne, *Op. cit.,* p. 154.
43. L. P. Jacks, *The Education of the Whole Man.* New York: Harper and Brothers University of London Press, 1931.
44. Erwin L. Lueker, Editor in Chief, *Lutheran Cyclopedia.* St. Louis: Concordia Publishing House, 1954.
45. Ralph Harper, "Significance of Existence and Recognition for Education," *NSSE Yearbook,* 54th. Chicago: University of Chicago Press, 1955.

46. Henry M. Wriston, Chairman of the Commission and responsible for *The Commission Report*. New York: The Spectrum Book, Prentice-Hall, Inc., 1960.
47. Jacques Maritain, "Thomist Views on Education," *NSSE Yearbook,* 54th. Chicago: University of Chicago Press, 1955, p. 77.
48. *Ibid.*
49. *Ibid.,* p. 186.
50. Wriston, *Op. cit.,* p. 22.
51. Bower, *Op. cit.*
52. *Ibid.,* p. 200.
53. *Ibid.,* p. 199.
54. *Ibid.,* Preface, p. vi.
55. Romans 1:28-32, Philip's Translation.
56. John J. Brubacher, *Modern Philosophies of Education*. New York: McGraw-Hill Book Company, 1939, p. 334.
57. John Dewey, *The Quest for Certainty, A Study of the Relation of Knowledge and Action*. New York: Minton Balch, 1929.
58. Herbert Feigl, "Aims of Education for Our Age of Science: Reflections of a Logical Empiricist," *Modern Philosophies and Education,* Nelson B. Henry, Editor. Chicago: University of Chicago Press, 1955.
59. George R. Geiger, "An Experimentalist Approach to Education," *NSSE Yearbook,* 54th. Chicago: Universiy of Chicago Press, 1955, p. 146.
60. *Ibid.,* p. 145.
61. *Ibid.*
62. *Ibid.,* p. 157.
63. *Ibid.,* p. 171.
64. Feigl, *Op. cit.,* pp. 304ff.
65. *Ibid.,* p. 304.
66. *Ibid.,* p. 306.
67. Arthur Moehlman, *School Administration*. Cambridge: Riverside Press, 1940, p. 45.
68. John S. Brubacher, "The Challenge to Philosophize about Education," *NSSE Yearbook,* 54th. Chicago: University of Chicago Press, 1955, p. 14.
69. Roy W. Sellars, "Teaching the School as a Major Social Institution," *Eleventh Yearbook,* Department of Elementary School Principals (MEA, 1939), Part I, pp. 45-47.
70. John 3:3.
71. Jeremiah 13:23.
72. I Peter 1:23.
73. Robert S. Cohen, "On Marxist Philosophy of Education," *NSSE Yearbook,* 54th. Chicago: University of Chicago Press, 1955, pp. 175-214.

74. *Soviet Commitment to Education,* Report of the First Official U. S. Education Mission to the USSR. Washington, D. C.: U S. Department of Health, Education and Welfare, Office of Education, 1959, Bulletin 16.
75. *Ibid.,* p. 1.
76. *Ibid.*
77. *Ibid.,* p. 3.
78. *Ibid.,* p. 36.
79. Cohen, *Op. cit.*
80. *Ibid.,* p. 182.
81. *Ibid.,* p. 182.
82. John Dewey, *My Pedagogic Creed.* Washington: Progressive Education Association, 1929, p. 306.
83. Charles A. Beard, *The Unique Function of Education in American Democracy.* Washington, D.C.: Educational Policies Commission, 1937, pp. 77-90.
84. *Ibid.*
85. Jeremiah 29:7.
86. Matthew 15:19.
87. Jeremiah 13:23.
88. John 3:5.
89. Proverbs 1:7.
90. Proverbs 3:5.
91. Proverbs 14:34.
92. I Peter 3:18.
93. Psalm 32:1.
94. I Corinthians 13:13.
95. Rudolph Karl Bultmann, *Jesus Christ and Mythology.* New York: Scribners, 1958.
96. Tillich, *Op. cit.*
97. Acts 1:8.

NOTES TO CHAPTER FIVE

1. Rev. Harold R. Hodgson, "The Ethics Needed to Confront Communism," The *Christian Economist,* March 17, 1964, p. 1.
2. Albert Van Del Ziel, *The Natural Sciences and the Christian Message.* Lutheran Studies Series, Minneapolis: T. S. Denison and Co., Inc., 1960, p. 211.
3. Virginia Held, *The Bewildered Age.* New York: Potter Inc., 1962.
4. Ruth Nanda Anshen, Editor of Credo Series. New York 18, N. Y.:

Simon and Schuster, Inc., *Moral Principles in Action: Man's Ethical Imperative*. New York: Harper, 1952.

5. Held, *Op. cit.,* p. 174.
6. Denis J. B. Hawkins, *Christian Ethics*. New York: Hawthorn, 1963.
7. Edith Kermit Roosevelt, "Totalitarian Mentality Lives On," *Christian Economics,* Vol. XVI, #6, March 17, 1964.
8. Exodus 20:1-17.
9. Hebrews 1:3.
10. John 14:6.
11. Acts 19:9 and Acts 24:22.
12. Proverbs 1:3.
13. Proverbs 1:17.
14. Ecclesiastes 12:13.
15. Ephesians 4:1.
16. Ephesians 5:15.
17. Ephesians 5:2.
18. Colossians 1:10.
19. Colossians 2:6.
20. II John 6.
21. Chr. Ernst Luthhardt, *History of Christian Ethics*. Edinburgh: T. and T .Clark, 1859. Trans. by W. Hastie.
22. *Ibid.,* p. 8, Preface.
23. Adolph Koeberle, *The Quest for Holiness*. Minneapolis: Augsburg, 1936.
24. Martin E. Marty, *The Hidden Discipline*. St. Louis: Concordia Publishing House, 1962.
25. James D. Smart, *The Teaching Ministry of the Church: An Examination of the Basic Principles of Christian Education*. Philadelphia: The Westminster Press, 1954.
26. C. F. W. Walther, *Proper Distinction Between Law and Gospel,* Trans. by W. H. T. Dau. St. Louis: Concordia Publishing House.
27. Theodor Graebner, *Borderline of Right and Wrong*. St. Louis: Concordia Publishing House, Revised 1956.
28. Epictetus, *Moral Discourses,* Trans. by Elizabeth Carter. London: J. M. Dent and Sons, 1910. Book II, Chap. VIII, p. 80.
29. N. H. Soe, *Christliche Ethik*. Muenchen: C. Kaiser, 1949.
30. *Ibid.,* p. 38.
31. *Ibid.,* p. 41.
32. *Ibid.*
33. Romans 2:15.
34. Soe, *Op. cit.,* p. 33.
35. Henry M. Wriston, Chairman, *A Report of the President's Com-*

mission on National Goals. New York: The American Assembly, Columbia University: Prentice-Hall, Inc., 1960, p. 23.

36. Apology of Lutheran Confessions, Triglotta, St. Louis: Concordia Publishing House, p. 335.
37. Soe, Op. cit., p. 41.
38. Ibid., p. 30.
39. Theodor Culmann, Die Christliche Ethik. Kaiserlautern, 1927. Preface, p. v.
40. Albert William Levi, Philosophy of the Modern World. Bloomington, Indiana: University Press, 1959, pp. 528-9.
41. Herman H. Horne, "An Idealistic Philosophy of Education," Philosophies of Education, 41st Yearbook, NSSE, Nelson B. Henry, Editor. Chicago: University of Chicago Press, 1942, p. 140.
42. Soe, Op. cit., p. 13.
43. Adolf Hitler, Mein Kampf. Trans. by Ralph Manheim. New York: Houghton, 1943, p. 174.
44. Denis Diderot, Encyclopédie. Paris: 1870.
45. Lawrence Sullivan, "The Moral Code of Communism," Christian Economics. February 21, 1961. New York.
46. "Dachau," The Encyclopedia Americana. New York: Americana Corporation Edition, 1959. Scene of Nazi gas chamber for mass execution of Jews and other political prisoners.
47. Bellshausen, prison camp similar to Dachau. Ibid.
48. Jeremy Bentham, The Utilitarians, An Introduction to the Principles of Morals and Legislation. Garden City, N. Y.: Doubleday, 1961.
49. Harold Hoeffding, Modern Philosophers. London: Macmillan, 1915.
50. Ibid., p. 150.
51. Francis Hackett, What Mein Kampf Means to America. New York: Reynal and Hitchcock, 1961, Forward, p. xiii.
52. Thomas Huxley. Lecture: Evolution and Ethics, 1893. Reprinted in Readings in Philosophy, John H. Randall, et al., New York: Barnes and Noble, Inc., 1946.
53. V. I. Lenin, Selected Works, Vol. IX, p. 477. Quoted in The Naked Communist, p. 304. Salt Lake City: W. C. Skousen, Ensign Publishing Co., 1958.
54. Radio Moscow, August 20, 1959.
55. Lenin, Op. cit., p. 478.
56. Karl Marx, Friedrich Engels. Communist Manifesto. Quoted in Communist Handbook, p. 35, and in Das Kapital, Chicago: Encyclopaedia Britannica.
57. Christian Economics, Vol. LLL, No. 7. New York: March 27, 1951.
58. Senate Document No. 125, Washington. 84th Congress, May 21, 1956.
59. Ibid.

60. Hawkins, *Op. cit.*
61. Ron Bailey, "This is Gracious Living," Chicago Tribune, October 8, 1961.
62. Illinois State Journal, Springfield, Illinois, September, 1964.
63. T. H. & J. Huxley, *Evolution and Ethics.* New York: Macmillan Company, 1893, p. 81.
64. Erich Fromm, *Man For Himself; An Inquiry Into The Psychology of Ethics.* New York: Rinehart, 1947, p. 7.
65. Walter Lippmann, *A Preface to Morals.* New York: Macmillan, 1929, p. 3.
66. *Ibid.*
67. Robert M. Hutchins, *The Conflict in Education.* New York: Harper and Brothers, 1953, p. 25.
68. John S. Brubacher, *Modern Philosophies of Education.* New York: McGraw, 1939, p. 336.
69. Immanuel Kant, *Fundamental Principles of the Metaphysic of Morals.* The Havard Classics. Collier, 1909.
70. *Ibid.*
71. Lucien Price, *Dialogues of Alfred North Whitehead.* Boston: Little Brown and Co., 1954.
72. Alan Fletcher Markun, *The New Revolution.* New York: Philosophical Library, 1963, p. 421.
73. *Ibid.,* p. 422.
74. *Ibid.,* p. 423.
75. B. P. Yesipor and N. K. Goncharov, A Textbook used in Teacher Training, Trans. by George S. Counts and Nucia P. Lodge. New York: John Day Co., 1947.
76. Thomas Henry Huxley, *Evolution and Ethics.* New York: Macmillan Co., 1893. Reprinted in *Readings in Philosophy,* John H. Randall, et al., New York: Barnes and Noble, Inc., 1946.
77. Jonathan Rinehart, "Mothers Without Joy," *Look Magazine.* March, 1963, p. 29.
78. Reinhold Niebuhr and John C. Bennett, "Federal Aid to Education: A Call to Action." In *Christianity and Crisis,* October 28, 1963.
79. Lippmann, *Op. cit.*
80. Hutchins, *Op. cit.*
81. Richard Katz, *The Solitary Life.* New York: Reynal, 1959.
82. *Modern Philosophies and Education,* 54th Yearbook of the NSSE. Chicago: University of Chicago Press, 1955.
83. Lin Yutang, *Between Tears and Laughter.* New York: John Day Company, 1943, p. 214.

NOTES TO CHAPTER SIX

1. Epicurus, "On Pleasure," *Treasury of Philosophy,* Dagobert D. Runes. New York: Philosophical Library, 1955. (Quoted from Runes' Introduction.)
2. W. Farrell, *A Companion to the Summa.* New York: Sheed and Ward, 1939, Vol. II, p. 192. Quoted in *A Catholic Philosophy of Education.* Milwaukee: Redden and Ryan, 1956.
3. Pius XI, *The Christian Education of Youth.* New York: The America Press, 1936, pp. 19-20.
4. Matthew 5:3-11.
5. John 8:31, 32, 36.
6. Ephesians 2:8,9.
7. Galatians 5:1.
8. John 4:34.
9. I Corinthians 13:13.
10. Romans 15:4,13.
11. Psalms 37:5.
12. Psalms 118:9.
13. R. M. Hutchins, *No Friendly Voice.* Chicago: University of Chicago Press, 1936, p. 24.
14. Aristotle, *Ethics,* VIII and IX, *The Nichomachean Ethics.* Trans. by J. A. K. Thompson. New York: Barnes & Noble, 1953.
15. *Ibid.*
16. Herbert Feigl, "Aims of Education for Our Age of Science," *Modern Philosophies of Education,* 54th Yearbook, NSSE. Nelson B. Henry Editor. Chicago: University of Chicago Press, 1955.
17. Bertrand Russell, *Education and the Good Life.* New York: Boni and Liveright, 1926, pp. 242-243.
18. *Ibid.,* p. 45. Quoted with approval by Arthur B. Moehlmann, *Schools and Administration.* Cambridge: Riverside Press, 1940.
19. Robert S. Cohen, "On the Marxist Philosophy of Education," *Modern Philosophies of Education,* 54th Yearbook, NSSE. Nelson B. Henry, Editor. Chicago: University of Chicago Press, 1955.
20. *Ibid.,* p. 204.
21. Charles A. Beard, *The Unique Function of Education in American Democracy.* Washington: Educational Policies Commission 1937, pp. 77-90.
22. Will Durant, *The Story of Philosophy.* Garden City, New York: Garden City Publishing Company, 1926, p. 108.
23. *Ibid.,* p. 109.
24. *Ibid.*
25. I Timothy 6:6-10.
26. Epicurus, "On Pleasure," *Treasury of Philosophy, Op. cit.*

NOTES TO CHAPTER SEVEN

1. Exodus 20:5-6.
2. Ezekiel 18:20-21.
3. Ezekiel 18:21.
4. Genesis 18:18-19.
5. Matthew 19:14.
6. Titus 3:5.
7. Ephesians 6:4.
8. Quoted by James D. Smart, *The Teaching Ministry of the Church: An Examination of the Basic Principles of Christian Education.* Philadelphia: The Westminster Press, 1954.
9. Decalogue: Exodus 20:1-17.
10. Sermon on the Mount: Matthew 5-7.
11. Genesis 39:9.
12. *Chicago Daily News,* February 22, 1966.
13. Psalm 112:1.
14. Ephesians 4:11-12.
15. Matthew 28:20.
16. I Corinthians 13:13.
17. 1 John 4:16.
18. Arthur A. Cohen, *Humanistic Education and Western Civilization.* New York: Holt, Rinehart and Winston, 1964.
19. John Courtney, Murray, S. J., *On the Future of Humanistic Education,* p. 231.
20. Mayer, (Op. cit. p. 230).
21. Galatians 5:19-21.
22. Galatians 5:22-23.
23. Boettcher, Henry J., *Instructor's Manual.* St. Louis: Concordia Publishing House. 1964. (Thirty-four Resource Units on God-centered Fundamentals. Usable for any age level, Kindergarten to Adult Classes.)
24. Boettcher, Henry J., *The New Life.* (Workbook activities For Junior High Level.) St. Louis: Concordia Publishing House. 1950.
25. Boettcher, Henry J., *Comprehensive Test on Fundamentals.* For Junior High Level. St. Louis: Concordia Publishing House. 1965.